"Morley's keen ol⸻ ⸻⸻ wry humor make him an ideal guide for a vicarious trek across a Canadian winterland—one full of warmth and a community of strangers."

—Ken Ilgunas, author of *This Land Is Our Land: How We Lost the Right to Roam and How to Take It Back*

"From the first page, you want to travel with Anders Morley as he skis off alone yoked to a sled with 100 pounds of gear. He is self-effacing and poetic, with a pitch-perfect ear for the friendly Canadians he meets along the way. There's plenty of snow and quiet and room for Morley's fierce self-questioning. This is a journey into the wilderness and homeward. He's moved by necessity. He's attempting it, not because 'it's there,' but because he is. Morley is a tough and tender voyager."

—Howard Mansfield, author of *The Habit of Turning the World Upside Down*

"The experience of winter, the world of white, is changing quickly. Anders Morley, crossing Canada, has chosen this moment well to chronicle his life on skis and his many unexpected encounters—both human and non-human. 'The purpose of winter is to reveal weaknesses in living things,' he writes. If you want to feel the snow stinging your cheeks, but prefer not to get your shoes wet, I highly and warmly recommend that you follow Morley's tracks across the map."

—Bernd Brunner, author of *Winterlust: Finding Beauty in the Fiercest Season*

"A fascinating story of a man who decides to break from his ordinary life and follow a lifelong dream to cross the Canadian wilderness on skis. With determination, courage, and a fine poetic awareness of the landscape that surrounds him, Anders Morley delivers a story that makes you want to pack your bags, leave civilization behind, and journey into the great unknown."

—Torbjørn Ekelund, author of *In Praise of Paths: A Journey Through Time and Nature*

"An epic adventure, and of a kind that may not be possible much longer. For those who love snow and winter, this is a good book to read by the fire on a cold night—perhaps it will persuade you to go to work trying to save that precious season."

—Bill McKibben, author of *Falter: Has the Human Game Begun to Play Itself Out?*

"*This Land of Snow* invites readers along for the glide, the trudge, the effort and ela- tion, and the ⸻ ⸻ ⸻ in winter. There are cold snap⸻ ⸻ ⸻ ⸻ ⸻ ⸻ nd a way forward becomes clea⸻ ⸻ ⸻ ⸻ ⸻ rating and vivid, a real pleasu⸻ ⸻ ⸻ ⸻ usand Miles Long

BOOKCLUB 796.93 MORLEY
Morley, Anders,
This land of snow : WITHDRAWN

12/02/2021

THIS

A JOURNEY

LAND

ACROSS THE NORTH

OF

IN WINTER

SNOW

ANDERS MORLEY

ROCKFORD PUBLIC LIBRARY

MOUNTAINEERS
BOOKS

MOUNTAINEERS BOOKS is dedicated to the exploration, preservation, and enjoyment of outdoor and wilderness areas.

1001 SW Klickitat Way, Suite 201, Seattle, WA 98134
800-553-4453, www.mountaineersbooks.org

Copyright © 2020 by Anders Morley

All rights reserved. No part of this book may be reproduced or utilized in any form, or by any electronic, mechanical, or other means, without the prior written permission of the publisher.

Mountaineers Books and its colophon are registered trademarks of The Mountaineers organization.

Printed in the United States of America
Distributed in the United Kingdom by Cordee, www.cordee.co.uk

23 22 21 20   1 2 3 4 5

Copyeditor: Ellen Wheat
Cover and interior design: Jen Grable
Cartographer: Bart Wright, Lohnes + Wright
Cover illustration: Jen Grable

Library of Congress Cataloging-in-Publication Data
Names: Morley, Anders, 1978– author.
Title: This land of snow : a journey across the north in winter / Anders Morley.
Description: Seattle, WA : Mountaineers Books, [2020] | Includes bibliographical references. | Summary: "A coming-of-middle-age story in which the author skis across Canada in winter"— Provided by publisher. Identifiers: LCCN 2020004781 (print) | LCCN 2020004782 (ebook) | ISBN 9781680512724 (trade paperback) | ISBN 9781680512731 (epub)
Subjects: LCSH: Morley, Anders, 1978– | Skiers—Canada—Biography. | Skis and skiing—Canada.
Classification: LCC GV854.2.M67 A3 2020 (print) | LCC GV854.2.M67 (ebook) | DDC 796.93092 [B]—dc23
LC record available at https://lccn.loc.gov/2020004781
LC ebook record available at https://lccn.loc.gov/2020004782

Mountaineers Books titles may be purchased for corporate, educational, or other promotional sales, and our authors are available for a wide range of events. For information on special discounts or booking an author, contact our customer service at 800-553-4453 or mbooks@mountaineersbooks.org.

♻ Printed on recycled paper

ISBN (paperback): 978-1-68051-272-4
ISBN (ebook): 978-1-68051-273-1

An independent nonprofit publisher since 1960

Per la Mau (1967–2013),
che era un pezzo di torta

Always the same, when on a fated night
At last the gathered snow lets down as white
As may be in dark woods, and with a song
It shall not make again all winter long
Of hissing on the yet uncovered ground,
I almost stumble looking up and round,
As one who overtaken by the end
Gives up his errand, and lets death descend
Upon him where he is, with nothing done
To evil, no important triumph won,
More than if life had never been begun.

—Robert Frost, "The Onset"

CONTENTS

Author's Note 9

Morley's Route 10

PART ONE: PACIFIC OCEAN TO TERRACE

1. Prince Rupert 14
2. Origins 20
3. Highway of Tears 30
4. Advance and Retreat 37
5. Terrace 45

PART TWO: TERRACE TO FORT SAINT JAMES

6. Finally Skiing 52
7. Over the Mountains 60
8. Lights in the Forest 66
9. Into the Babine 78
10. Among Loggers 83
11. End of the Earth 92
12. Christmas 99

PART THREE: PRINCE GEORGE TO SLAVE LAKE

13. Great Divide 108
14. Peace Country 120

15. McLennan 125

16. Cold 132

17. Winter 136

18. Lesser Slave Lake 141

19. Edmonton 150

PART FOUR: EDMONTON TO LAC LA RONGE

20. Paradise Below Zero 154

21. In Cree Country 161

22. Maps and Dreams 166

23. Canoe Lake 169

24. The Cossack 173

25. Pinehouse 178

26. The Pearl Necklace 186

27. Ordeal by Ice 192

28. La Ronge 200

29. Lac La Ronge 203

30. Trails 208

PART FIVE: LAC LA RONGE TO WINNIPEG

31. The Sunless City 216

32. On the Shield 225

33. Zoë 230

34. Dad 237

35. Thaw 245

Acknowledgments 251

Suggested Reading 253

AUTHOR'S NOTE

The events and conversations in this book are told as I remember them. Most were carefully set down in my diary within a day or two of happening. I have taken some small liberties with chronology for the sake of clarity, and a very few names and minor identifying facts have been altered to protect privacy. What has changed significantly in the years between the first and final drafts is perspective. For any resulting discomfort or hurt feelings all I can offer are apologies and regret.

Although Canada officially underwent metrication in the 1970s, throughout most of this book I have preferred imperial units. The reason is partly practical: more Canadian readers will be familiar with the imperial "system" than US readers will be with the metric. For those of us raised using miles and Fahrenheit degrees, moreover, metric units have a way of flattering us with an inflated sense of our own strength and accomplishment, especially in the context of a self-propelled journey made in winter; metric feels like cheating. Twenty miles may not sound like much—but thirty-two kilometers gets respect. Conversely, while on the centigrade scale it's below zero for half the year in much of Canada, in Fahrenheit "below zero" is still a meaningful expression. It means winter is finally starting to tighten its grip.

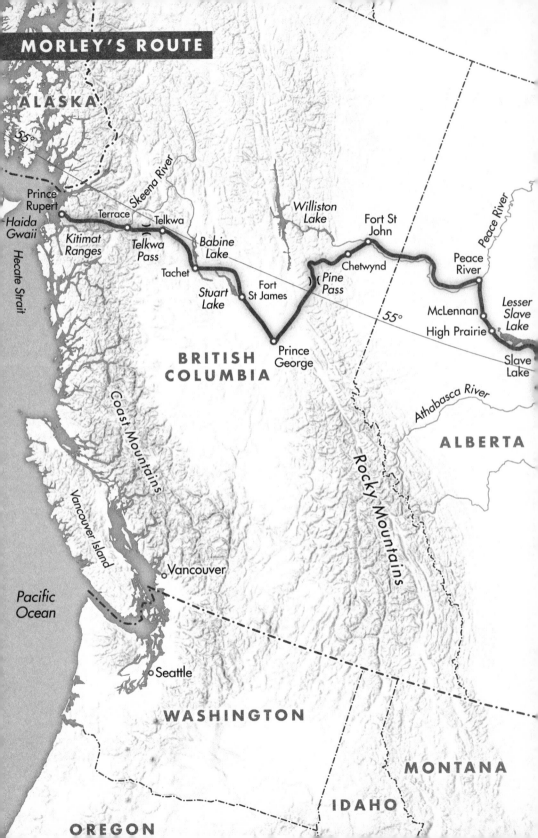

MORLEY'S ROUTE

ALASKA

55°

Prince
Rupert

*Haida
Gwazi*

Hecate Strait

Terrace

Skeena River

Telkwa

*Kitimat
Ranges*

*Telkwa
Pass*

Tachet

*Babine
Lake*

*Stuart
Lake*

Fort
St James

*Williston
Lake*

Fort St
John

Chetwynd

*(Pine
Pass*

Prince
George

55°

Peace River

*Peace
River*

McLennan

High Prairie

*Lesser
Slave
Lake*

Slave
Lake

BRITISH
COLUMBIA

Coast Mountains

Athabasca River

ALBERTA

Rocky Mountains

Vancouver Island

Vancouver

*Pacific
Ocean*

Seattle

WASHINGTON

MONTANA

IDAHO

OREGON

PART ONE

PACIFIC OCEAN
TO TERRACE

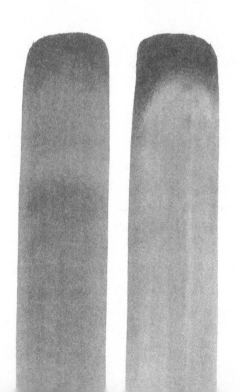

1

PRINCE RUPERT

I awoke to gray Pacific light falling through a sea-sprayed window onto the inside deck of the MV *Northern Expedition*, where I lay sprawled among maps and my duffel bag. The ferry makes a twenty-two-hour passage between the northern tip of Vancouver Island and the top of the British Columbia coast, calling at remote communities in the middle of the night. My body ached for rest, and the boat lulled as best it could, but my sleepless brain yearned to make land, the better if covered in snow. I wanted only to be skiing toward the center of the continent while breaths of cold air oxygenated my coursing blood. Body and mind had struck a compromise near dawn and let me sleep a couple of hours.

I stood up, stretched, and climbed topside. The ship was lumbering up the Inside Passage, the channel that threads through islands up the coast of British Columbia to Alaska. A chill rain tickled my thinly bearded cheek. To east and west, where steep mountainsides met the sea, wisps of mist hung with surreal clarity. The slopes were thick with dark, ancient forest. Everywhere were waterfalls forever cycling water from land to sea. They reminded me why the stretch of land between Northern California and the southern Yukon is sometimes called Cascadia. When I returned to the top deck a few hours later we were approaching Prince Rupert. The sun blazed across the sky and the mid-November air was bracing.

In port a young fisherman I had been traveling beside for the past forty-eight hours offered me a lift into town. He had nearly sunk far offshore a few days earlier, and I badly wanted to think of him as swashbuckling, but the soft glow of his Canadian niceness precluded it. Still there was something; he said he was coming home to Rupert to find a staid government job and to hell with the ocean, but the way he ate, as though the contents of his plate were an enemy that must be shown no mercy, wouldn't let me believe him. He helped me heave my duffel bag into the bed of a neighbor's truck, to be left at my lodgings later. The two of us went in a van with the rest of our gear and a number of the fisherman's sisters, who had come out to welcome the ship.

They dropped me at the Pioneer Hostel, where I had stayed once more than a decade earlier. The year after university I hitchhiked to Prince Rupert from California with a copy of Tom Robbins's *Even Cowgirls Get the Blues* in my jacket pocket. The journey was a crash course in Cascadian ways for a New Englander naturally bent toward the Old World. There was allure in the sense of freshness and impermanence. This time the only staff member on duty at the hostel was a woman in her forties with long sandy hair. She had a slight accent and I asked where she was from. She said Sweden by way of Oregon. An easiness filled the space between us, like we were old housemates, because I was the only guest in the dorms. I floated in and out of the common room, snacking nervously and flipping through books. I imagined that being Scandinavian made her sympathetic to my strange ambition. "What are you doing with all this stuff?" she had asked me in the afternoon, when I kept returning outside for more. Heaped on the wood floor were a backpack with a shotgun strapped to it, an orange polyethylene sled, wooden snowshoes, a ballistic nylon duffel bag, and a pair of Norwegian expedition skis with a stern portrait of explorer Roald Amundsen emblazoned in red on each tip.

"I'm skiing across Canada," I said.

WALKING THE DARK STREETS OF Prince Rupert that night was something I had long been waiting for. For some reason the town had a haunting magnetism, and I wondered whether this expedition was not simply an excuse for me to go back to it—back to a place that felt like it might fall off the map, cease to exist. Why was I drawn to such places, especially if they were cold and rain-soaked? Even now I know I must return. To think about it pulls me there. It's like a gray autumn day, saturated with a sense of loss but infinitely rich. Prince Rupert is said to out-rain every place on earth. Sarah de Leeuw, Canadian author of a collection of essays on northern British Columbia towns, has written a dismal homage to this one: "The rainfall in Prince Rupert is unparalleled, but it does not drown monsters."

There was something desperate on the night air. I felt the damp snap of wind against my skin. It carried the disquiet of cold mountains and deep ocean. I looked over the water at darkness. Prince Rupert, like so many northern places, must be felt to be believed. At a distance it is hard for me to think there is actually such a place.

THE NEXT MORNING I AWOKE in a panic. I didn't know where I was, so I racked my brain through a photo album of images but couldn't turn up the right one: dark place, low ceiling, drafty windows. I knew from vague recollection of other displaced awakenings recently that I was somewhere early in my expedition to the land of snow, which had dominated my imagination for more than a year. Vancouver came to mind, then the Pacific, then Prince Rupert. The hostel. Top floor of the hostel.

I dressed and went down to the kitchen, where I ate what fresh food I had left—carrots, broccoli, and some leftover fried chicken I had craved on my midnight walk. In an alcove I noticed a young couple I had seen several times since leaving Vancouver on a small ferry three days before. They were quietly enjoying their breakfast, but when our eyes met I walked over to greet them. The pair were from Halifax and were touring Canada. The husband spoke with a French accent. He had noticed my luggage and was curious to hear my story.

"Aren't you worried about grizzlies?" he finally asked from behind his tidy brown beard.

"Not really," I said.

"Well, you should be." The reply was unexpectedly peremptory.

"I figure in a week I'll be into winter weather, and they'll be asleep. I'll take precautions. Until then I'll mostly be near the road."

"Ha!" he said with a dismissive sneer. "You tink so? Dey will have you for breakfast." With gums bared, he tore a piece of bacon from his fork and chewed it vigorously.

"I have bear spray," I offered, "and bear bangers." Bear bangers are noise-making flares used by backcountry travelers to scare off troublesome animals without harming them.

"Do you really *tink* a big grizzly bear fears such tings?"

As I was walking away I remembered something and turned back toward him. "I nearly forgot," I said. "I also have a twelve-gauge shotgun. And a handful of rifled big-game slugs." He stared at me. "That ought to spook them. Don't you think?"

I lingered in the kitchen, nursing cup after cup of coffee and washing other people's dishes. This is how I procrastinate in my day to day, and the procrastination here, with hundreds of miles of cold beyond the front door, was for the ages. Another lodger, a sturdy middle-aged woman, came in. Her long hair, brown surrendering to gray, hung in large frizzy curls. She looked old-fashioned. I might have guessed she was a Baptist or a homesteader from Idaho. She was neither, as it turned out, but she was American. Amy Lasalle was in Prince Rupert from Flagstaff, Arizona. When I asked what brought her there, she didn't answer right away. "You see, I don't usually tell people, because if you don't believe in astrology, you'll think I'm weird," she said.

"I'm not generally regarded as normal myself," I countered, "if that's any encouragement."

"As a matter of fact," she went on, "you're the first person I've told." She sounded relieved, although she hadn't told me anything yet. "Every year I take a birthday trip for my solar return."

"I'm sorry?" I said.

"My solar return."

"Is that like when the sun returns to the position it was in when you were born?"

"Exactly. Where you are on your solar return is important. It sets a tone for the year to come."

The idea that the configuration of the solar system in the instant we are born is part of the baseline of our identities was compelling. But there are differences between the natal moment and each solar return, Amy said, and she tried hopelessly to explain in the cryptic language of astrology. The earth may float in the same relation to the sun, but stars and moon and planets are aligned differently. The solar return is therefore a kind of rebirth into a new, somewhat shifted, world. It was a refreshing thought, if not so different from the feeling others of us might get from watching the days or the seasons come around. Amy told me she seeks out places for her solar return each year where things will be aligned in a way that she likes, but added that perfection was out of reach. This year she wasn't thrilled with the position of Uranus. I wondered whether perfection meant to turn the clock back and hold it there.

She went to her room to fetch a diagram showing the alignment of sun, planets, and stars for Prince Rupert, British Columbia, N54°18′44″, W130°19′38″, at 5:06 a.m. It was November 19, 2012, the day of her solar return and, for me, the beginning of a journey through winter. The diagram showed concentric circles representing natal alignment and return alignment and gave a coordinate in degrees meaningless to me. When I told her that my thirty-fourth birthday was coming up, she asked if I was a Capricorn or a Sagittarius.

"Now it's your turn to think I'm strange," I said. "I can never remember my sign."

I gave her my birthdate, and she told me I was a Sagittarius. "That's why you're skiing across Canada," she said. "Sagittariuses are *very* adventurous. Then again, you might do it if you were a Capricorn too. But for different reasons. Capricorns are ambitious." Of course they are, I thought.

I HAD THINGS TO GET ready, so I told Amy I needed to go. Suddenly I felt an unaccustomed urge to give her a hug. We embraced awkwardly, then I said goodbye. I spent the rest of the morning condensing luggage and running last-minute errands. I bought gas for my brass Primus camp stove and spare lighters to stash in various pockets.

In spite of its high latitude, Prince Rupert has a mild oceanic climate. There was no snow, and I sent my sled and skis ahead by bus to Terrace, ninety miles to the east, the next town I would come to. The day was radiant, windy, and cloudless. It was not a Prince Rupert day. Back at the hostel I found the Swedish woman outside giving orders to a man on a ladder. He knew who I was, because he climbed down to shake my hand. He shook his head slowly and laughed and said in a lilt, "You're fucking crazy."

I went inside to fetch my backpack and braced myself for the momentous first step. I shouldered an outrageous ninety pounds and descended the steep flights of wooden stairs between my dormitory and the front door. Amy Lasalle was on her way in from taking photographs and I almost bowled her over. "Do you want me to take a picture of you before you go?" she asked. She took one in front of the hostel and another of me walking up the road. I heard the shutter click behind me and waved without looking back.

At the end of the street I turned east. The morning's sunny sky had given way to a consuming gray. Walking out of the grim Cascadian town stirred a faint memory of an early scene in *First Blood*, the debut Rambo movie, complete with antiheroic strains of soundtrack. Because thoughts come in trains, and the cars in this one were cinematic and absurd, I thought next of *What About Bob?* in which Richard Dreyfuss plays psychiatrist to a neurotic Bill Murray. Dreyfuss advises Murray to approach his daunting everyday tasks in baby steps. "Baby steps up the road," I muttered to myself. "Baby steps out of Prince Rupert. Baby steps to Terrace. Baby steps across Canada."

2

ORIGINS

I clearly remember my first time on skis. I was five years old. My father and I were at the local ski hill, and my dad bought himself a lift ticket and walked me to the base of the bunny slope. "Go up and down here for a while," he said. "I'll come back and see how you're doing in an hour." He showed me how to carry my skis over my shoulder and said I could walk up and ski back down. He didn't think the fifty-yard rope tow was worth the price of a ticket. My dad clipped his skis on and skated off to a chairlift, while I started walking up the side of the rope-tow track, where other kids twice my size were being pulled uphill at five times my speed.

In a few minutes I was at the top of the run. I stepped into my bindings and took on the shallow grade without fear and, as it turned out, without event. When I got to the bottom a few seconds later I thought the descent seemed much too short. On my next walk up I decided there was no good reason for me to stop at the top of the bunny slope, so I slogged past the lift attendant's warming shack and up the side of an intermediate run that followed a line of tall white pines. I was about three-quarters of the way up the hill when my dad spotted me on his way down. He taught me how to snowplow and to turn in a wide S behind him, and soon he was congratulating me at the bottom of my first real ski run. So began my love affair with skiing.

I was fortunate to grow up in a place where snowfall was abundant, exclusion from private property was frowned upon, and outside my door were thousands of acres of forested hills to explore. By the time I was ten my feet were as big as my mother's, and I pinched her leather cross-country ski boots and a set of wooden skis and poles from Finland that had stood neglected in the cellar for years. I never had any instruction in Nordic skiing technique, but as soon as I pushed off it was obvious that this was an easier way to move about in the winter woods. To this day I have a hard time thinking of skiing as a sport and have felt self-conscious the few times I've skied in prepared tracks among the athletic and sleek-suited crowd that frequents Nordic centers. For me skiing is just the way you walk when there's snow on the ground. It's walking in cursive, and I love to walk.

IN THE SUMMERTIME WE WALKED everywhere when we were kids. I had three brothers—twins named Matt and Dave a year behind me, and Jon a year behind them. By the time we were all in elementary school together we may as well have been quadruplets, although I never lost a sense that I was the oldest and somehow a conduit to the adult world. I was the least rebellious of the brothers and sometimes had to defend myself against charges of treason in three-on-one brawls. But we moved quickly beyond our differences. We were best friends, and almost always a friend to one brother became a friend to all four. We walked for miles along old forest paths or along quiet dirt roads that wended into the hills toward the Monadnock region of southwestern New Hampshire. At night our dad would read to us for an hour, sitting on the floor in Matt and Dave's room, where we made our way through books by Mark Twain, James Fenimore Cooper, Jack London, and John Bunyan.

These readings fueled our imaginations, and periodically we would announce to our mother that we were fed up with her rules and were running away from home. She never appeared to be bothered by our threats and almost seemed happy we were going. Finally she would have some peace and quiet. "Do you need help packing?" she might ask Jon, who was easily distracted. We'd stuff matches, twine, and a few snacks into our rucksacks and stomp off into the woods, where we would improvise on lessons we'd learned from Tom or Huck or Chingachgook. We bent straight pins into fishhooks, tied them to twine, and dropped them into the stream that ran in the woods behind our house. Then we built lean-tos on the bank and sat by a campfire while we waited for the fish to rise. They never did.

Once, before we understood the laws of buoyancy, we took a toboggan and piled onto it everything we thought would be necessary for a long voyage over lakes and rivers. Our plan was to eventually set sail from an island in the upper Saint Lawrence River, where we spent part of each summer in a family cottage, and head west across the Great Lakes for the interior. I was particularly taken with this idea. Alone in my room at night I carefully drew up lists of the supplies we would need and then penciled our route onto the wrinkled pages of the family road atlas, which had a photograph of a sunset over a lake on its cover. One day we persuaded our mother to drive us to the local river so we could test our vessel. We loaded our cargo and dragged it down the sandy bank. When we pushed it into the water we watched it sink in three feet of current before any of us could climb aboard.

Winter was different. It was dark when we went to school and dark again an hour after we got home. There was usually no time for elaborate escapades. I occasionally fit in a short ski in the woods before supper. On weekends our dad would take us downhill skiing—sometimes at hills near home, but more often in the White Mountains in northern New Hampshire. Of all the brothers I loved skiing best. It was my one childhood passion. While my brothers sometimes preferred to stay at home and see their friends on weekends, I never missed a chance to join my father on the slopes. Skiing therefore became a special bond between us, and I spent hundreds of hours trying to imitate his distinctive style. In the early nineties my brothers all went over to snowboarding. I kept on skiing.

When I was about thirteen my dad decided I was ready to tackle Tuckerman Ravine, a glacial cirque on the eastern slope of Mount Washington, New England's highest summit. Descending one of its couloirs is a rite of passage for northeastern skiers. It meant packing our skis up three miles of trail, spending the night in a tent, and then bootpacking up the last 800 vertical feet of the steep cirque with our skis on our shoulders. At the top of a route called the Right Gully, where I had to cut a ledge into the snow so that I'd have a place to step into my skis for the descent, I lost my balance before getting them on and peeled off the side of the mountain at a terrifying speed. I tumbled head over heels and could see rocks and snow and people speeding past me, one second right-side up and the next upside down. Hundreds of feet below me was a mass of boulders, and I could find no way of stopping myself as I accelerated toward it. But then I caught a glimpse of a skier off to my left racing down the gully in a wide arc. He leaned hard into a turn toward me and a second later I felt a great crash. Suddenly I was pinned against the snow in my father's arms, safe and immobile. I had never seen my dad ski so fast before. I knew only his slow, graceful sweeps—like a calligrapher drawing brushstrokes down the mountainside. Once he had made sure I was all right, we climbed together back up to the top of the gully to retrieve my skis. "Always keep your weight into the mountain," my father said when we got back to the ledge. Then we pushed off and skied down together.

IN JANUARY 2003, EIGHT MONTHS after my first visit to Prince Rupert, I moved to Europe for graduate school. In Germany I met an Italian woman named Elena and fell madly in love—more in love, I still think, than I've seen anyone else fall. She was the most beautiful woman I had ever laid eyes on. She taught Greek and Latin at home in Italy and had come to Germany for a few months to improve her German, which was much better than mine. We went for long walks along the grassy paths of Baden-Württemberg and talked until my halting German became passably fluent.

Elena was older than I was, and I found her at once intimidating and the most natural person in the world simply to exist beside. Even though we had different native languages—and had never spoken a word to each other in any language but German—it was as if we had a more direct way of communicating. It didn't matter that some of our interests were different and that we were happy to pursue those things on our own. We agreed on fundamental things, like the importance of always seeking what is true and what is beautiful. And although we were both rather serious people, it seemed significant that we laughed at the same things. We often laughed at each other. From the moment I decided I wanted to be with Elena, everything else in my life became secondary.

Within two years I had taken up residence in an Italian city, was living an Italian life, and was taking in the world through the lens of the Italian language. I worked for what seemed like a long time as a teacher and translator. In 2007 we acquired a puppy from the local shelter. He was a black cairn terrier cross who looked exactly like Toto from *The Wizard of Oz* except for his floppy ears. We named him Beowulf because I was studying Old English at the time, and he became my companion on hikes and ski tours in the nearby Alps. Elena and I were married along the way. As lives go, mine was good. But especially late at night, when I went for walks with Beowulf, I missed the restful silences of home, the pure air, the dark skies, the whisper of wind in the trees, and the need, sometimes, of being far from other people. I missed the feeling that I could walk out the back door and keep on walking, practically forever. This longing was bound up with a vague sense that my life was incomplete or in some way lacked enough of my own imprint—that in my single-minded quest to be with the woman I loved I had left something out.

In the spring of 2011 I bought a copy of *National Geographic* at an Italian newsstand. As I flipped through the pages my eyes landed on a foldout photograph of a man leaping across a semifrozen mountain river with a pair of cross-country skis in one hand. He was bundled against the cold, looked a little battered, and was carrying a backpack. The picture immediately stirred something inside me latent from childhood. It was attached to a story about Andrew Skurka, the man it depicted, who the year before had spent 176 days making a giant circuit of Alaska and the Yukon—on skis, in a packraft, and walking. The expedition had a seductive sense of completeness to it; its perfect form was its justification. When I read that Skurka was twenty-nine years old, a restlessness took hold of me. I was only thirty-two, but suddenly I felt that slipping sensation that initiates a midlife crisis.

In the fall of that year I told Elena I wanted to spend the winter of 2012–13 traveling across northern Canada on skis. The words "northern Canada" were enough to make most Italians I knew shiver, but I didn't think the plan should come as any surprise to my wife. She knew how I had grown up, and I still spent much of my free time hiking, camping, and backcountry skiing. Before we got married I even asked her for a promise that, once we were married, she would not stand in the way of my lifelong dream of someday making a months-long self-propelled journey on my home continent. Since such rustic ambitions were far from her civilized experience, at the time I had given her the Appalachian Trail as an example of what I meant. She consented to as much, doubtless imagining me sauntering under the summer sun from village to village through a friendly eastern Arcadia. She was a reasonable person, and there was nothing offensive in such a plan. I lived in her country, after all, and although I didn't dislike it, she knew I had a powerful connection to the woods and lakes and hills of home, and was often sick for them. It was only fair.

But what I proposed now was a different beast. "Why does your trip have to be you, alone, in northern Canada in the winter?" she asked. She worried that the cold and the sparse population made death or disappearance so much more likely. It didn't *have* to be Canada, I had reasoned to myself before unveiling my plan. I could ski across the continent, dropping down out of Canada every so often to touch snowy American places like Minnesota or northern New England. But when I looked more closely at long-term snow cover trends, Canada was obviously the safest bet. And I had always had a special fondness for Canada. My father was Canadian, and I took pride in telling kids at school that I was only "half American"—that I was equally a Canadian. Canada stood in my mind for an earthier kind of freedom than the abstract "liberty" of the Pledge of Allegiance we recited every morning. Since I had spent my childhood bouncing back and forth across the invisible border, I considered the whole continent an extension of the woods that stretched away from our house to the north and west. It was all in some way home. A few months in Canada struck me as the perfect medicine for my diffuse sense of nostalgia and civilizational glut.

That it would be winter was part of the point. What better way to skim off the dross of soft urban living than to remove all possibility of comfort? Winter added an element of the remoteness I sought as well, since snow and cold make wild places harder to encroach upon, although I was equally interested in the settled places I would come to. I wanted to learn something about how people lived at the edge of the wilderness and in places where winter was long and hard. I had grown up in the southern part of the snowbelt and had always felt something pulling me north. My upbringing—as well as my education in an alternative public school system where Thoreau, Aldo Leopold, Wendell Berry, and Annie Dillard were the canonical writers—had instilled in me the idea that the unbuilt world had lessons to teach us that were transferable to our lives in built society. So Canada it had to be, and it had to be winter. As to the matter of my going alone, a casual survey will reveal how few of anyone's circle of acquaintances would happily join in spending the four coldest months of the year living outside—traveling on foot all day and making a new camp every night—in places where North Dakota is considered southern.

Finally there was the skiing itself. Norwegian arctic explorer Fridtjof Nansen understood its magical appeal as well as anyone and described it in 1890 in *The First Crossing of Greenland*:

> *Where can one find a healthier and purer delight than when on a brilliant winter day one binds one's [skis] to one's feet and takes one's way out into the forest? Can there be anything more beautiful than the northern winter landscape, when the snow lies foot-deep, spread as a soft white mantle over field and wood and hill? Where will one find more freedom and excitement than when one glides swiftly down the hillside through the trees, one's cheek brushed by the sharp cold air and frosted pine branches, and one's eye, brain, and muscles alert and prepared to meet every unknown obstacle and danger which the next instant may throw in one's path? Civilisation is, as it were, washed clean from the mind and left far behind with the city atmosphere and city life; one's whole being is, so to say, wrapped in one's [skis] and the surrounding nature. There is something in the whole which develops soul and not body alone.*

Elena was convinced that the reasons I gave were not the real reasons. She thought there was something deeper that I wasn't being honest with myself about. This and the fact that she seemed to doubt my ability to stay alive in the cold made me feel like she didn't trust me. I resented it. What hurt her most of all though, she said, was that I had made the decision without first discussing it with her. I had made it by fiat.

In the end it was my insistence on going by myself that tipped the scale. I remember a time of embarrassing scenes of public berating. Our decade-old relationship had been such a happy one. No couple I knew got along as well as we did or seemed so in love. But now this surface chop was exposing turbulence deep down that I hadn't known existed. For the year leading up to my departure we lived parallel lives. In my free time I either shut myself in the kitchen to plan every fine detail of the journey I had resolved to undertake, or I took to the Alps with an intentionally light sleeping bag to train myself to sleep through increasingly intense states of shivering. Elena, meanwhile, poured herself more and more into her work. There were a few happy moments, but my memory of that year is mostly of reciprocal resentment, argument, and silences.

All this only made me hunker down. I ruminated on the contrasts that seemed to define my world. The easiest kind of contrast to see is the kind found on a photographic negative, where everything is either black or white, visible or invisible. The contrasts I noticed in my everyday existence began standing out to me in this kind of ungraded starkness. I started to see the world as a set of oppositions between urban and rural, civilized and wild, loud and quiet, coweringly gregarious and boldly solitary. The shorthand for this became Italy versus me. Every little grievance went toward bolstering a worldview, held by a party of one, that owed something to environmentalist thinking but was angry and at odds with my longstanding sense of the importance of the past. My journey became the tip of a massive iceberg of sophistry, and there was no telling what damage it might do.

When I hatched the idea of traveling across a season and a continent, one of the things I was genuinely interested in was how people made lives in places where winters were long. I had settled on the boreal forest of subarctic Canada as the perfect laboratory for my curiosity. The boreal forest (alternatively called the taiga or the snow forest) is the evergreen ecosystem, sometimes sprinkled with birch or aspen, that girdles the northern hemisphere between roughly 50° and 70° latitude. In my mind it represented the space where wilderness and civilization met to negotiate their differences. To the north were the barrens and the tundra. To the south were the prairies or northern hardwood forests. It was a place where you could travel for weeks without seeing another person, but also a place where there were modest-size communities linked together by single-lane roads (which sometimes saw no traffic for days). It was home to a spread-out population of Canada's First Nations and home as well to bears, moose, caribou, wolves, and millions of smaller fur-bearing creatures that historically made it the heart muscle of the Canadian fur trade. The rivers of the Precambrian Canadian Shield—the exposed geologic backbone of the North American continent—once pulsed with the canoes of voyageurs, the rugged French-Canadian couriers of the Hudson's Bay and Northwest Companies, which were the key players of the trade. Small farms poked the southern edges, hemming off tiny fragments of the endless forest with fences, but mostly the land was too cold and nutrient-poor for agriculture. Had I been seeking only solitude, I would have set my sights from the beginning not on this peopled wilderness of the Near North but on the Far North, where population is so sparse that for a traveler on foot the land is effectively empty. Nevertheless, by late summer 2012 a colleague could suggest that my reductive thinking habit was making me into a misanthrope—and perhaps not be far off the mark.

A journal entry made about a month before my departure illustrates the tenor of my mind at the time:

September 24, 2012

Bergamo

Yesterday Elena and I went for a hike from home up to a prospect overlooking the small town of Olera. Even here I have a hard time using the word "village" because of the layout of even the smallest Italian communities. They are like shrunken cities, differing from their giant counterparts only quantitatively. The smallest Italian town up in the mountains is a dense cluster of brick, stone, and cement. It may have a population of thirty, but its population density will be exactly thirty persons per acre, and you will hear your neighbors arguing, and the barking of their dogs will resound off the stone walls of the house across the narrow lane so that it sounds as if the dog is barking six inches from your ear. There are bars on all the lower windows. Anyway, up on this prospect, a few hundred meters above the town, was a shrine, the endpoint of a grueling Via Crucis [a devotional walk along which Christian believers stop to pray at fourteen Stations of the Cross, images representing Christ's sorrowful steps between his trial and execution] that climbs up from the valley floor. The shrine is emblematic of the European, and perhaps especially Italian, understanding of history and material culture that I've been contrasting with those of the original peoples of North America. One finds a solid little shrine, built of stone and cement, with a terra-cotta roof. Behind its barred window, shut with an armored padlock, is a portrait of the obscure object of devotion—Tommaso Acerbis, Capuchin friar (Olera, 1563—Innsbruck, 1631), called The Mystic of the Heart of Jesus, whatever that means. So this fellow lived four hundred years ago, along with hundreds of thousands of others, and probably very few people, even in his little hometown, know anything about him— and who can say how much of what is known is apocryphal? Yet here is his monument, lest we forget him. Why not give our atten- tion to virtuous things or people of our own times, about which we can know something useful? But apart from the permanence of the building and the ... attempts of certain humans to make the man's reputation permanent, there are the ... devotional knickknacks: fake flowers and a light-bulb candle. Fake flowers because real ones wither and die; fake candles because real ones melt away and burn out—perhaps both things that poor Father Acerbis and his mem- ory ought to be allowed to do in peace. I read, perhaps in Paulette Jiles's North Spirit: Sojourns Among the Cree and Ojibway, *that Native cultures in northern Ontario do not remember individuals for more than about three generations.*

My fatal flaw had always been intransigence. Elena's was an inability to rein in her anger once unleashed. She said at least once that if I went alone into the north I needn't bother coming back.

3

HIGHWAY OF TEARS

People who have never been to Prince Rupert, which is most people, don't realize that, like Montreal and Manhattan, it is an island town. Unlike its crowded metropolitan cousins, however, Prince Rupert occupies only a small corner of Kaien Island. Even the least ambulant citizen can walk from the heart of town into the bush without motorized aid. Wolves haunt its neighborhoods. An hour of walking along the highway, the only road out, and you've left the last stray signs of commerce and human habitation.

In a mile or two I came into a ruddy world of muskeg. The plants carpeting the ground were magical pinks and oranges and crimsons blotted with shades of coniferous green. Shadows were purple and snow was on the distant interior mountains. It dawned on me that Alaska lay only a few miles over the northern hills. The force of its name, pronounced at my lips when I knew the real place was so near, was enough to send a shiver down my spine. A bush plane roared low overhead.

By evening I made the mainland. I walked a mile east from the turn for Port Edward, a tiny community once known for packing more sockeye salmon than any place on earth, and followed a dirt track into the bush. I pitched my tent near an inlet called Morse Basin that wraps around the east side of Kaien Island from the Pacific. It was getting dark, and already I had broken a promise to myself that I would always make camp by sunset. Being out after nightfall in the thick of grizzly country where winter can be so mild that the bears don't hibernate made me uneasy.

To keep the scent of food away, I made supper sixty yards downwind of my tent. Before setting off I had spent several days dehydrating meat and vegetables and mixing them with couscous, rice flakes, or pasta. I stuffed meal-size portions of various combinations of these ingredients into plastic bags. By cutting up a reflective windshield sunshade, I made a double-layered cozy that fit snugly around my cookpot. To make my evening meal on the trail all I had to do was boil water, pour these dry ingredients into my pot, usually with an inch or two of butter to boost the calorie count, and nestle the pot into the cozy, where in five or ten minutes the meal would cook on its own using the retained heat. This method enabled me to save fuel for a task that would be vital once I moved inland from the temperate coast: melting snow into drinkable water. While I waited for my meal to cook the first night, I fired a bear banger to make sure the pen-size launcher worked. The bang and the sparks were exhilarating in the night silence. After supper I stuffed all my food into a nylon bag and hoisted it up onto the longest tree branch I could find that was high enough to be out of a bear's reach. Later, while I wrote the day's happenings in my tent, I heard a rustling from the direction of the tree. I stepped outside to investigate and found a porcupine looking for a way up the dangling rope.

"Get out of here!" I shouted, practicing the menacing voice I'd use if it really were a bear.

The next morning, after I'd walked a few hours through low terrain, a truck drove past me and slowed to a stop a hundred yards farther on. I would have run ahead to keep the driver from waiting, but my burden was too heavy for anything but walking. At the truck a curl of smoke slid from the window, and inside were a man and a woman, both Native.

When I approached the driver's side window the man looked at me but remained silent for a long time. He had high cheekbones and an austere expression. He wore a baseball cap and a heavy red flannel shirt. "So where ya' goin?" he eventually said.

"I'm going to Terrace now. Going to try to ski across Canada." Then, to head off any charity he might offer, I told him I wasn't hitchhiking.

"Yer not hitchhikin'?" He looked puzzled.

"No. I'm walking."

He chewed on the idea for a minute, looking into the distance. Then he said, without turning his head and through a smile so subtle it could only be heard, "I never seen 'at before." It was hard to know whether he meant walking across Canada or refusing a lift to Terrace.

Then, as if finally getting some savor from this lean conversation, he continued. "I seen ya' yesterday."

"Oh yeah?"

"Yuh."

There was a long pause, and I had nothing to fill it with.

"Looked like you was freezin'," he said.

"I'm all right," I said.

A baby cried in the back of the cab. The wife looked blankly at me.

"Well," said the man. "Have a safe journey." He drove off and pressed the horn twice.

THE MOUNTAINS GREW AROUND ME. I walked past lakes and began a long and slow but, for the weight, not effortless climb. My legs were getting sore and my step felt out of kilter. I couldn't find a compensation to make it feel any better. I was wearing thick leather boots I'd brought from Italy, hand-sewn and designed for long-distance travel on backcountry skis. I chose them because I'd reckoned I would be walking a lot, and I wanted to carry only one pair of boots. They weren't stiff like downhill ski boots, or even cross-country ski boots. Except for the duckbill toes that fit into the simple three-pin binding on each ski—a design not improved on in a century—they were more like hiking boots. They felt comfortable, and I didn't know what was causing the soreness. I knew I was carrying too much weight, but I'd been walking for little more than a day.

The temperature fell as the elevation rose. The road pass between Morse Basin and the Skeena River was only about 600 feet high, but it was suddenly winter. Dry snowflakes shot sporadically out of the gray sky. A wind rushed from the east, making progress harder. At the pass itself, oddly called Rainbow Summit, a white van slowed down and a young man with wire-rim glasses and a foot-long beard asked me if I wanted a lift to Terrace. "No thanks," I said, "but I appreciate you offering." As the van pulled away I read on the back window, in screaming letters, JESUS SAID: FEAR HIM WHO CAN DESTROY BOTH BODY AND SOUL IN HELL. It reminded me of a sermon I had heard in Saint Giles Cathedral when I was a student in Edinburgh. The minister had recalled his clerical apprenticeship among the old fire-and-brimstone believers of Scotland's northwestern isles. "Fortunately," he said, "they did not practice what they preached."

Once I had cleared the pass the wind became stronger, the atmosphere more wintery. I thought how glad I was to have cut my teeth winter-traveling in New Hampshire's hills. Few frequented places could be as rugged as the bleak and stunted White Mountains of my childhood. It was a place I seemed to think of in some form nearly every day, whether I wanted to or not, the way my brothers almost always appeared in my dreams.

I came down around the flank of a small mountain into a wind shadow and saw the Skeena River below. I heard another car slow down, only this one stopped behind me. I turned, ready with my explanation, but noticed that the car was backing away. It must have lost something out of the window. But in a minute it was there again, so I turned once more, and again it backed away. When it happened a third time, I watched.

I saw an older man get out of the car in filthy clothes too big for him. He walked around the car, opened and closed the trunk, and returned to the door. This was no answer, but I was uncomfortable staring. The rigmarole repeated itself several more times, each time at the limit of my peripheral vision, pricking my nerves. Until now I'd given no thought to this highway's reputation. The 450-mile stretch of lonely road between Prince Rupert and Prince George is often called the Highway of Tears. Since 1969 some forty people have disappeared along it. Most have been indigenous women, and many have vanished without a trace.

Finally the presence became so nerve-racking that I cast politeness aside and stopped to see the entire cycle: there was a woman in the passenger's seat who told the man when to stop; he would then back up, get out, scramble into the ditch, and emerge with soda and beer cans; he would open and close the trunk every time, perhaps not wanting to risk an open-container-law violation, and toss the cans in before moving on. To see such poverty moved me, especially the thought that this penny-wise scheme likely only impoverished the pair further as they drove endless miles along the endless road. When I spotted a beer can at my feet I bent for it, careful not to tumble, and winged it to their side of the road.

I QUIT WALKING JUST AFTER sunset, when I reached the north bank of the Skeena. The river was more than two miles wide where I camped, opposite the ghost town of Port Essington. Before the Grand Trunk Pacific Railway was built to Prince Rupert, in the years leading up to 1914, it was the most important town in this remote corner of British Columbia. Now Port Essington is a memory. That is what happens to towns that are never more than fishing or logging or mining camps. Yet their persistent aura casts a strong spell on those of us who gaze at old maps.

The Skeena, which flows down from the Sacred Headwaters on the remote Spatsizi Plateau in far northern British Columbia, is as mighty as any river. In its lower reaches it has the breadth and majesty of the Columbia, but it flows in too obscure a corner of the continent to have become widely known. It has a road—no interstate but a modest two-lane affair—on one side only, and its banks are effectively uninhabited. In all of British Columbia, the Skeena is second only to the Fraser River in length and ability to produce sockeye salmon. To the speakers of the Tsimshianic languages who inhabit its watershed, its name, whence ours is derived, means "water from the clouds."

There is not much room in the valley, if not for water. On the narrow strip of land between the precipitous mountainsides and the river, nearly all the free space is occupied by a thin ribbon of road and rail. I pitched my tent in a cottonwood grove a few feet from the railway. In the fifteen hours I was there, ten trains must have passed, many of them a mile long. I knew Prince Rupert was important. Canada's northernmost Pacific port is the deepest ice-free natural harbor in North America. I also knew that the powers that be wanted it to become even more important, so that other Pacific countries could more easily draw on interior Canada's embarrassment of riches. But I also knew that Prince Rupert was a small town on a small island. As the trains forged through the night making my tent shudder, I wondered how they could all fit there when they arrived, these mile-long chains of steel boxes. And how could they unload them as fast as needed? And how could they keep filling them and sending them west one after another? And why were there so few trains going the other way? All I could think was that there was too much happening, more than should happen. So it seemed to the mind of a tiny walker picking his way across the continental vastness. The long silences between trains restored order to the world until each new one came.

The next day I put one foot in front of the other as the weather around me worsened. My neck and shoulders were as sore as was to be expected, but by dark my knee had become so inflamed I couldn't bend it. I hobbled for hours, disheartened but not wanting to stop lest my leg seize up entirely.

There is a broad, straight stretch on the Skeena about halfway between Terrace and the mouth where the valley musters a mighty wind. I let my pack fall on a flat spot by the edge of the storm-battered water. I lay in my cold tent not ten yards from crashing waves. My map told me I had made only ten miles. The last five or six were made in a stiff limp, and I was seriously discouraged. I had experienced the same pain twice before, both times on long bicycle rides. I hoped it was only sore muscles and would pass with conditioning. But my knee hurt badly and I didn't know if I would be able to walk the next day. I was still fifty miles from Terrace and had little more than a day's food left.

The gusts around my tent beside the river must have reached seventy-five miles an hour in the night. In the morning I awoke unable to move my right leg. I lifted it with my arms and was surprised, never having lifted a leg, by how heavy it was. I lay still in my sleeping bag for two hours listening to the woody *clock-clock* of raven voices outside. My sleeping bag was a sophisticated piece of equipment, made especially for deep cold by a cottage manufacturer in New Hampshire, who was, ironically perhaps, a committed naturist. One of the bag's many distinctive features was the fact that it had two top flaps of unequal thicknesses, each with a vapor barrier designed to block sweat condensation from the invaluable goose-down insulation layer. Depending on the temperature, I could choose whether to use the thinner top, the thicker one, or both together.

While the wind and rain thrashed my tent, I faded in and out of damp childhood scenes of black rivers racing through the New Hampshire woods, and tried to make a decision. During the night, when it was easy to discount physical limitations, I had thought the best thing was to rest for a day and then see how my knee felt. But later I remembered that I was low on food and had a long road to Terrace. It was clear that at some point I would have to hitchhike. I decided for sooner rather than later and set about the chore of striking camp in the maelstrom. Then I swallowed my pride and at that roadside put out my thumb.

4

ADVANCE AND RETREAT

An hour of idleness in a warm car was enough to undermine any immunity I had built up to the cold. I stood outside the Greyhound station waiting for it to open so I could pick up the gear I had shipped. It was only a few degrees below freezing, but the wind lent bite to the chill. Driven snow lashed my heat-softened cheeks. Somewhere between where I had slept the night before and the town of Terrace, winter had taken hold in a way that gave no sign of letting go. My pack rested against a wall of cinder blocks. Others who had business at the station waited in the heat of their idling trucks and looked at me like I was insane.

Once the station opened I collected my equipment and asked the clerk to call a cab for me. In the meantime I asked him if he knew of a cheap motel in town.

"Cheap!" he chirped. "Not anymore. You'll be lucky to find a goddam room. With all the shit that's going on around here the hotels are always booked. And they've all jacked their prices up. Cheap! Good luck."

"Cheap motel" was about all the English my cab driver knew, but it was enough. He left me at the Cedars Motel, The Spirit of Northern Hospitality, run by a pleasant South Korean couple. I asked for one night, thinking it might become two. In my head was the voice of an old camping friend, who the night before I left the East Coast uncharacteristically gave me a piece of advice over the phone: "If you feel pain, any pain at all, stop and wait for it to pass. These things have a way of piling up." I only wished I could ask him now where the line stood between negligible discomfort and pain.

In my room sipping instant coffee, I felt sorry, even ashamed, for having compromised my resolve to walk every inch of the way. I told myself dangerous precedents were being set. When I talked to Elena on the phone, she said she felt reassured that I had made a wise decision. I was not convinced.

That night I took a hot bath with Epsom salts and swallowed ibuprofen tablets. I rubbed menthol on my knee and read a book by Velma Wallis that retells an ancient legend about two old Athabascan women who are left for dead by their community in the depths of winter. They survive by quietly applying hand-me-down knowledge. In the end, their freezing and starving evictors come to them, begging rescue from winter's ruthless assault. The old women know the risk they run but forgive and help them anyway.

In the morning I did logistical things about Terrace: mailed redundant supplies farther east; bought hard-plastic totes to stow food and gear in my sled; read my email at the public library; and in the motel bathroom melted wax into the bottoms of my skis and trimmed a pair of climbing skins to size. Climbing skins—so called because they were once made from sealskin—are strips of fabric that adhere to ski bases and, because of the backward orientation of the synthetic fur sewn into them, make it possible for skiers to slide forward but not backward. They are indispensable for skiing uphill and for pulling heavy loads.

Two nights in Terrace gave me sound sleep, but I had no rest by day. Ibuprofen had become a dietary staple, and I was stretching my legs wherever I had the room, attracting censorious looks in public spaces. My knee hardly felt improved, but I was more and more anxious and intimidated. I knew I was growing soft, that my subconscious mind was deploying sophisticated avoidance tactics. I needed to get moving.

WET SNOW WAS FALLING WHEN I called a taxi to take me out of town. The driver had bleached-blonde hair in a bowl cut. He must have been my age but looked like he had walked off the page of a surfing magazine from circa 1986.

As I filled his cab with my unwieldy traveling equipment, he stood by in his summer-weight duds, shoulders hunched in that irrational reflex to precipitation, and watched. He was friendly enough, more than happy to talk as we rolled out of town. Despite having lived in Terrace all his life, he knew almost nothing of the terrain beyond its downtown. The Copper River, my destination ten minutes up the highway, rang only the most muffled of bells—and that's if he wasn't bluffing.

It took patience to convey to him what I was up to. He had trouble wrapping his mind around some aspect of the journey. The idea of skiing tripped him up. "No, no, no!" I seem to remember lecturing, as wet snow splatted against the windshield, "not behind a motorboat. The kind where you slide over the snow." But he also stumbled on the geography involved. "You're right," I conceded, "the road *does* go to Smithers, but the distance is shorter over the mountains, where the road can't go."

"Did I see a gun in your stuff?" he asked at one point.

"Yes, you did," I said.

"Cool! What's that for?"

"Grizzlies, maybe."

"No way! Grizzly bears?"

"I hope they're sleeping now, but these mountains are full of them."

He stopped to think. "Seriously? Crazy! I guess they would be, wouldn't they? I never thought of that."

I saw where a logging road went into the bush, just south of where the Copper River met the Skeena. "Do you mind pulling in here?" I asked.

"No problem," he said.

He drove in fifty yards to a place wide enough to turn around in and stopped. "Here we are," I said. I paid the fare and we both got out. As he watched me unload my equipment he said, "Hey, this is like a movie or something. I mean, like, I might be the last guy that ever sees you."

"Thanks, buddy!"

"Oh, sorry. But, uh, just in case, what's your name?"

"Anders Morley."

"Andrew Swirly?"

"No, A-N-D . . . I mean, yes. Andrew Swirly works." I thanked him for the ride and took down his number in case I ever needed a lift back to Terrace.

When the cab driver was gone and the exhaust from his car had dissipated, to be replaced only by the steam of my breath, it was deathly quiet. The snow settled down so inaudibly it was deafening. I looked at my gear strewn on the white ground. I looked at the wall of forest and at the mountains behind mountains and mountains beyond that, all of it white. I sensed in my bones that there was a continent beyond those mountains, clenched in frost and covered over with crystals of snow that would sting. "What am I doing? I don't *want* to do this," I said into the silence. "Do you realize what you're getting yourself into?" I was suddenly aware that I had not considered this particular question before—that I never really, until now, could have. I had a towering premonition of the discomfort and pain that I knew must be my almost constant company for months to come.

But then I felt cold. I learned very quickly that living outside in the wintertime leaves no time for standing around thinking. Movement is the creed of the northern winter, and until movement generates fire, it must be ceaseless—so I briskly set about assembling the hauling system for my sled and loading my food and camping equipment. I had never pulled the sled before, I would have been embarrassed to admit. (I had read a book the year before by another snow traveler who made just this admission and thought, "What a rookie! Could you imagine such a thing!") I decided to try first without using skins for traction. I rubbed grip wax into my skis, slid into my harness, and pulled. But nothing happened. I thought of Buck, the invincible sled dog in the Jack London story, and tried again, but the suggestion did nothing to make my sled budge. There was no precedent for this in my skiing experience.

I dug out a pair of special half-length climbing skins, thinking they would be sufficient for the shallow grade ahead of me. I put them on the bottom of my skis and, as if the skis had only been teasing me before, I was off and running. My skis were designed by a small Norwegian company for long expeditions over varied backcountry terrain, which was exactly what I expected to encounter. They were 187 centimeters long, and their width went from 67 millimeters at the tip down to 57 millimeters at the waist and back up to 62 millimeters at the tail. In other words, they were shorter than ordinary cross-country skis and about as wide as alpine skis were when I grew up in the 1980s and 1990s. These dimensions gave them the right balance of maneuverability and stability for mixed conditions. They were moderately cambered, an important feature of ski design that gives users more or less spring each time they lift their feet, and also had a modest sidecut, the thinning at the waist typical of alpine skis, which makes the skis easier to control on downhill turns. Unlike most cross-country skis, my skis had metal edges, making them more responsive to aggressive footwork. Finally, two invisible slits in the bottom of each ski permitted me to attach the half-length skins I had just put on. These short climbing skins were a unique accessory—and a relatively new invention—that gave me some of the grip of full-length skins while leaving the skis more of their natural glide. The skis were mostly black but had a photograph of polar explorer Roald Amundsen as an old man transposed in red on each tip. It was a relief to be moving so much weight without feeling like I was being pushed into the ground by the sum of my belongings. There would be no more hustling back and forth to fetch a second or third load. It was still a hundred and forty pounds, but now at last I was skiing.

I was gloating over the breakthrough when I felt a sudden jerk from behind, as a dog on a short leash must feel when it tries to give chase. I turned and saw that my sled had capsized. I unclipped my harness and skied around to set it right-side up again. It flipped over ten more times that afternoon, spurring me to sling expletive after expletive into the unhearing wilderness in a decidedly uncharacteristic manner.

Between these fits of pique, however, I couldn't help but take pleasure in noticing that I was being engulfed by a canyon that rose higher and higher, following the steady course of the Copper River as it rushed down from its source. The unimproved road was not plowed. It had just enough snow cover to ski on, and it showed the long twin impress laid by the passing of a single truck. The misty river ran free of ice in the relative warmth of early winter. Wet snow clung to the boughs of spruce and cedar that stood straight up in defiance of the diagonal of the canyon wall. The road was cut and graded level into the slope, but the forest was huddled so thickly around it that the steepness of the surrounding land didn't give me any feeling of vertigo.

After four miles of climbing, when the sun was about to set, I slid into a clearing to pitch my tent. My knee had begun hurting again, and for the last mile I had propelled myself forward with an ungainly one-sided kick that reminded me of an ancient skiing technique I half remembered reading about that relied on one ski for pushing and one for gliding. That night I sat inside my tent with my feet on a folded tarp to keep them off the cold ground. I ate my dinner feeling distressed. I hoped against reason that the terrain between here and Telkwa, seventy miles to my east, would not become any rougher. My knee had done well as long as the grades were mild.

The thought of stray grizzlies out for a late-season binge before they knocked off for winter also made me uneasy. I laid my shotgun within reach, a cartridge nearby, and hoped that I would be able to get my wits about me if rudely awakened. Now that I was idle and warm in my tent the doubts I'd had at the trailhead resurfaced: *What was I doing here? The winter would be long. The winter would be cold. What exactly was I doing here?*

In the morning there was no question of discomfort. My knee was in unmistakable pain. I decided to stay put for the day. It was wet, and the snow sank into itself but did not melt. I felt bored and lonely. I limped half a mile up the canyon to find better exposure to the sky and put a satellite call through to Elena but got no answer. Back at the tent I decided I would spend another night in the same place. I took out my journal and made notes on my time in Terrace.

I decided to treat the day as a Sunday. I melted snow for drinking and cooking, then made an early dinner of rice and dahl, a spicy Indian lentil stew. I worried about running out of food if I had to go through Telkwa Pass more slowly than planned. I hoped my knee would somehow be better the following day. I felt assailed by doubt already, so early in a journey that was supposed to last for months. I tried to reason with myself, to parse the situation by thinking out loud—which only showed me that much more than my knee was at stake: "The reason I called Elena was that I wanted to hear someone else's opinion," I wrote in my journal that evening. "But I also called because I am lonely and wanted to hear a human voice. I miss Elena. I don't know if it's because she's my wife and I love her and therefore miss her, or if it's because I am lonely and she is the closest person to me, and so it's natural to miss her."

After dinner I had a cup of tea. The teabag was one of those that had a little pearl of wisdom printed on the dipping tab, like a fortune cookie: "Those who are in tune with the unknown find peace in the known." What did it mean to be in tune with the unknown? I stuffed it into my odor-proof plastic garbage bag.

THE NEXT DAY I MANAGED to talk to Elena and to my brother Matthew, who is known in my family for his level-headedness. They convinced me that the only thing was to return to Terrace and wait until my knee felt better. My main worry was the expense, but they put it into perspective: I might be out a few hundred dollars, but the alternative was being forced to quit and the tremendous sense of waste that would follow.

Skiing back down the valley, I met a man in a truck crawling slowly uphill. He was a driller for a gas company and very affable. He looked strong and had the rugged face of a prairie-bred Scandinavian. "Where ya' comin' out of?" he asked.

"I'd planned to ski through to Telkwa," I said, "but I'm going back to town for a while because I hurt my knee. I hope to pick up again in a few days."

The man said he was a snowmobiler and that friends of his had reported six feet of snow on the other side of Telkwa Pass. I wasn't sure whether this was good news or bad. It would depend on the snow. But I wasn't going to let it worry me now. It could be a different world by the time I got there.

When the driller was about to drive on, he narrowed his eyes and stared at the toque on my head. It was a ratty woolen ski cap I had worn on every trip I'd made in the last fifteen years. I was deeply attached to it and considered it a talisman. It was decorated with a thin band of Norwegian flags. I couldn't remember, but I may even have bought it on a trip to Norway. I have a mild anarchist streak and don't like flags, but I made an exception for this cap, which I wore as a quiet tribute to the great nation of ski tourers.

The driller said, "You're lucky I'm even talkin' to you with that Norwegian hat on. I'm Sveedish. We got no use for you guys." He drove off before I had time to tell him, for what it was worth, that my ancestors came from Britain.

A mile from the main road the snow that had covered the trail two days before had all but disappeared. I strapped my skis to my sled and pulled it over what traces of snow remained on the side, walking on the gravel road like a mule on a towpath obliquely hauling a barge. My knee gave me no trouble any of this time, and it was hard not to turn around and head back into the mountains. When I reached the asphalt road I turned to see the driller in his truck rolling down out of the bush. I hobbled over to ask for a lift to town. There was plenty of room in the bed of the truck.

"You can put your stuff in the back, sure," he said. "But as for you, you'll have to run along behind and bark like a Norwegian."

5

TERRACE

Ensconced once more at the Cedars Motel, I got to know the owner, Jun Chu, who had moved north from Vancouver ten years before. He marveled at what I proposed to do. During my days there, he would often accost me in the hallway, or even call my room, and after a ceremonious preface ask me about some particular of my plans. Jun was a recreational skier. "Cross-country ski help me survive long winter here. If I no cross-country ski, I stay inside, I get . . . I don't remember word."

"Cabin fever?"

"Yes, yes," he said nodding energetically. "Cabin fever! That's da word."

Jun carefully photographed all my equipment, so he could show it to his friends at the ski club. He solicited explanations of why I had chosen each component of my kit and how it all worked. His enthusiasm was such that he insisted on giving me fifty dollars. "I wanta suppawt you. I wanta help. Only thing I know is make money contribution." He took the cash out of the register—where it would return a few days later.

One evening I walked in from the cold and stopped to talk with him for a few minutes. When afterward I went upstairs and heard the phone ringing inside my room, I hurried to open the door and answer.

"Anders?" said a man's voice on the phone.

"Yes."

"It's Jun."

"Hi, Jun. What's up?"

"I notice you have little bit saw troat. You want me turn up temperature?"

IN TERRACE I THOUGHT A lot about what I was carrying and concluded that purging was in order. The snowshoes, although they gave backwoods flare to the load on my sled, would go. So would most spare clothing. Books that I judged anything but indispensable would be given away. Rain gear was no longer necessary: in all likelihood liquid water would from now on be found only in my cooking pot.

The one thing I doubted was my shotgun. If I could get rid of the gun and ammunition it would mean ten pounds less to drag across the country. I wasn't sure how to do it legally, so I walked to the nearby Royal Canadian Mounted Police headquarters to ask. Thinking I'd have no time to pursue other outlets, I said to the officer on duty, "Can I just give it to you?"

"Sure you could. But we would destroy it."

"Destroy it? Is that just a way of saying it would be irretrievable?"

"No. We would quite literally take a hacksaw and cut it up into little pieces."

I grimaced. "That seems like a shame. It's a pretty nice gun."

"I agree, but that's the law. If I were you I'd put an ad in the buy-sell section of the paper. If no one buys it, you can always bring it back here."

"And can I sell it to anyone without filling out any special paperwork?" I asked.

"Sure thing, as long as they've got a possession and acquisition license."

I thanked the Mountie and went outside. I didn't think I'd have time to sell the gun through the newspaper, but on my way to the library, where I would look into the matter, I noticed a hunting and angling shop. I went in and asked the man at the counter if he was interested in buying a single-shot twelve-gauge.

"I might be. Why don't you bring it by?"

An hour later I was back. I laid the gun on the counter.

"I'll tell you what," I said after explaining myself. "As far as I'm concerned you can have the thing. I just want to find a home for it."

"No, no," he said. "It's a good gun. But to be honest there's not much demand for a single-shot breechloader anymore."

"Then just give me a few bucks for it," I said.

He turned it over and held it slightly farther away. "I'll give you thirty bucks."

He handed me the money, and I gave him the box of slugs.

After the transaction he said, "So are you looking to kill yourself? That's some lonely country you're going into, and it's damn cold. I mean cold. You know what cold is? You ever feel fifty below? I have. And I use a wall tent and a woodstove. It's still cold."

I had never felt fifty below. The coldest I clearly remembered was twenty-five below, unless you were the sort of person who took into account "wind-chill factor." And I am not. "I think I'm prepared," I said, trying for a properly modest tone. But there's no getting around the hubris inherent in a winter journey.

"Look," the man said, "do what you want. But if I were you, I'd call it off. Come back in the summer. I'll take you fishing."

I talked to him for two hours. When he'd accepted that my intentions were quite serious, he was ready with advice. He made calls all over the north of the province to ask after conditions of logging roads, lake ice, and bush trails. We examined maps of the immense area between Babine Lake and the Rocky Mountain Trench. He persuaded me that I would probably wind up dead if I followed my planned route carrying only two weeks' worth of food, and he was good enough to propose several alternatives. I asked him to talk slowly and took notes so that I could mark my own maps back in my room.

"Should I be worried about grizzlies?" I asked him candidly. "Will they be asleep yet?"

"Grizzlies aren't true hibernators," he said. "Closest run-in I ever had with one was in January. Just give 'em a wide berth and be careful around clear-cuts. That's where they like to look for food."

"Should I have kept my gun?"

"No," he said. "Around here we've been finding lately that gunshots at this time of year attract bears better than they keep them away. The grizzlies have learned that gunfire means a shot moose—which to them spells free food. So it becomes a race between the hunter and the grizzly to see who can get to the kill first. When they hear a gunshot, that's the dinner bell. I wouldn't worry too much about grizzlies. If there's an animal you need to be concerned about, it's wolverines."

"I thought they were elusive," I said.

"You see them out there. They mostly keep their distance, unless you got something they want. Mean sons-a-bitches. And persistent too. I once lost a whole night's sleep defending my food from a wolverine outside my tent."

"How'd you do that?"

"I had a metal rake, and I kept whacking it at him all night long."

"A rake?"

"Yep, a rake."

I didn't think to ask what he was doing in the middle of the northern British Columbia wilderness with a rake.

WHEN I LEFT THE OUTFITTER'S shop, the man's face seemed to wonder whether I'd ever be seen alive again once I skied into the woods. My knee continued to be a source of anxiety. I bought a pair of sneakers for three dollars from the Salvation Army thrift store, thinking that they were better for walking in town than my heavy ski boots. I kept up my regimen of ibuprofen, baths in salt water, and knee exercises I'd gleaned from library books. But really I wished I had a voice of authority, someone knowing, who had seen my leg.

I went to a clinic, where I had been told over the phone to ask for a Doctor Lennox Brown. In the examination room I told Dr. Brown my story and my symptoms, and he had me pull up my trouser cuff so he could examine the knee. "I can't see what's happening inside," he said. "From what you've told me, however, it sounds like what you're doing is the best course of action. We could order an X-ray, but it would have to be sent south to a specialist for interpretation, and the costs would start adding up. It would take time." He sighed and said, "The life of a doctor in the north."

He had an accent, and I asked what part of Scotland he was from, adding that I had spent a couple of years there as a student. That seemed to engage him slightly. He told me to rest for as many days as I could afford and keep taking ibuprofen. I realized that was all anyone could tell me. I thanked him and went out to pay my bill. As the secretary was putting my particulars into the computer, the doctor told his next patient to wait a minute and leaned into the office.

"Do you have insurance, young man?" he said. "I seem to remember you mentioning you don't live in Canada."

"No, I don't. I was just going to pay in cash."

He turned to the secretary. "This young man studied in Edinburgh. There'll be no charge for him."

After ten days in Terrace, during which it snowed almost without interruption, I was ready to move. Disjointed dreams of exertion brought painful sensations to my knee that were so sharp and sustained they jolted me awake. Yet each time I woke up, I could move my leg freely and felt not even a trace of discomfort. Whatever they meant, my psyche was obviously playing tricks on me.

"How you doing?" said Jun when I walked in one evening from the spin-driven snow.

"I feel good, Jun. What are you doing the day after tomorrow? Can you drive me to the Copper River?"

"Oh-h-h-h!" he responded, in long, guttural reverence. He was fighting the urge to bow. "You betcha!"

PART TWO

TERRACE TO FORT SAINT JAMES

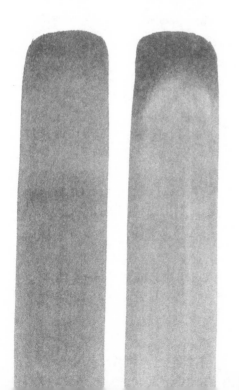

6

FINALLY SKIING

Jun Chu gripped the steering wheel. Sweat beaded along his hairline. He smiled nervously and looked around at the trees and snow. They were a pretty stage curtain hiding a forbidding winter wilderness he would probably never know. "You can leave me here," I said. "You don't have to drive me up the road. A kilometer or two isn't going to make much difference."

But Jun insisted on taking me as far up the Copper River logging road, covered in six inches of new snow, as his old blue Isuzu Trooper would go. "I wanna suppawt you as much I can," he said again.

A mile in, the road roughened. There was a loop of tracks from a truck that had turned around, so I suggested Jun stop and follow them home. We got out, and Jun opened the hatch. Unlike the cab driver of ten days before, he was eager to help. While I pieced metal fittings together and deftly shifted weight around in the sled, taking care to keep snow out of my containers, he looked on in wonder. "This gonna be lotta wok," he said.

"Yes," I granted. "A lot of work."

We shook hands awkwardly. I took a mental impression of Jun in khaki pants, a creamy orange merino sweater, and winter boots. When I had skied a hundred feet, I turned to make sure his truck was moving along and watched him disappear around a bend. It was midday. The conditions for travel on skis were almost perfect. A few inches of fresh snow covered a base lightly compacted by a few trucks and snowmobiles. I swished along easily.

Dark was looming when I had gone twelve miles. I found an adequate site to pitch my tent and settled into supper and a book. Most of my suppers were food I had cooked and dehydrated myself, but into each supply drop I stuck two or three freeze-dried meals that I had persuaded a camp-food manufacturer to donate to my expedition. My plan was to save these tastier suppers for moments when I needed encouragement or had cause to celebrate. The day had been a success. My knee had made no trouble. I ate freeze-dried lasagna.

I moved at a respectable hour the next morning. I went slowly up the long valley following the side of the river. I saw no one and heard only the sounds of my slipping skis, the rippling river, and the occasional plop of snow sloughing from the short boughs of the tall spruce trees. Low forested mountains flanked the valley. In the afternoon I saw two dedicated fishermen who had driven as far as their truck would take them and then marched through the snow in their waders to a secret spot on the Copper River. The road had effectively ended where their truck stopped. No wheels would overtake me now.

I skied a few hours into the night but covered less than sixteen miles. The grade steepened after dark. A sense of vertigo brought on by the shadowless night and the still unfamiliar feeling of a weight trying to pull me backward made the going hard. The trail was less compacted now too; only a few snowmobiles had left their mark. Near the top of a steep section a sharp pain exploded from my knee and raced up my leg. Then it was gone. I decided to make camp.

Lying in my sleeping bag I thought about my increasing distance from other humans. The mountains were getting bigger. The next day, I expected, I would be flanked by glaciers. Before sleeping I wrote in my journal that I hoped to come through the pass before making camp again. During the night a pang, identical to the one I had felt earlier, woke me up. It almost brought on tears—not the pain but the thought that it could spell an end to my journey. It passed this time too, though, and two weeks would go by before I felt anything more.

I woke and got dressed. I had decided before setting off on my journey that I would always sleep naked. It was a way of keeping myself from sweating at night, and moisture from sweat is the chief enemy of anyone traveling for more than a day or two in winter weather, because it adds weight, diminishes the insulation value of clothing, and turns to ice when allowed to cool. Once ice has formed in fabric there's no way of getting rid of it. The trick to sleeping without clothes on was to wait until I had reached a comfortable temperature before allowing myself to drift off. That way I wouldn't wake up cold and, indulging the weakness of the midnight mind, put so much extra clothing on that I would wake up sweating half an hour later. Sleeping naked, however, brought with it a morning ritual of fumbling in my sleeping bag to find the clothes I'd peeled off the night before, and then trying to slither back into them without letting too much cold air into the sleeping bag. Once a base layer was on, I slid out of the bag as fast as I could and pulled on the rest of my clothes. On this morning I breakfasted on granola.

Before breaking camp I collected snow data. It was something I did in the early days, because I wanted to understand something concrete about this season and about the medium I was moving over. At my tent site that morning, on a north-facing slope between two and three thousand feet above sea level, the snow was still only nine inches deep. It had a surface temperature of 39°F, and at the ground-surface interface, where the soil was stiff mud, the temperature was 32°F. It was December 8, 2012, my third day on the trail to Telkwa Pass.

Striking camp is the bane of winter travel. You want nothing more than to move, because it's the coldest time of day, but you can't yet. I often whiled away the sheer boredom of the task by speculating that it was the hassle of breaking camp that ultimately made our hunter-gatherer ancestors abandon the wandering life, plant seeds, and trade tents for houses. The worst part of breaking camp, for a winter wanderer, is every day seeing more and more condensation getting folded into the tent that you've worked so hard to keep dry.

Once I was back on the trail the climbing started immediately. This meant whole miles of sapping herringbone steps. Climbing in herringbone steps is usually a last resort for skiers, a tiring and awkward technique for going over short stretches of terrain that are too steep to skin up. But with a heavy sled at my back, I sometimes had to advance this way for an hour at a time. This time, it was early in the day so I relished the effort. The landscapes were stunning. I knew I was the only human on all the land I could see. The mountains were beginning to look like real peaks, masses of rock and ice that soared above tree line. Unimaginably tall yellow cedars, also called Nootka cedars, towered around me, their lime-green sprays of needles glowing as brightly as the snow. The trees were laden with snow but seemed calm and at rest. The sun striking them made a kaleidoscope of glinting colors.

During a cruising descent after a three-mile climb my mind eclipsed itself so that it was nowhere else. The uphill struggle had so absorbed my mental energy, drawn me so deeply into the weave of the winter world, that I was in a state of pure perception. The intensity had begun as pain but, without lessening, had morphed into pleasure. A flock of pine grosbeaks came in over my left shoulder and started making noise. I kept an eye on them as I slid effortlessly downhill, and in a minute it occurred to me that they were dressed the same as I was: red heads and breasts, black beaks, black and white wings, and spindly black legs. They flitted from tree to tree beside me, as if stepping down the hillside to keep me company. It would have been no great leap to believe I was picking up odd words among their piping, the way one does in a language one has studied only a little.

On the higher sides of the valley were massive clear-cuts, of a size and steepness you could never really quite believe unless you have been in British Columbia. The patches were cut from the sheer flanks of mountains and were not contiguous with lower cuts. It was hard to imagine how it could be worth the cost and effort required to take timber out of such inaccessible places.

The climb into Telkwa Pass really begins thirty-three miles up the road from the mouth of the Copper River. Here the last of the snowmobiles had turned toward home. I would be the first, and probably the last, traveler until the snow melted in April. This was wilderness. I made my own tracks now.

I came almost immediately to a fork in the trail. My map showed a single dotted line through Telkwa Pass, but the local diversions one always encounters when following bigger trails were not shown. A steep-sided notch ahead, the only likely way through these mountains, had been visible for a few miles, and I was sure both trails led there eventually. I chose the branch on the right, which started steep, reckoning it best to face the worst right away. The sun had set now too. It would be another night of skiing in the dark.

The next hours were spent tracking up a rugged ascent that seemed endless. From above, Cassiopeia's bright stars urged me onward through the dark. The profile of the enormous face on the south side of Telkwa Pass was a shadow, my only land reference. My skis made a pleasing *swish-swish* as they shuffled through sugar-like ice granules. It was cold after dark at three thousand feet, so I wore my jacket, with its ruffed hood over my head. I didn't wear my headlamp, even though there was no moon. An eerie white blaze through the bush was guide enough.

The night culminated in the steepest and longest climb, which brought on hallucinations of bobbing calories: visions of flying licorice Allsorts danced unreachably in my imagination. I'd been proceeding in spurts of thirty herringbone steps, after each of which I would stop to breathe. These spurts were now reduced to six or ten steps, with longer breaks between. The last rise took me an hour to climb. I thought I could see the top, and then over a shallow hump, more hill. Finally it leveled out, and I stopped then and there, lest another rise dare me on. I rifled my food box for a frozen-solid energy bar and devoured it as fast as my cold-stunned jaw would allow. Then I set about pitching the tent, unloading the sled, and boiling water I had got by breaking the ice on a stream earlier in the day—the last liquid water available for some time. I drank hot powdered lemonade while sitting in my tent and waiting for supper to cook. Afterward I sipped hot chocolate from my thermos, inaugurating a nightly tradition. Sitting in the pitch black sipping, I contemplated the probability that there were no humans but me for thirty miles in every direction. The country felt wild.

It had been my first day of hard travel. My brothers Dave and Jon and I had once paddled a canoe nearly eighty miles in a single day. We started early and finished hours after dark on a summer night. Exhaustion brought us close to a three-way fistfight. It had gone beyond the possibility of alliances, every man for himself. But today surpassed that. On my reckoning, I skied only twelve or thirteen miles, although they were uphill and in deep, unbroken snow, with 120 pounds pulling backward and my legs still not in shape for skiing.

Yet the day was easy compared to those that followed. The trail ran higher and the snow got deeper. As the approach steepened and it became more difficult to pull the sled, it occurred to me eventually that I should switch out my half-length climbing skins for full-length ones. They would provide better traction. The changeover gave me the same sense of relief as when I had put the half-skins on at the outset.

The peaks of the Howson Range, jutting skyward to the south, were daunting. Sometimes they were horrifying. They were massive, steep rocks. I had climbed higher mountains, but under much different circumstances. Mountains, when they are big enough, make their own weather, which here was a ravaging din of wind and flying snow. I skied first past Preterition Peak, then past Redemption Peak. I wondered what had gone through the head of the trembling Calvinist who named them.

Once I entered Telkwa Pass, which is laced across with a chain of small lakes, I had to traverse a row of talus slopes that angled like buttresses where the mountains met the narrow valley floor. I had to cross one slope up high, because alders had smothered the trail below. I proceeded nervously across what I knew might be a twitchy snowfield: alone, and with an anchor tied to my waist, my chances against an avalanche were hopeless.

Suddenly the white side of Redemption Peak peeled away in front of me, and a boom hit my ears. Powder billowed out from the steep slope of the 8500-foot mountain. It exploded hundreds of feet into the sky, as if a buried charge had been set off. I stopped in my tracks, knowing I would have to cross the path of the avalanche in minutes. Turning around, my only other option, would mean going back across a slope that hadn't let go—that for all I knew could spring, like a trap, the moment my ski grazed it. At least the one ahead had already discharged. The sun was going down, and this was certainly no place to sleep. I snaked my way cautiously but with all the confidence I could muster over the tortured drifts that drowned the summertime trail to the pass. Sometimes the drifts had sharp sides that dropped five feet, suddenly, like an ocean wave stacking. But my sled tracked beautifully and would swoop down them behind me in a graceful collapse, like a duck landing on water. The sense that every facet of my environment was working together gave me enough peace of mind to move along with calm focus. Still, I made a mad dash when I reached the densely piled snow of the avalanche path, and came to the other side safely.

When darkness fell—before four o'clock in early December—there was no suitable place to camp. I realized now, too, that whatever trail lay ahead was obliterated by the avalanche fallout. I suspected it lay across a small river that was still running, but I had no strength to test my theory so late in the day. When snow moved in from the west, I decided to stop where I was. It was a fraught place, only feet from the base of a steep slope that held back the weight of a snowfield a thousand yards long—another avalanche in the making. Above, white storms shrieked around the peaks, like a baleful orchestra warming up to score the nightmares stalking my enfeebled consciousness. For the first time I was afraid, but I had little strength left to counter the fear, and I knew it would be a pointless waste of energy anyway. I know I ate, only because I always do, and then I crawled into my tent, resigned to the possibility that I might never wake up, except for a split-second flash of blunt trauma, or maybe suffocation. I was serene. I only thought of Elena and Beowulf, whom we loved as much as any child. I clung to them inside my sleeping bag, knowing I had no way of escaping whatever happened, and drifted off.

THE NEXT DAY WAS MY thirty-fourth birthday. It became the most miserable day I had lived through until then. A few minutes of reconnaissance in the morning persuaded me that I'd been right, that my trail was on the other side of the river. The river looked no deeper than my thighs, so I decided to strip below the waist and carry my equipment across. I dismantled my sled kit and ferried across four or five loads, careful not to lose my footing in the current, and tossed skis, sled, boxes, boots, socks, pants, underwear, and duffel bag onto the high bank of snow on the far side. Then I climbed up through the deep snow, which squeezed between my toes, and sat in the sled. I lay back, kicked my legs in the air, and rubbed them briskly with my hands. I wanted my skin to be completely dry before I dressed again. Once I'd run my fingers between all my toes, hunting out the last pockets of moisture, I carefully put my clothes back on, reassembled my kit, and started skiing east. The trail picked its way through a thicket of water-loving alders and was buried beneath four feet of heavy snow. Rain began to fall.

The route wandered to the north side of the narrow valley and started climbing again. My ascent through rain-soaked snow was even slower now than the slog of the preceding days, because the snow clung to my skins in thickening clods, so each ski weighed five pounds, then ten, then fifteen. I took one step up, then leaned forward to pull the sled up behind me. I took another step up, then leaned forward to pull the sled up behind me. Every two or three such steps, the sled would capsize, and I would scream at it that it was a good-for-nothing son of a bitch that should never have been born. This had no effect, so I would take off my harness and sidestep carefully down the slope, turn the sled upright, and make sure the load was still tight. I would climb back up the slope, holding the sled to keep it from backsliding, and wiggle back into my harness to carry on. Then I would take another step up, then lean forward to pull the sled up behind me. A minute later it would happen again—and again and again, for an entire hell of a day. I had no trouble believing my map when it told me in my tent that night that I had gone less than two miles.

While early winter days in the mountains of northwestern British Columbia can be rainy, nights freeze. Apart from my boots—whose dryness I always fanatically ensured by applying regular coats of mink oil—every inch of me and my clothing was soaked through. Arms and legs and teeth and hands rattled wildly as I tried to write in my journal that night.

The next morning my castoff clothes were frozen solid in freakish shapes—I had to break them down to get dressed. The climb outside my tent that day was what had determined my resting place the night before, and I was in no hurry to face it. So I took my time over a breakfast of granola, dried fruit, and coffee—a belated birthday present to myself. The rise might have looked like nothing to someone who had simply appeared there, but it was so steep I had to take off my harness, attack the trail in sidesteps an inch or two apart, and draw the sled up by its straps in a tug of war against gravity and collapsing snow. Each pull, equal to about six inches of progress, required its own rest afterward. When I was halfway up, I sensed motion from the corner of my eye, and turned to see a fisher leaping across the hillside, twenty feet away, unfazed by my presence. I envied it its lightness on the snow. When I had made the hundred yards to the top of the rise, half my day was gone.

7

OVER THE MOUNTAINS

From the look of the sky through the trees I thought there was a lake to my south. If my hunch was right I was approaching the high stretch of land between the Bulkley River and the lower Skeena River watersheds. When the trail flattened out it crossed a broad swath cut to take powerlines over the mountains. There were no trees to delineate the trail anymore, and it disappeared. The powerline swath, which I might otherwise have followed, went northeast over impassably craggy terrain. So I unhitched my sled and went searching for my onward course.

The tops of young trees poking above the surface of the snow gave me the idea that the snow was eight or nine feet deep, and it sometimes sloughed down into pockets among the branches if I cut too close to them. Skiing for a few minutes without my sled brought a feeling of sprightliness, reminding me of the fisher. I slipped along the swath to a rise with a long view westward, so I could check the land against my map. I took off my skis and climbed a transmission tower for a better view. I could see that Top Lake, the last lake in the series striding the pass, was behind me. It meant I was on the height of land, but it was as though the trail had dead-ended.

By skiing east along the south side of the swath, I figured I had to hit the opening of the trail at some point. Clutching this invincible nugget of logic, I darted along the edge of the clearing, still fisher-like, for ten minutes. It started snowing in lush, unearthly flakes. The silence imbued peace into every shimmering molecule of the hermit universe surrounding me. Amid the hush, suddenly a soundless puff of snow burst at my feet. My heart leapt, startled by the bursting thing. There was something whiter than the enveloping whiteness levitating higher and higher.

The rise morphed into flight. It took me longer than it should have to register what it was, and the ptarmigan made for an opening in the trees as if to show me that the path was there. The bird blended back into the white and was gone. I retrieved my sled, seemingly weightless now, as if I were a ghost transiting the solid world. I pictured myself as the subject of a Chagall painting, an Old World skier floating upward to chase a ptarmigan across the white sky, and felt almost at home in the snow. In minutes I was beyond the pass.

REVERSALS COME SWIFTLY IN THE winter wilds. For the first few minutes east of the pass I was ecstatic. The sun came out as if to announce that I was beyond the reach of the gray Pacific. The snow was deeper now and waved out in oceanic drifts, some at least twelve feet deep. I took a new series of sled turnovers in stride and thought only on the bright side, cheerfully switching out my short climbing skins again when I found that the longer ones were the only way I had any purchase in the thigh-deep fluff.

But as the sun sank below the high ridge at my back I came to the edge of a brook set down in a gully. It wasn't good for my spirits. Unloading and reloading the tightly packed sled was tedious, cold, and never welcome work. Getting across the deep trench with a few feet of fast water flowing down its middle posed a concrete challenge. I poked around and discovered where a tree had fallen without being uprooted, so that it hung slantwise halfway across the gap. If I could climb far enough up it, I could manage to jump to the other bank. First I took small loads of gear up the trunk and tossed them to the far side, where they landed in the soft snow. Then I made the leap. On the other side, however, I found the trail was gone. I stood face to face with a wall of dense wood. Discouragement washed over me, drowning the high feeling of a few minutes before. But I knew there had to be a trail somewhere on this side of the brook. I had seen proof only moments before that a trail this far from the world doesn't just run out: it leads somewhere. Out of the food box I grabbed a snack for energy and to lift my mood, then abandoned my sled again to explore on my skis what lay ahead.

It wasn't heartening. I squeezed into a thick tangle of alder and hemlock. The maturing hemlock trees, some as thick as my arm, said that someone had been this way, but perhaps not in decades. Hemlocks grow slowly, especially here, at the extreme eastern limit of their range, which is seldom more than sixty miles inland. The snow was still deep and lay in monstrous drifts riddled with small tree wells. I wove my way through, and after half an hour broke out on the other side, where something like a trail reappeared. I felt mild comfort to see a faded piece of flagging tape on a branch.

I now realized I would have to bring my sled through this maze. The thought reduced me to tears on the spot. It seemed stupid to waste energy trying to fight the tears, so I decided to start skiing back and let myself keep crying. Schlepping along in regular steps, I became conscious of the rhythm of my breathing. Then I slowed it down and steadied it, bringing it into time with my feet, and this eventually brought the tears under control too.

I skied the half hour back to the stream, loaded half my gear onto the sled—a full load was too bulky to slither through the narrow gaps between trees—and started through. With a half load the sled performed miracles, snaking along behind me like a bobsled, skimming over drifts. Ecstasy came back, and soon I was shouting maniacally. I professed my undying admiration for the man who had designed and built my sled in a far-off Minnesota garage, recompense for the flood of curses I had called upon his unknowing head over the preceding days. When I came to a point where I could find no gap between trees wide enough to pass through, I teetered on the verge of another breakdown, but my better half won out and I took out my hatchet and felled a thick tree. The adrenaline blitzing through my system made it like slicing through butter.

Once I'd brought my duffel bag through I returned for the food box and whatever else remained. By the time I was done it was pitch dark. I still wasn't convinced I was on a trail again, and the doubt was unsettling. I knew it wouldn't let me rest, so I decided to push into the night, following an opening in the trees that I hoped would keep opening upon itself for miles and miles.

The opening led straight and clear for perhaps an hour. I came to a place, though, where it seemed to branch, with one part bending left and the other running straight. I investigated the bend first. It ended, after a few minutes of skiing, in a racing stream sunk in banks of snow. I went back to check the other trail that had appeared to continue straight ahead, but it vanished also in an army of full-grown trees.

I went back to the stream and carefully scanned the other side. I saw a break in the trees around a bend that looked vaguely promising. A frail ice bridge that looked like it might hold a house cat extended across the stream upriver. I was desperate, and the brook could not have been very deep, so I decided to risk crossing without dismantling my kit.

The ice held, and the gap I had seen was a trail, unmistakably. It began with a steep climb that required herringbone steps, even with my long skins on, but eventually I was back on a wide trail that defined itself clearly against the bush, like the one I had been following the days before. Soon the trail intersected an even larger one, which was so broad and straight I knew it had to be a logging road, although it lay under feet of snow and would obviously not be used this winter. I looked around and found one of the numbered posts that mark every kilometer along bush roads, so that trucks using them can call their locations into the radio and drive more attentively when they know other vehicles are nearby. Finding this confirmation made me shout with excitement. By looking to the North Star I could see that this section of road ran north to south. I wanted to go east, so I wasn't sure which way to choose. By some midnight reasoning I chose south, and soon I came to a descending kilometer board. I was heading toward the beginning of the road—and closer to civilization again.

The stretch was covered in unbroken snow that lay deep on the wide open trail. It seemed unending. I repeatedly lost awareness of what I was doing, as if I had fallen asleep shuffling heavily along. I remembered that at a certain point in my early twenties I had concluded once and for all that staying up until dawn was never worthwhile. I now argued back with myself that at least once on this journey I had to ski through an entire night, and that already I had hours invested in this one. For the first half of the night the stars were out brightly—Cassiopeia and the Big Dipper at first, Orion making his appearance a little later. But then clouds washed the stars out of the sky, and I felt genuinely lonely.

Not much later, though, animal tracks converged on the trail and marched in file down the middle. There were weasels, wolves, a bear, and following the trail for mile after mile were the tracks of a single caribou. At first I thought it was a moose with a deformed hoof, but then, remembering there was a caribou herd that lived on the east side of Telkwa Pass, I understood why the form of the track was rounder than a moose's, resembling a horseshoe with a gap in front, and why there were drag marks between the hoofprints. Unless snow is exceptionally deep, long-legged moose don't usually drag their hooves.

I was excited to encounter this trace of the Telkwa caribou herd, which is a tiny vestige of the vast herds of northern woodland caribou that once ranged all over the mountains surrounding the Bulkley Valley. In the middle of the twentieth century, when helicopters were brought into the area for forestry and mining exploration, the range of hunters expanded drastically. The herd was nearly wiped out by 1966. Snow compaction on roads by backcountry motor vehicles also made hunting easier for natural predators, especially wolves. A ban on hunting the caribou in 1973 led to a partial recovery of the population, but by the early '80s the local herd teetered on the verge of extinction. Therefore females and one male were brought in from another herd. The Telkwa caribou still exist, but they're gravely at risk. I was lucky to cross paths with one of their number.

After several long hours and about six miles on the road I came to a junction and saw snowmobile tracks. The dawn gloaming tinged the sky. My mind had all but quit functioning. Basic reasoning powers had long since gone to bed. My legs would probably have kept scissoring along, if central command had ordered them to, but I couldn't begin to work out which way was which—and then which of those whiches was the direction I wanted. So I stopped.

As soon as I ceased moving I felt the gnashing cold. When I bent to begin making camp I realized that all the soft fabrics encasing my body were hard as rock. The zippers on my clothes and duffel were intractable without brisk rubbing. With the most intense stinging pain I'd felt yet—the pain of cold air biting nerves—I got my tent up and crawled in. I lit the camp stove to melt snow for water, then to save time downed one of my special freeze-dried meals and slid into my sleeping bag for as much rest as my body would take. The dawn was cold and I woke up shivering. I pulled the outside layer of my double-layer sleeping bag over me and was soon warm enough to drift off again.

8

LIGHTS IN THE FOREST

I don't know what woke me first, the bright sun striking the red and yellow walls of my tent or the distant whine of snowmobiles. I hurriedly pulled some clothes on in case any of the approaching riders came calling. A minute later a swarm of them tore past either side of my tent. None stopped.

Outside the air was limpid and stinging cold. Packing up my ice-stiffened tent was a miserable task. I was still dazed from sleep and thoroughly disoriented. The sun wasn't far off the horizon, and the thought that sunset was approaching distressed me.

After a few minutes of skiing in the direction the snowmobiles had come from, clarity seeped into my mind again. I took out my compass and discovered that I'd been wrong: the sun was in fact above the eastern horizon. By dumb luck I had chosen the right direction, and it was still morning. I had probably slept for less than an hour. The prospect that I might make it to a place inhabited by people before my next sleep put vigor in my kicks.

The terrain east of the pass was more pleasing, or maybe I just welcomed the change of scene. The land was gentler. It spread out before me under a cozy blanket of snow and evergreen trees. The trees were smaller and gave the land a sense of horizontal extension, so that it appeared as a rippled plain tilting away toward the invisible Bulkley River. The green of the trees was lighter; there were lodgepole pines in the mixture, which I couldn't remember seeing among the spruce, fir, cedar, and hemlock west of the pass.

Five and a half miles from that morning's camp I came to a spot where the snowmobilers had left four or five trucks. It meant I could count on finding fast, compacted snow for the rest of the day. A signpost told me I was at kilometer 20 on the logging road, which meant I had 12 miles to go until I reached the outermost municipal road of the village of Telkwa, where I might begin to meet more vehicles. From there it would be only a few miles to the village center.

Later that afternoon the first of the homebound snowmobilers stopped his truck to talk.

"What are you doing out here?" he said.

"I'm skiing across Canada."

"If you're not a good skier already," he said, "you sure will be when you're done, eh?"

"That or I'll never want to see a pair of skis again," I said. I'd had moments already when the thought crossed my mind. Now I remembered a story my father used to tell us of a young Austrian ski racer named Toni Matt who in a 1939 ski race called the American Inferno sped down the side of Mount Washington in six and a half minutes. He is estimated to have touched ninety miles an hour on his schuss of Tuckerman Ravine's legendary Headwall. Matt had so terrified himself, my dad would say, that at the base of the mountain he laid his skis down in front of his car and ran over them, leaving behind the useless splintered planks when he drove off. While the story of the race is historical fact—hard as it is to believe for anyone who knows Mount Washington or has seen what skis looked like in 1939—the ending was entirely a product of my father's imagination. I have often wondered what insight inspired him to tack this poetic coda of pure apocrypha onto an episode of canonical New England ski lore.

"Do you want a lift into Smithers?" the man said. He sounded like the serpent in the garden.

"Believe me, I'm tempted," I said, "but I promised myself I'd ski all the way down to Telkwa. Thanks for offering though."

"Have it your way," he said. "Take care."

He accelerated, but after a few seconds he braked and pulled over. He got out of his truck and reached behind the seat. When he straightened up he was holding a can of beer. He jogged toward me and pressed it into my hand. "You look like you could use this," he said. "Good luck."

"Thanks" I said. When the man had driven off again, I stopped and put the beer in my food box, where I knew it would quickly turn to ice.

The other valley-bound snowmobilers offered rides too. They got harder and harder to refuse, but I managed, until no more trucks but only darkness came. And again I was alone.

Skiing in the dark again I started to feel tired and a little bored, so I decided to introduce a rewards system. I always carried several pounds of hardtack for camp food, which I had made in an enormous batch before setting off. It was no ordinary hardtack—the baked white-flour rations of soldiers and sailors—but was made with whole-grain flour and sweetened with molasses and honey. The way I had to suck on it for a few minutes before it was soft enough to nibble at made it a drawn-out pleasure to eat. I had made the pieces small enough that I could hold one entirely in my mouth, which let me keep both hands on my poles and eat on the move. That evening I pressed on by allowing myself one piece of hardtack for every kilometer marker I passed. (Traveling in Europe and Canada I had always loved the sense of ease and speed I got from ticking off distances in kilometers. A good argument for maintaining the English mile is that it breeds mental toughness.) The steady stream of nutrients made my progress seem leisurely.

After a few hours, through a web of tree branches, I saw an electric light for the first time in more than a week. It came from a small cabin hidden in the bush. The sight sent a pulse of warmth through me—to think here were humans, a species of which I had not felt especially fond in recent years, inside warm walls, keeping company. I knew deep down that my skis were not a home. Nor was a tent dragged around on a sled. I was sure a home was somewhere beyond the rugged existence I was now leading, but not so far beyond it as the rest of civilization had gone toward comfort and convenience. There was a balance, and this soft light in the woods seemed to represent it. I wanted just so much physical hardship that enjoying things like closeness, warmth, and light would still retain a measure of bliss. More forest dwellings cropped up in the succeeding miles, and I could see people in them. I felt envious. The farther down the mountain I came, the bigger the houses grew, but none were so big that the charm of the people around the hearth was lost. They were small refuges in the wilderness that did not offend the wilderness.

From the end of the logging road it was still four miles to Telkwa. Sand started to mix in with snow, indicating heavier vehicle use, but I could still ski on it. When I came to the outer limits of the village, I stuck my thumb out whenever a car passed, in case anyone was going to the larger town of Smithers, ten miles north. I had decided I would check into a motel, dry my things, and buy provisions. This leg had taken me longer than expected, and I was almost out of food, with no mail drop planned for another week.

I stood at the corner of the Telkwa Road and Highway 16 with my gear piled up beside me and my thumb over the empty highway. I jumped up and down to stay warm. In half an hour a little car turned toward Telkwa and drove past me. A few minutes later I saw it coming back down. It stopped and a woman in her thirties with Japanese features stepped out.

"Where are you headed?" she asked.

"I'm hoping to get to Smithers to find a place to sleep," I said.

"Where did you come from? You're not hitchhiking along the highway with all that gear, are you?"

"No. I just skied over Telkwa Pass from Terrace."

"Are you kidding?" she said.

Her name was Mika and she had just got off work in Smithers. It had been a long day, and she wasn't keen on driving back to town. "But if you want, you're more than welcome to come back to my place," she said. "My husband and I have a trailer behind the house, so you can even have your own space. You can hang your stuff to dry by the woodstove."

"That's really kind of you," I said. "It sounds better than a motel in Smithers."

It was obvious that my equipment wasn't going to fit into Mika's car. She said she had a friend nearby and pointed to a house a hundred feet away. "She won't mind if we leave some of your stuff in her yard." I took my duffel bag and food box off the sled and stuffed them into the back of Mika's car, then the two of us carried skis, sled, and whatever else remained to her friend's yard, where we left it.

Mika drove five miles back up the hill I had just come down, back up among the dwellings in the woods I had admired. Snow was falling. It squeaked under the slow-rolling tires. It must have been quite cold, but I was so glad to be back among people that I had barely thought about it standing by the roadside. We turned into the woods and moved up to a timber-framed mountain house. In the flame-colored light of the kitchen window I saw Mika's husband washing dishes. He smiled to see her headlights coming and gave a playful wave he might not have given had he known a passenger was in the car.

When we stopped I started to unload, while Mika ran upstairs to tell her husband she had dragged home a strange man. Next thing I knew I heard a furious thumping on the stairs, and the husband charged through the outside door. He ran at me in the dark and grabbed my hand with both of his and pumped it excitedly. "Holy shit, man! Holy shit! Are you fucking crazy?"

I didn't know how to respond to such enthusiasm. It was a yes or no question, but a simple yes or no wouldn't suffice: "No, I am in full possession of my senses" or "Yes, I am in fact, although the preferred term is 'mentally ill.'" Perhaps it was my difficulty producing a response that made him apologize for swearing. "I'm sorry, dude. I hope I didn't offend you. My name's Nick."

"I'm Anders," I said. "And you didn't offend me."

"I don't really think you're crazy," he said. "It's just that it's so cool you're here. I've honestly been waiting for something like this to happen." He told me that a few years before, a long-distance cyclist traveling from Alaska to Patagonia had passed through. Mika had met him in Smithers, but she hadn't thought to invite him home. Nick had regretted it ever since and told her to invite all such stragglers home with her in future. He loved to collect stories, and such people had them to tell. At last she had reeled one in.

Nick went out to the trailer to turn on a space heater while I spread my tent and clothes around the woodstove in the walkout basement. Upstairs I was given a glass of red wine that sent another surge of warmth through me. Never had I been so happy to be in company, but Nick and Mika didn't seem like just any company. They were supremely friendly and supremely easy to talk to. I had forgotten how easy it could sometimes be to talk to people. It was like being a kid among friends at school again. And to look at the space they had created around themselves, they seemed to see the world the way I did. Having lived for years in a place that had left me feeling increasingly foreign, this tasted of homecoming. Hot food was brought out of the oven. We sat around an island counter and ate and drank and talked and talked and talked. I had not talked so much in years.

A sleepy-eyed child wandered in, a two-year-old daughter. She wondered what the noise was. Mika and Nick said she had never done anything like this before. The way they said it made my arrival into an advent. The daughter insisted on giving goodnight hugs to all three of us. Then Mika got up and carried her back to bed, while Nick and I went on talking.

"I see a ring on your finger," Nick said. I could never imagine being so forthright. I admired him for it. "Are you married?"

"I am," I said, "but my marriage is on the rocks."

It was a formulaic phrase, the kind that colonizes your native language when you're more used to speaking another, and it sounded that way as soon as it left my mouth. "On the rocks" was a perfectly natural idiom, of course, but in this instance the words were marked because they brought me back to a specific place and time. Elena and I had happened to be sitting on literal Mediterranean rocks the summer before, when she encountered the phrase in a novel she was reading and asked me what it meant. "It means someone is going through a marital crisis," I said.

"Are we 'on the rocks'?" she asked, half joking.

"Yes," I said, and she turned very sad. I had never understood the phrase to denote total ruin, but now that I thought about it the prospects of a ship caught on a shoal are not good.

I told Nick the story of how I had come to be in his kitchen, as I understood it then. I said my years in Europe had sometimes left me feeling tense and claustrophobic. I was realizing now that I stood at a fork in the trail. What had begun as a circuit leading back to Italy started to split. Nick and Mika's life seemed to point in a new direction. It was a direction that had something familiar about it though—something that reminded me of growing up in the woods, and also of the poems and essays by Henry David Thoreau, Aldo Leopold, and Wendell Berry our teachers gave us to read in high school.

Nick had grown up on a potato farm on Prince Edward Island, where his father had moved from New England as a young man. We talked about Prince Edward Island and New England, which seem close when you are in the west, and about Canada and the United States, since we were both citizens of both countries. We talked about what home meant, about the joys of children, about work, and even about the sore subject of love. Nick told me about a downhill-skiing accident he'd had a few years before, which left him with a serious head injury. The experience changed him completely, he said. He came out of a coma and left his girlfriend. The decision cost him his house, but he believed that the accident was subconsciously deliberate—a push in the direction he needed to go but would not—nature's inscrutable way of forcing a transition to a new phase of life. Then he told me about the time he was in a sweat lodge back east and had a vision of a raven. He understood the vision to mean that he needed to go to Haida Gwaii (formerly known as the Queen Charlotte Islands), homeland of the Haida Nation, in whose mythology the shape-shifting, forever-meddling Raven is a central figure. Nick drove across the continent to Prince Rupert and took the ferry across Hecate Strait, off northwestern British Columbia, to Haida Gwaii. On his first night there he met Mika, who was from near Vancouver, and fell in love instantly. "We made love in my van for three days straight," he said, "and the rest flowed out from there."

After Haida Gwaii, Nick and Mika settled in Smithers, where they had both worked as tree planters, eventually opened a little coffee shop called the Bugwood Bean, and had two children. Bugwood is a name for timber that has been riddled by mountain pine beetles, vital members of British Columbia's forest ecosystem that in recent years have become a plague. These small insects normally help maintain healthy forests by attacking old or weak trees so that young ones can mature in their place. Winter cold spells, which can kill larvae, have historically ensured that pine beetle numbers are kept in check, but now milder winters enable more larvae to survive, while warmer summers mean longer breeding seasons. The result is too many hungry beetles. Affected lodgepole pines die within weeks of attack, and whole forests turn from green to rust to gray in a few years. Forestry practices that fail to take into account the complexity of ecosystems have accelerated the cycle. In British Columbia, a total of nearly 62,000 square miles of lodgepole pine forest—an area the size of New England—has been destroyed by mountain-pine-beetle infestation. The wood, if harvested early enough, is good enough for timber framing, and the grooves chewed by the beetles make whimsical arabesques on the posts and beams of Nick and Mika's coffee shop on Main Street in Smithers.

Once we had finished eating supper, the three of us moved downstairs—where the woodstove, the master bed, and the entrance to the house were—so as not to wake the two children. We sipped our wine and talked for a while longer. When we all started fading Nick walked with me out to the trailer, carrying a heavy wool blanket he had warmed by the fire, and wished me goodnight.

Alone in the trailer, I sat still for a moment before stripping down for bed. I thought about the homey lights I had seen as I came down the mountain and how remarkable it was that I had wound up in one of those very homes. I thought about Mika and Nick's kindness and easy generosity. I thought about their smiling faces and their working together—how they'd made a life that gave them time to be with each other and with their kids. I thought about the tiny breathing bodies of their little ones as they slept in their beds, and about the tender affection with which Nick had looked at them as we passed by when he showed me to the bathroom. I thought about the very design of their house, with no doors separating any of the spaces, so that everything was connected. Not even a door on the bathroom, just a thin curtain. "There's not much privacy," said Nick, "but we don't mind. Hope you don't."

I thought about how wonderful all this was, and how it seemed an almost perfect embodiment of ideas about life and home that I had fostered for years but had somehow let slip to the back of my mind or be put on hold. And I thought about myself and how I was alone out here, by choice, and how I had someone but something wasn't working. Was it because our ideals had clashed? Was this journey nature's way of leading me back to what I really wanted from life, and back to the half-wild places where I was sure that whatever that was must live? In a process over which I felt I had little control, I was beginning to think that this journey might be a step along the way to a new beginning. I thought about how change is sad, but also about how failure to change when change is called for is sadder still. I thought about the fire of the woodstove. I thought about the warmth inside the trailer. After a quick stretch I lay down, covered up, and kept on thinking these things, smiling in the darkness, until I drifted off.

I slept until daylight and then wandered into the house, waking Nick in the process. After a long and delicious breakfast with lots of good coffee, we drove to Smithers, where we would meet Mika, who was working the morning shift at the coffee shop. We all had lunch and afterward I went off to replenish my food stores.

Smithers is a pleasant and vibrant town. It's as close as you come in the north to the kind of mountain town you find farther south where city-bred people with rustic tastes can live without feeling deprived. Here the tribe is smaller, limited to those willing to drive a couple of days, or fly, to reach a real city. In a pinch they settle for Prince George in four hours. Yet Smithers retains enough of its rough northern character. The holiday spirit was palpable. Everyone walking the snow-clad sidewalks seemed remarkably happy, the way they often do in nice towns that haven't been "discovered" yet.

I found time that afternoon to call Elena on my satellite phone. She was planning to join my parents and fly across the continent to spend a few days with me at Christmas. They would land in Edmonton and then drive to meet me at some yet-to-be-determined place near my route. It was December 13 and time we started discussing where that might be. I stood in the street while the late-day sun beamed down on me over the shoulder of Hudson Bay Mountain.

On the phone there was a feeling of irreducible distance between me and Elena. Whenever I had talked to her since my departure I had a feeling of melancholy. She sensed this, but at the same time there must now have been a layer of joy in my voice from my having successfully made the first leg of my journey and spent such a wonderful evening. She asked me if I still wanted her to come at Christmas. I evaded the question. I didn't want her to come, not because I thought I wouldn't enjoy her company, but because I had started to see this journey as a way of forcing distance between us. If we would only let it, this might be the twist of fate—like the skiing accident Nick had told me about the night before—that steered us down different paths. I wished she would just stay home, let me go my own way, and time and distance would take care of the rest. I had never learned to have hard conversations though.

"Tell me that you don't love me anymore and I won't come," she said.

"I would be lying if I told you that," I said. "It isn't that simple." It felt as though she was trying to force me to see the world through a lens she had cut for me. Love had nothing to do with it as far as I was concerned. I said I would work out the Christmas details with my parents and ended the awkward conversation.

I walked around Smithers some more and in the darkness of late afternoon rode home with Mika. In the car we talked about language. Mika's parents were immigrants and she was raised speaking English and Japanese. I had spent most of the past decade speaking languages other than my own. I shared a hunch that in learning to express ourselves expertly in different languages, we risk creating new personae, alternative versions of ourselves: the English-speaking Mika might be different from the Japanese-speaking Mika. I was afraid that the English-speaking version of myself was different from the Italian- or German-speaking one, and that this in part had provoked the clash that was making this journey into something far more momentous than I'd ever intended it to be.

Back at the house we had another lovely dinner. In the meantime Nick's father had arrived. Although he still lived on Prince Edward Island, he now came west for months at a time to see his sons, who had all migrated to British Columbia. Nick was glad, he said, because his dad had lived a life of constant giving and got little in return. Only in his sixties had he learned to take a little space for himself. I admired his sense of sacrifice—even envied it slightly—but at the same time felt an aching sadness for what he might have lost. He was a sweet man. He had the rough appearance of a farmer but refused the hand I extended before setting off the following day, insisting on a hug instead.

In the morning Nick presented me with a pull saw from Japan as a gift. "To make it work right you have to remember that it only cuts on the draw," he said. He picked up a branch in the dooryard that was as thick as my forearm. "It's a lot smaller than that buck saw you're dragging around with you, and it cuts about ten times as fast." He got down on his knees and with three or four decisive tugs halved the branch. I took my old buck saw out of my duffel bag and handed it to Nick, then thanked him as I put the new saw in its place.

The gravel Smithers Landing Road runs east from Smithers to Babine Lake. It gives access to a sprawling network of smaller logging roads east of Smithers and north of Houston, home to the largest lumber mill in the world and immediate destination of most of the timber cut in the district. Only a fraction of these smaller roads are used often enough to be maintained regularly; when a new block of trees is slated for harvest, the road leading to that block is cleared of obstacles and, if necessary, graded smooth enough for trucks to drive on. As a major artery, the Smithers Landing Road sees a lot of heavy truck traffic—more than one hundred log trucks a day in winter, when the frozen ground makes it easiest to haul trees out of the woods. I was concerned both about the volume of traffic and about the effects it would have on the snow. We decided it was best for Nick to drive me a few miles east along the main road to a place where I could peel off on one of the unused bush roads.

After lunch I packed my things into Nick's Toyota truck and we were off. He called our position and direction of travel into the radio at each kilometer marker as we made our way into the bush, so that the log truck drivers would know to look out for us at the bends in the road. Meanwhile the evidence of intensive logging activity all around brought us to armchair polemicizing about the politics of resource extraction.

Nick worked for years in and around the forestry industry. My impression as an outsider was that then Prime Minister Stephen Harper's federal government was rather cavalierly auctioning off chunks of Canada's territory to immense and far more powerful geopolitical interests, especially China. For now the risks involved might be containable, because the Americans' Monroe Doctrine affords Canadians a disproportionate geopolitical confidence. But will the United States always be in a position to tough-talk the Chinese? China's economy is enormous, and it is hungry. Its population is nearly five times that of the United States, and its power grows by the minute.

Nick and I both admired Norway. Here was a resource-rich country that at least sometimes acted with restraint and foresight, a place where ethics was considered neither subordinate to nor discrete from economics. North Americans, we agreed, had much to learn from Norway. But instead Canada was pursuing, and continues to pursue, an aggressive approach to the use of its natural resources. Nick grew heated as he talked about the cutthroat world of British Columbia logging. Enormous and expensive machines are required to keep pace with demand. Consequently, more and more must be cut to pay for the machines. All it takes though is one broken piece of equipment to drive a whole company under, the competition is so fierce.

"But what's the rush?" said Nick. "Every new resource industry fails to learn from the mistakes of the ones that have come before it. When we've taken all the fish out of the ocean we simply move onto the next resource, but do we think at all about how to avoid exhausting the next thing? It's time to slow down. We have so many resources, so much space, a small population. We are in a unique position. Canada really has a chance to shine, to bring a new economic model to the world stage. But here we are mowing down trees as fast as we possibly can."

At the sight of the first promising road I told Nick to stop. He snapped a picture while I packed my sled. Then he put his arms around me and said a heartening word. As I skied off I repeated Nick's question out loud: "What's the rush?" I thought only of felled trees and not at all of the axe I held squarely aimed at the trunk of my own existence.

9

INTO THE BABINE

It was three o'clock in the afternoon, and I was seventeen miles from Granisle, the nearest named place on my map. After saying goodbye to Nick I quickly hit my stride. My rhythmic advance spooked a bull moose, who bolted across the road very nearby and slipped tracelessly into the bush. It was dark in an hour. I slid swiftly along the road with no sense of up or down. At moments I was conscious of making minimal physical effort, yet I could see the dark forms of tree tops racing past backward, as though I were a small child looking up and out the window of a moving car. It was the only indication I had that I was going downhill.

I came into Granisle in a snow squall. "Granisle is the real geographical center of British Columbia," a man in Smithers had told me. "Vanderhoof's claims be damned." The village was an apparition, a short string of muffled sodium lights and scattered buildings lashed by an unremitting wind that moaned banshee-like from Babine Lake, invisible in the darkness to my east. The only life was a loaded Dodge Caravan that crept past, tires spinning on the snowpack, keeping its distance. The passengers turned their heads slowly to watch me, a phantom emerging from the wilderness in the stormy midnight. They looked like zombies. The sides of the road near town were crisscrossed with snowmobile tracks, but these disappeared within yards of the last building, and again it was me and the snow.

I pitched my tent in deep snow two and a half miles south of town near a place called Red Bluff. On my compact crank-driven radio I picked up an AM broadcast of the CBC and learned that more than twenty people had been gunned down at an elementary school in Connecticut.

In the morning I skied into Tachet, a Dakelh community of the Lake Babine Nation, at the mouth of the Fulton River. From there I hoped to board a ferry for log trucks that would take me into the remote area on the east side of Babine Lake. Babine is British Columbia's largest natural lake. It is exposed to high winds and in mid-December is not yet frozen. Even when it does freeze, the ferry still runs thanks to an air hose underlying its course that sends up bubbles to maintain an ice-free channel.

Tachet at first was dead silent. It felt like the most dismal kind of Sunday afternoon. There were sporadically audible wisps of a snowmobile without a muffler revving in the far distance. I came into the village and saw rudimentary houses but still no human activity. First a dog ran barking at me, but its wagging tail assured me of friendly intentions. Then another, and another, and finally a pack of village dogs fell in behind me. They variously barked and howled and yelped, their ranks expanding with each lifeless dwelling we passed.

Eventually I came to what looked like an ordinary house, except that there were bars on the windows and a single old-fashioned gas pump in front. I went inside. It did not look like a store. There was a small domestic kitchen. The shelves were stocked with snack foods. A refrigerator was full of margarine when I opened the door. In among it were a couple of pounds of butter. I grabbed one, having forgotten mine in the fridge at Mika and Nick's. I picked up four Mars bars. I could use the calories. An old woman behind the counter eyed me with suspicion.

"Do you know when the barge runs?" I asked her at the till. I had somehow learned that the locals called the ferry a barge and thought using the local term would work in my favor.

"No."

"Is there any way you could find out?"

She thought for a moment and then picked up the telephone and put in a number. "Hi. It's me. There's a young man here wants to know when the barge is running."

She hung up. "Monday to Friday."

There was a sign that said NO LOITERING.

"Do you mind if I stand inside and eat a candy bar and drink some water?" I asked.

"Go ahead."

At the barge landing were two men welding logging equipment. I surprised them. They confirmed that the next ferry would cross the lake on Monday morning at four. It was now Saturday morning.

"Can I put my tent here?"

"No."

I hadn't expected that answer. "Do you know some place where I could put it?"

They thought about it, but said, "Why don't you go sleep in one of them cabins at the rez campground?"

"Where is it?"

"Right over there." One of them pointed toward a string of plywood buildings 300 yards down the shore. I turned to ski off toward the buildings.

"Hey," called one of the men after me. "Where'd you say you came from?"

"Prince Rupert."

"Holy fuck."

I chose a cabin at random and went in. There was no insulation and no stove, but it was better shelter than a nylon tent. It had a window to the lake. There was a covered porch and an outhouse nearby. What more could I want? I spent Saturday and Sunday reading, writing, eating, skiing down to the lake for water, standing outside in the sun. I saw no one, heard no one.

On Monday morning I rose at three twenty-five. My things were all packed the night before, but even so, as I skied along the shore toward the landing I saw the ferry pull away into the darkness. It would be back in an hour. At the landing it was fourteen degrees. A gruff man in his sixties who looked Scottish to me with his formidable white muttonchops shifted the newly fallen snow around in a large yellow grader. He wore only jeans and a thin cotton tank top.

While I waited, empty log trucks lined up for the ferry, whose sole purpose was to facilitate the extraction of timber from the Babine district for milling in Houston. When the ferry came back, I skied onto the snow-covered deck with my sled, and saw one of the welders from Saturday. He invited me to come up to the crew cabin to get out of the cold.

In the cabin old newspapers lay around. It smelled of coffee and tobacco. A huge man sat in the corner, and behind me a few other men came up the stairs, including Lyle, the muttonchopped grader operator. Coffee was poured.

"Are you trying to kill yourself?" someone asked.

I took out my maps.

"Holy fuck," said the man from Saturday.

I showed Lyle the route I proposed to take, which ran east and skirted Stuart Lake all the way to Fort Saint James.

"Impossible."

"Why? There's a road on the map."

"There's been no cutting there in years. Road's not maintained."

"That's good. No trucks."

"The snow's too deep. It's hundreds of miles. No one could find you."

"But is there snow on the roads you guys are hauling on?"

They smiled. "Yes."

Lyle pointed at the road on the map.

"Holy fuck," repeated the man from Saturday, who stared at the map, then at me, then at the map.

Lyle explained. "Take this road to kilometer twenty-five." I scribbled notes on an old envelope. "At kilometer twenty-five turn right on the Austin Road."

"You don't have a gun?" one of the men asked.

"Holy fuck."

"The wolves are gonna get you. They're fucking huge. There's big packs of 'em in them mountains over there. Do you know where you're going? There ain't nothin' on the other side of this lake. Nothin'." I told them I wasn't worried about wolves. I didn't bother saying that no healthy wolf has ever been known to kill a human adult in the history of North America. That would only have been further proof of my insanity.

"Are you running from the police?" asked the man in the corner.

"No." I laughed.

"Don't worry. We won't tell them we saw you. Unless you did something really bad."

"Holy fuck," came the refrain.

"If the police are looking for me," I said, "please tell them where you last saw me."

I double-checked the route with Lyle, bolted another cup of coffee, and thanked them all. As I clambered down the stairs I heard something from behind me.

"Holy fuck."

BEST

4000

Pickup By:
12/22/2021

**This land of
snow : a
journey across
the north in
winter**

31112021087362

10

AMONG LOGGERS

The ferry landed at a pitch-dark spot on the far shore of the lake. Five or ten trucks drove into the interior and were swallowed up. The ferry too retreated into the darkness. Now the stories of the wolves tickled my imagination. I skied briskly along the white line.

After fifteen miles of hard travel I came, as promised, to the Austin Road. I turned east and found the road narrow, tortuous, and heavily sanded. I had to ski the next six miles atop the snowbank along the roadside. Every hour or two a truck passed, carrying logs home, then vanished so quickly I forgot it was ever there. By dusk I was pleased with my progress and made camp on high ground back from the road. The infrequent traffic had long since ceased, so it was a quiet night. After supper I took off my sock and peeled back a bandage on my foot to check on an open blister I'd had for a few days. The wound was soft and green. It looked scarily like an infection to my suggestible eye. I cleaned it with alcohol, squirted some antibiotic cream onto it, and put a new bandage on.

I dug out an introduction to winter ecology I was carrying and began to read aloud. Like a religious enthusiast who lets his book of scripture casually flop open and then assigns prophetic value to the first words his eyes fall on, I read, "Winter is an energy bottleneck, a constraint on the lives of organisms.

Reduced solar radiation during the winter leads to a plethora of forces that act harshly on plants and animals, reducing their chances of survival." I was getting cold, so I climbed into the main compartment of my tent to stretch before sleeping. Then I burst out weeping uncontrollably. "Why am I doing this?" I cried. After stretching, I calmed down and got into my sleeping bag. I jotted a brief note in my journal: "Despair. Loneliness. Cold."

Traffic on the logging road started at two-thirty in the morning, so my sleep was occasionally interrupted and I did a lot of thinking during the night. My understanding of my journey was evolving. I asked myself, "Do I have to ski every single mile of the way across the country?" That principle had already been violated. "Do I have to make it all the way to Quebec?" Now that I had spent a few weeks traveling across the map, it was plain how impossible that would be. Northern winters are long, but not that long. "Does the journey need to have some unifying sense?" Of course. Perhaps it was more about a season than a physical space. Probably I would not know the real sense, if I ever did, until long after the journey was done. I could ski until the spring equinox, skipping sections as dictated by fate—running out of food and having to hitchhike to the next town, say, or just finding bad conditions for travel on skis. Yes, mid-March. Ninety more days in the cold. I had a number, no longer an endless icy abyss stretching out before me. Now I could sleep.

IN THE MORNING I LAY in my sleeping bag for a long time thinking. I still felt depressed and shaken. But I was soon lifted up by an unlikely thing—the tenderness of loggers. As I lay there, not wanting to brave the cold but knowing it was getting late, I heard through the ice-crisped air a truck stop and a door open. I realized someone was coming to see if I was still alive. Jerking at the frozen zipper, I quickly opened my tent door and popped my head out. A man in his fifties was slogging through the deep snow toward my tent.

"I'm okay. Just being lazy today," I called out.

"That's okay," he replied. "As long as we know you're all right." I was touched by the "we," as if the loggers and truck drivers were collectively concerned for this stranger skiing through their wild territory. I dressed and went outside. By the side of the road, where my tracks from the day before turned into my campsite, was a brown paper bag. The lunch consisted of a sandwich, pizza, cookies, an orange, and a fruit bar. All of it was naturally frozen solid. My mood shifted completely, the way it so often did on the trip. I took it as a cosmic vindication of my more casual way of thinking about the journey.

When I had almost finished breaking camp, a truck halted on a rise and a man got out to adjust his chains. He waved and then pulled up to where my tracks met the road. I recognized him as one of the pair I'd seen welding on Saturday, the one I hadn't seen on the boat. He pulled a well-used thermos from the cab. "Want some coffee?"

"Love some."

"It's vanilla-flavored. I hope you don't mind." It could have been flavored with sulfur and I would have relished it.

"Mike," he said, as we sipped coffee and looked out over the spiky hills.

"Anders."

It was as rich a conversation as we needed.

Soon I was skiing through fog that the sun was doing its best to burn off. The frosted branches crowning the aspens that stand lonely in clearcuts were translucent, their beauty too ethereal to think of trying to capture with a photograph. I had a camera with me, but I seldom took pictures. At moments like this, the idea seemed almost a desecration. At other times I couldn't be bothered keeping batteries warm or simply felt too cold to stop and fiddle with buttons and switches with my bare hands. I skied all day along the ridges of the plowed snowbanks, since the narrow road was sanded, but did not mind. I waved and received waves in return from every log truck that passed. I made only ten miles but felt at the end of the day that it had been a good one.

Near my camp at dusk a pickup came barreling down a hill. The doors flung open in a way to strain the hinges and three men spilled out. They landed wearing enormous grins and each held a sloshing can of beer. They ran over to where I had come to greet them. Steve, Randall, and Darryl were their names.

"Did you like your lunch?" one of them asked.

So these were my benefactors. They said they would bring me lunch again and I thanked them as profusely as I could, muttering something about needing all the calories I could get. They were enthusiastic and said the next day they wanted a picture with me. They offered me a beer, which they unexpectedly allowed me to refuse, and were gone.

That night I ate chili, enlivened with exotic ingredients like hemp seeds and cacao nibs that my Smithers friends had given me. I savored it in slow silence, smiling to myself at the thought of the big bad wolves.

Come morning I had still heard no wolves, but as promised I did find lunch outside my tent, this time with buttery muffins that powered me through the first few miles. I was up at five-thirty and traveling by seven. I still felt that I was wasting too much time breaking camp but so far had not hit on a way of speeding up the process. The mornings were getting colder too. I had to remember that it was easier to get up a few hours before sunrise, the minutes around dawn being the coldest of the day. But it wasn't easy to convince the flesh when I was warm in my sleeping bag.

Even with the sinking cold, however, I was still able to get up, stretch, and break camp wearing just a thin shell for a jacket and fleece gloves. Striking the tent usually required a bit of bare-handed work followed by sessions of brisk rubbing of palm against palm under my jacket, but I wanted to prolong the period of light clothing as much as possible so that I still had an ace up my sleeve when it started to get really cold.

It began snowing in earnest and continued that way all day. Though falling snow can at times be irksome, as when you flip your hood and a load of ice crystals falls down your neck, here it was to my advantage, because it meant that Larry, who drove a plow the fifty-five miles between the ferry and the cutting block each day, could not keep pace with the snowfall. One side of the road always had enough snow cover for me to travel over it without scraping the bottoms of my skis.

At the crest of a hill I stopped for a snack, and in my lunch bag, which I'd been keeping in my jacket pocket, was thrilled to find a cold but not-quite-frozen omelet. While I chewed, an empty truck stopped and the driver rolled down the window. He told me there was a maintenance shop at kilometer marker 716 where I might be able to find a warm spot for the night. It was a little over three and a half miles away and I had an hour of sunlight left. It would be perfect.

Much of the way was downhill, so I arrived faster than expected. There was a cluster of five trailers, most with harsh fluorescent lights burning inside, and the hum of generators filled the air. It was getting dark fast, still snowing hard. These perennially humming modular micro-cities, abandoned when work crews are not present, are scattered across the north and have something haunting about them. To Berkeley's question about the tree falling unperceived in the forest they seem to give a squalid affirmative answer. They are sometimes the only foothold of civilization for hundreds of miles in the vast northern wilderness. I went to the biggest trailer and gave a few sharp taps on the door with my ski pole. No answer came.

While I waited for a response to my second knock a pickup came careering into the pullout through foot-deep snow. Out sprang Randall, Steve, and Darryl, already in mid-conversation before their feet had landed.

I told them I was knocking around in hopes of getting a floor to sleep on. This they already knew from the radio. I could certainly sleep there if I wanted to, they said, but why didn't I come back to camp with them, sleep in a bed, have supper? "Tonight's steak night," said Darryl.

First they insisted on taking a few pictures using Randall's smartphone. Darryl, who was fifty-five but seemed older, tried but couldn't make the camera work, so one of the others had to trade places with him. We stashed my sled, skis, axe, and fuel cans under one of the trailers, lifted my duffel and food tote into the pickup bed, and were off on the sixty-mile drive to camp at breakneck speed. Randall, a certifiable madman, was at the wheel guzzling beer, along with the others, and soon me. He held up his beer and looked at me in the rearview mirror: "This is one thing we're allowed to do over here that you can't do on the other side of the lake." He seemed to honestly believe the law ended on the far shore of Babine Lake.

Darryl enthused over the fact that tonight it would be steak and prawns in camp, this being Wednesday, and did I like steak? Instead of prawns there might even be crab legs, this being the week before Christmas, and didn't I think crab legs were even better than shrimp? "Oh, you'll eat good tonight, Anders. Sandy, she's the camp cook, she puts on a first-rate feed, she does. She can be hard to get along with, but she lays out a real nice spread."

Darryl told me they'd been dying to meet me since the first day I'd been in the district. "'Who is this guy?' we thought. 'We gotta meet a guy who can ski thirty-five kilometers uphill pulling a sled.' Stevie here can't even make the drive out to the block without falling asleep."

"Fuck you," said Steve.

"We weren't sure what you'd say if we invited you back to camp," Darryl continued. "We thought maybe you was antisocial, like Mudgy here. So we talked about it and decided we'd ask, just to see what you thought." Mudgy was Randall.

"I'm glad you did. I could use a good meal and some company."

Randall asked if I had a gun. I said no, that I'd had one but sold it in Terrace. He said he would have brought one, but Darryl agreed with me that wolves would leave me alone. "They don't know what you can do with those ski poles." I told them I had bear bangers, and they all said to each other, as if they'd made a wager beforehand, "See, I knew he had something. Didn't I tell you yesterday, 'I bet he's got bear bangers or something like that'?" This seemed to put them at ease.

Darryl appeared to be getting antsy. "Are you guys gonna get some pot going around?" he asked the two in the front seat.

"Well," said Steve, sounding like he was speaking in court, "I wasn't sure how to bring up the whole marijuana subject. I didn't know what the feelings might be."

I told them I had no objections and out came a ready joint. They thought that because I had called myself a teacher when asked about my profession that I might disapprove. As the joint made its way around the vehicle Steve told the story of one of his old teachers. "The guy'd always give me a hell of a time at school. For years he made me toe the line. But then I ran into him a few years later and smoked a joint with him. I swear the fucking guy never wore jeans a day in his life, but holy shit did he smoke pot like a motherfucker!"

Darryl provided a running commentary in his slow rolling voice. "We always like to smoke a little pot on the way into camp. It piques the appetite, eh. And it helps us unwind." He sighed. "Now, mind you, Anders—she's a six-beer drive in from the back, so we find that a little dope makes the drive easier. Sorta takes the edge off. Course these guys make me sit in the back, being the old-timer. But we're quite a crew, Anders, we're quite a crew. Isn't that right, fellas?"

"Yes, we are," said one of the others with an indulgent laugh.

"I can see that," I said.

Darryl continued. "In the morning I drive, o'course. Stevie there, he sleeps in the back, and Mudgy and I bullshit up front. We're not bad guys, eh. Just a buncha dope-smokin' redneck loggers."

Steve objected from up front. "Not too redneck."

"Speak for yourself, Stevie!" said Darryl. "I'm pretty redneck. I can't even run the cell phone."

Steve and Randall were giggling like a pair of stoned teenagers up front, and I was doing the same in the back. "We're quite a crew," Darryl said over and over, and often reiterated that the six-beer drive from the back block entailed great hardship and required that the very best use be made of it, because camp was dry.

Another leitmotif was Randall's antisocial personality. "Once this guy's in camp he never leaves his room," Darryl said. "Brings a week's worth of food so he doesn't have to go to the cafeteria. Every time he goes there he gets in a row with someone. He's not a bad guy. He's just antisocial. And, like I said, we thought you might be antisocial, out here skiing by yourself and all. So you fellas ought to get along."

"Mudgy!" he said imperatively. "Why don't you get Anders here set up with a room when we get into camp? I'm an old-timer. You know how I am. I've got to eat."

Then later: "Mudgy! You gonna eat with us tonight, seein' as we got a guest?"

"No," said Randall. "No offense, but I wouldn't go eat with that bunch of assholes even if the Queen herself was coming into camp tonight."

Darryl whispered in an aside to me, "Mudgy's a good guy. Really is. He's just antisocial."

Randall did seem well-disposed toward me at least. But he had a look in his eyes—like when he walked into a room the chances of a fight breaking out were pretty good. And even if he was skinny, you could see that he was tough. If a fight broke out you'd want him on your side. Steve, on the other hand, was a giant of a man, and only twenty-three. He was known in camp for the immensity of his appetite, and later that night I would eat him under the table.

We arrived in camp and went straight to the mess. Never having been in a logging camp, I was surprised at how good the food was. Sandy the cook indeed gave the impression of having a chip on her shoulder, but I tried to imagine the harassment she must have received constantly and didn't hold it against her. She greeted me curtly and agreed to give me supper but said it would be impossible for me to sleep in the bunkhouses; I was a stranger and the rooms weren't locked. I didn't much mind sleeping in the truck and was far more interested in the food, but Darryl persisted in his plea and soon a foreman I'd met briefly the day before added his voice to the cause. Eventually a choir of brawny loggers was supplicating the seemingly omnipotent Sandy. In the end she broke down and gave me a room. I kept myself awake long enough to write her a thank-you to leave on my pillow in the morning.

I was up at 2:20, and at 2:30 Darryl banged on the door and said in cheerful tones to come to breakfast. In the mess I stuffed a paper bag full of sandwiches and snacks for the day, and by 3:05 we were in the truck with Darryl at the wheel, Randall in the passenger's seat, and Steve dozing next to me in the back. "Mudgy!" shouted Darryl. "Give Anders your number." And Mudgy did, with instructions to call once I was safely through to Fort Saint James.

When we reached their winter block, which was near where I'd left my things, they gave me a brief tour in the truck. It was the middle of the night, so I could see only what was revealed by the bright halogen lamps that hung on the bunchers and processors. Feller bunchers are machines that reach into a stand of trees like a giant hand, cut them at their bases, and gather them into bunches of four or more, like plucked dandelions, before laying them on the ground. A processor comes along behind the buncher, lifts each felled tree and slides it through a processor head that simultaneously delimbs and swings it through the air on a boom, before finally cutting it in lengths that are dropped in neat piles called decks. Darryl and Steve, who operated processors, pointed out their giant stacks of timber with pride and told me each represented only a few hours' work.

Darryl, testing the patience of his supervisor, had agreed to take me as far as he could toward the Middle River. We had heard a rumor of a truck forcing a way through the unplowed road a few weeks before. We learned very soon though that a rumor was all it had been. The road was plowed to just a few yards beyond the block and shortly gave way to two or three feet of snow. Darryl insisted on strong-arming through a few hundred feet of this, snow flying up over the hood like waves crashing over the bow of a storm-tried ship.

Every few feet he would get out and wipe the windshield clear with his shirt sleeve, refusing to let me help him, then back up and take another ram. But when the truck started to overheat I told him to stop.

He was relieved to learn that I had a satellite phone with me. "Don't forget to check in every now and then with Randall," he said. "Mudgy's a worrywart, you know. He's antisocial, but he's real concerned about you."

It was five o'clock in the morning, snowing, and as dark as the inside of a cave when I began my eight-mile trudge through two feet of snow. I was skiing north, not far from the western bank of the Middle River, to a bridge crossing. There was a parallel logging road I needed to reach on the far side of the river just a mile away, and I wished I had wings. The first three miles were unrelentingly uphill, a bedeviling slog that I sometimes attacked in spurts of thirty feet. Eight hours had passed when I made the lonesome bridge. When I took off my harness and went to get some food, I discovered that Darryl had loaded my duffel onto the sled backward, with the weight in the front. Rather than press down the snow ahead, so that the load would float on top of it, the nose of the sled had been driving down into the snow like a plowshare, which explained why I felt like an ox that had just turned eight miles of soil.

11

END OF THE EARTH

I was at the southern end of one of the remotest stretches of British Columbia. The slender fingers of Takla Lake reach from its outlet at the Middle River, which I had just crossed, into a roadless north. A railroad from Fort Saint James to Dease Lake, in far northern British Columbia, was planned and begun once, but construction was abandoned in 1977, and now the tracks lie buried under snow along the Middle River and the train cars wait rusting outside Fort Saint James. East of Takla Lake are the Nation Lakes, a latitudinally oriented chain along whose length I had originally intended to ski before I was advised not to by the hunting guide in Terrace.

Farther east lies Williston Lake. It is a marvel of engineering, pooling the waters of the Parsnip and Finlay River systems where they converge as the Peace River, before funneling them east and then sharply north to the Arctic Ocean via the Slave and Mackenzie Rivers. (The Slave River takes its name from the so-called Slavey people, a subgroup of the Dene. As with many demonyms, the name was given by their neighbors, the Cree, who once enslaved Dene captives in times of war. The Cree word first entered French as *esclave* and later English as *slave*. The Slavey prefer to call themselves the Dene-Tha' and Dehcho Dene. The Mackenzie River takes its name from Scottish explorer Alexander Mackenzie, the first European to follow it to its outlet in 1789. Four years later, or twelve years before Lewis and Clark reached the mouth of the Columbia River, he became the first to cross the North American continent from Atlantic to Pacific north of Mexico. The Peace River, according to Mackenzie's account of his travels, is named for a place called Peace Point near where it joins the Slave, which commemorates a historical boundary between Slavey and Beaver, or Dane-zaa, territories.) Williston is British Columbia's largest lake. It lies astride the Rocky Mountain Trench, and its shores have seen very little in the way of roads or settlement. Northwest of this cluster of lakes—Babine, Takla, the Nations, and Williston—is a wilderness that stretches to the Yukon with little interruption. South of it are a few logging roads that converge at Fort Saint James. Locals in "the Fort" give these directions to visitors from Outside: "Go to the end of the world. Then turn right."

Fort Saint James was where I would spend Christmas. To me, as I traveled southeast, it seemed like the center of the world. Any human being I should chance to see now would doubtless be headed there. The road I emerged on after crossing the Middle River bridge is known as the 300 Road. It runs from northwest to southeast and its snow was clean. The clear-cuts here were more numerous and bigger. A cold wind ripped down the side of a mountain and sliced through my jacket. I quit shortly before sunset, having covered five miles since coming over the river. The snow was deep and fine, and I had to take special care to prepare my tent site.

The routine of making camp was a constant of my journey. I would choose as flat a spot as I could find, ideally about thirty feet long. I needed enough room for both the tent and the terminal guylines that extended a distance beyond it. With my skis on I would sidestep the length of the area, slide forward the length of my skis, and then sidestep back to the other end. This made the area of my platform some thirty feet long by two ski lengths wide. The snow was still very fluffy at this point, so next I would herringbone up and down the area, covering every track at least twice—once down, once back. I might do this more than once. From there I would go to one corner of my rectangle and ski across the width, pressing down as hard as I could on my skis. When I reached the far side, I would flip my lead ski 180 degrees, follow it with the other, and ski back, again applying the same weight and making sure to overlap the lead track from my previous line so that virtually all the snow was compacted. It was like coloring in the shape with a marker, line by line.

This treatment was sufficient in the first part of the winter, but on the evening in question the snow was so collapsible I had to go farther. I returned to the initial sidestep, this time adding pressure and taking care not to let any snow squeeze out over my skis. I took one run up the middle and one up each side. When I skied on the surface it always felt very stable. Next I spread out my groundsheet, aligned the tent on top of it with the door facing north so that I could unzip a wedge and peek out at the northern constellations for a few seconds every night before going to sleep, and took off my gloves to fasten the two together with tiny plastic hooks. I inserted the poles that would give the raised tent its volume. It was here that I always removed one ski, stuck it through a loop at the end of one of the terminal lines, and drove it into the snow at the end of the platform. Now I had to get to the other end of the tent. Even with the snow compacted, the foot without a ski still tended to posthole, so I would skip-slide gingerly to the far end, keeping most of my weight on the ski. There I would remove it, put it through the loop in the line, and sink it. The tent had its tunneled shape.

Then I would walk around the tent and "deadman" six wide stakes at the corners of the tent wall by burying them horizontally. This was the coldest part of the routine, as it often involved putting my hands under the snow. It was also done without skis on, so my feet often sank so deep that snow would sneak in through the tops of my gaiters. But shelter—the prize—was close at hand, and I could accept the inevitability of sinking. I tamped out a knee-deep chute connecting the vestibule door to my sled, and with a few runs back and forth I had everything inside. Then I would carry my camp stove and a fuel canister a few steps away from the tent, put on the headlamp whose battery pack I'd warmed against my skin for the final hour of skiing, and fill the stove.

After crawling into the tent's large vestibule, I dusted out as much snow as I could, heat-primed my stove by igniting a dab of alcohol jelly smeared on top of the brass fuel reservoir, and set up my kitchen while I waited. On this particular night it was close to zero degrees, so I donned my parka for the first time and spread my jacket over my crossed legs. And with that, camp was made. The rest was cooking, eating, and preparing for sleep.

IN THE MORNING I SLEPT again until sunrise and was angry with myself for it. To make matters worse I wasted nearly an hour looking for a signal for my phone to call Elena.

That afternoon I saw a pickup with a man my age at the wheel. He stopped, introduced himself as Eldon, said he operated a log loader, and asked a lot of questions. He had just loaded a final truck and was on his way home for Christmas. He said no one else would be coming down this road and handed me a hard-boiled egg left over from his lunch. I popped it straight into my mouth before it could freeze. Five hundred yards up the road his pickup stopped. He walked around to the passenger's side and appeared to check the tire before driving on. When I reached the point where he had stopped I found a tangerine in the snow with five granola bars planted around it like the spokes of a wheel.

Eldon had mentioned that there was a logging camp at kilometer zero on the 300 Road. It was sixteen miles from where I saw him in the late afternoon, but knowing that the road would see no more human life for nearly two weeks left me feeling alone. So I resolved to reach the camp that night. If there was a watchman, I would ask for a place to sleep. If not, I was sure I would find an open door.

Soon it was dark. I couldn't tell whether my skis were scraping gravel or broken ice, so I reluctantly dug out my headlamp, the first and only time I would ever ski with it, to spare my equipment unnecessary wear. It was a gradual climb through flecks of white shooting out of the darkness into the bright cast of my lamp. With the light I could see nothing outside what was immediately ahead of me, and the resulting boredom seemed to slow time down. To make it pass, I counted to ten thousand, counting one beat for every four strides, then started over. Eventually the realization that I was counting to ten thousand for a second time seemed to swell the sense of boredom, so I ordered my body to keep up kicking legs, poling arms, and following a straight line, then switched off my lamp.

A pinpoint of light flickering behind tree trunks in the distance suddenly brought me back to normal awareness. The camp was all it could be. It was the only light in tens of miles. It grew closer and closer until finally I skied into its jarring glow. I saw movement in a trailer marked REC ROOM, skied up to it, and unclipped my bindings. When I stepped off my skis for the first time in more than twenty-five miles, pain ripped through my right knee so sharply that it felt as though my leg had been twisted around a crankshaft. The leg folded, and I caught myself with my arms on the ground. I'd have screamed had I not been in a furtive state of mind. I limped up the porch, shook my leg out, and knocked on the door.

When it opened there was a tall man across the threshold. He seemed surprised that the knocking in the night had been anything more than his imagination. He must have been doubly surprised to see a man wearing a long beard drawn down by icicles standing in the dark as the snow settled soundlessly, and no vehicle in sight, but only a sled and a pair of skis.

"Can I come in?" I said.

He waved me in.

There was another man inside. Both were in their thirties. Aerosmith came from a pair of speakers, drowning out the sound of a flickering television. "We're working on getting drunk," said the man I had not met, a blond bearded fellow who, were he not sitting slumped in a reclining armchair, would have fit in a Wagner opera. He wore shorts and raised a gallon of Smirnoff as a visual prop. It had a pump-action handle on it, so you could squeeze shots into your glass like ketchup. He fingered the nozzle cap lovingly. On a coffee table lay a platter of cold bacon and onion rings that the two men picked at.

"You gonna spend the night?" the tall man said.

"I would appreciate it. I'll sleep anywhere. I'm just grateful for the roof."

"No one's in camp besides us. You can sleep in any room you like. Do you want a cup of coffee or something?"

"That sounds perfect."

The tall man went to fetch me a cup of coffee, and I sat on a corner of the couch to talk to the bearded man. He told me that his friend, Neil, was camp cook, while he, Thorfinn, was only visiting. They came from Campbell River, on Vancouver Island. Neil would work for twenty-nine days straight in camp, and then he had thirteen days off, during which he would drive the 750 miles home and the same distance back again. He always drove. Camp was vacant now, for Christmas holidays, but someone had to keep an eye on things, so he and Neil were here playing video games, eating cold bacon, and building their alcohol tolerance.

Thorfinn spoke as if he were talking to himself. He rambled. At one point his monologue veered off into a Scandinavian language. "Are you speaking Norwegian?" I said.

"*Joooh*," he said in a resonant voice. He rattled another sentence off, which I took to mean, "Who's asking?"

He told me, in English, that his father was Norwegian. He was a Norwegian citizen himself and had lived in Norway for a few years. He'd even been in the Norwegian Army. Neil came back and joined what conversation there was, which was soon reduced to Thorfinn's deranged soliloquizing in Norwegian, peppered with English expressions of marvel at the genius of the vodka spout.

Neil had the good grace to ask if I wanted to retire to a bunkhouse and showed me the way, stopping in the kitchen to fill a bag with snacks for me. In my narrow room, consisting of a bed, metal wardrobe, and television, I ate a sandwich and then went to the drying room, a fixture of every bush camp, to spread out all my gear. In the bathroom I washed my cooking utensils. I turned on the CBC, in camp via satellite, when I returned to my bedroom. December 21, which had ended minutes before, had been prophesied doomsday by the Mayans, the newscast reported, but the prophecy had apparently been wrong. I imagined how my day might have differed if the world-ending events *had* happened and concluded that things would be about the same. I might even be here in camp with Neil and Thorfinn, one of the last three men on earth. Human extinction would only be a matter of hours after that.

In the morning I packed everything up neatly, as if I were back at the beginning of my travels, and smeared a fresh coat of mink oil on my boots. My knee felt better now, but I went through my stretching routine anyway. I found Neil and Thorfinn in a bedroom strumming guitar chords and looking like two men who had drunk a bottle of vodka and eaten cold bacon before going to bed. Neil put on a brave face and told me to take anything I wanted from the kitchen; there would be no workers in camp for two weeks, so all the food would have to be thrown away. I drank a pot of coffee and a glass of chocolate milk, ate five bowls of cereal and some fruit, rested for a few minutes, and then faced winter again.

The Leo Creek Road, which trickled southeast toward Stuart Lake, was gritty, covered in a thin dusting of snow. It scraped the bottoms of my skis and sled. After four miles of this a pickup pulled up alongside me. "I was wondering if I'd see you," the man inside said.

He had hit a wolf the night before. It fell dead, so he stopped and heaved it into the bed of his truck. In the morning, where he had hit the wolf the night before, he saw another one by the side of the road. He said it looked to be sleeping. It didn't move when he drove up. He took his .308 from the back seat, walked over, and shot it. The two beautiful black wolves lay dead on top of a pile of cordwood in the bed. Some of the wood had shifted and now pressed on their muscles and rich, glossy coats. I touched one of the wolves, but withdrew my hand suddenly, either from respect or fear.

"I'll be the last person coming out of here for at least a week," the man said. "If you need a lift, this is your last chance." Knowing the road conditions would only get worse, unless it started snowing hard, I decided to go with him. I put my skis and sled on top of the already debased wolves, making a silent apology. I locked eyes with one of them, which minutes ago had been alive and whose corpse still emitted steam, and imagined I saw it twitch.

The driver, Dave, was a welder by trade who had spent the last few years logging. He lived in Vanderhoof, ninety miles to the south, but worked all week in the bush. The two wolves he had killed in the past twelve hours were the only two he had ever seen, and he had never lived anywhere else. He said he had a trapper friend who would pay him five hundred dollars apiece for the pelts, but he was thinking of having one mounted. I suggested he take the money. When Dave dropped me off in front of a motel just outside of Fort Saint James he said he would pray for me.

12

CHRISTMAS

I spent the next morning catching up on my journaling while I waited for a supply drop to be delivered by a man who kept a hunting and fishing lodge north of Fort Saint James. My change in plans put the lodge out of my way, and it was a happy coincidence that the man was coming to town for supplies. I had managed to track down several such helpers along my route months before setting off, usually through inquiries sent to local cross-country ski clubs, and arranged to have food shipments sent to them, preferring a personal touch to a post office wherever possible.

Eager to explore, in the afternoon I stepped onto my skis and pointed toward town. I had taken the skins off, since I had no load to pull, and could move along quickly. Past the grocery store I slid down a hill onto Stuart Lake, which from the small grid of streets at its eastern edge stretches forty-five miles west into remote and unpeopled country. I skied toward two distant figures fishing through a hole in the ice. They were teenage boys who had yet to catch anything. I wished them luck and continued down the lake in vague search of a pub Dave had mentioned as the best bet for Christmas dinner.

I skied ashore and continued west paralleling a quiet rolling road. After twenty minutes a car came along and slowed to my pace. It was conspicuous for not being a truck. The driver was a lanky man in his forties with blond hair and blue eyes. He looked European and, when he spoke, had a slight accent. "You should be skiing on the golf course," he said.

"Where is it?" I said.

"It's over there." He nodded across the road. "I set ski tracks on it with my snowmobile. You should use them."

I told him I would give his tracks a try, although I wasn't in town for long, and asked if he knew anything about the pub.

"What are you doing here?" he asked.

"I'm on a long ski trip," I said. "I'm supposed to meet some family for Christmas in Fort Saint James."

"A long ski trip? Can you meet me at the pub in one hour and twenty minutes?" he asked.

"If you tell me where it is," I said.

I SAT AT THE BAR alone drinking coffee and looking around. A woman sat alone at a nearby table doing roughly the same. After we had made uncomfortable eye contact several times she stood up and walked toward me. "Did you meet my husband, Paul?" she asked.

"I believe I must have," I said. "Is he a blond-haired Dutchman who skis?"

"That would be the one." She invited me to her table and told me Paul was on his way.

Kelley Inden grew up in Vanderhoof, although she was born in Oregon. Her disenchanted parents moved north to homestead when she was three years old. At a time when thousands of American back-to-the-landers and draft-dodgers were settling in the salubrious Okanagan Valley of southern British Columbia, where vineyards and fruit trees grow, or on the mild Sunshine Coast above Vancouver, Kelley's father decided to take his family five hundred miles north.

Growing up, Kelley wanted to be a Mormon. There were a lot of them in Vanderhoof, and it was her way of trying to fit in. She outgrew the idea eventually but found that the Latter-day Saints wouldn't let her off the hook so easily. "They still won't leave me alone," she said, almost thirty years later. "Anyway, it's the same way with the U.S. government. My parents left the country for good when I was three. It's as if I had never lived there, so why should any of us have to file income tax returns?" It's a common complaint in a country that's home to hundreds of thousands of dual U.S. citizens, born to families, like my own, that have sometimes been straddling an almost imaginary border for generations.

Paul, who appeared in minutes, had grown up in the Netherlands reading books about Alexander Mackenzie and David Thompson (well-known explorers of Canada's western interior), the Hudson's Bay and Northwest Companies (the two major fur-trading groups), and the lives of the trappers and voyageurs (the tough French-Canadian woodsmen responsible for transporting traded furs thousands of miles from the interior to Montreal by canoe). He emigrated at nineteen and had long since ceased to regard any place other than Canada home. Employed as a government forester, he spent his free time plying Stuart Lake in small unmotorized boats, riding his bicycle, and cross-country skiing. He returned to the Netherlands periodically to see his mother and always came back with the latest innovations in cycling. He sometimes thinks Fort Saint James is too crowded now and dreams of going north to one of the remoter lakes.

In the pub we talked about skiing. Paul was forever trying to promote it by setting tracks on the lake and throughout town, but no one used them. The wellness-minded northern European in him couldn't understand why people wouldn't ski in such an ideal setting. With its rolling terrain and evergreens, Fort Saint James looked like Norway, where everyone skis—even old ladies in long skirts toting shopping bags. The land cried out to be skied on. I told Paul I took a practical view of the matter and have never seen myself as an athlete, that I felt skiing was the most sensible way to move on foot in moderate depths of snow, and the most elegant. We dreamt out loud of snowbelt towns with winter infrastructure based on this idea, towns with unplowed roads, where cars were garaged from December to March and you moved about on skis, snowshoes, or snowmobiles. Imagine the fuel these towns would save! Fort Saint James, Paul told me, was one of the only municipalities in British Columbia where snowmobiles were permitted to drive in town.

Before we parted, Paul and Kelley insisted that my family have Christmas dinner with them. When we stepped outside I was pleased to see that Paul had come on his snowmobile. "I'll show you the fastest way to the lake," he said. He straddled the smoking machine and before I had my skis on had sliced through a snowbank at the back of the pub and was sailing downhill through a meadow, leaving a mist of snow for a wake. I kicked as hard as I could and held his taillights in view. Every so often he looked back for my headlamp, which I'd put on for just this reason. We ran along a winding trail into the woods, crossed a snow-covered road, and finally lurched down a long dip onto the lake. Paul slowed only enough to bid a clipped winter goodnight and sped northwest along the unlit shores of Stuart Lake. I killed my light and turned southeast to diligently follow the tracks set to town.

ELENA AND MY PARENTS LANDED in Edmonton on Christmas Eve. They would spend the night in a hotel there and drive to Fort Saint James early Christmas morning, hoping to arrive in time for dinner. After spending all day Christmas Eve organizing, I needed some physical activity and fresh air, so I decided to ski out to Kelley and Paul's A-frame along the lake, just so I would know where it was. I skied west through the preserved wooden buildings of the old Hudson's Bay Company post that represented the historical kernel of Fort Saint James. It had once been the hub of the HBC's New Caledonia district, which corresponded roughly to the strip of British Columbia I was traveling across. On the lake I picked up more of Paul's tracks. West of the trail to the pub, houses popped up in isolated clusters. The effect reminded me of the little houses I had seen coming down from Telkwa Pass—soft light in the forest, people living in the woods without offending the woods. After an hour of skiing under a partly cloudy but moonlit sky, I came to the only A-frame, right on the water, just as Kelley had described.

I didn't go ashore or try to get anyone's attention. If someone had been standing at the window I probably would have, but I didn't want to be a pest. I just followed Paul's loop around and bore back toward town. I wandered off track and out to the middle of the lake, hoping to shorten the distance by not following the bays, but there was water under the snow. It froze to the bottom of my skis and stole their glide. I took them off to scrape away as much ice as I could and angled back toward the track, skiing only half as quickly as before for having ignored Paul's tacit advice.

It was now below zero outside. I cooked couscous in my room without triggering the smoke alarm and afterward lay on the floor all evening listening to a Christmas concert on the CBC. When existence is pared down, I thought, civilization's simplest pleasures are set against a backdrop without distractions. The salience makes them shine like distillations of their every-day selves: classical music on the airwaves becomes a front-row seat to the Berlin Philharmonic; a rocking chair turns into a gem-studded Persian throne; a cup of Red Rose tea is a glass of vintage Calvados; and your own thin voice reading aloud morphs into the gravelly baritone of Jeremy Irons.

I spent Christmas morning fashioning cards from topographical maps I had already skied across. I made the room festive by hanging wool socks across the kitchenette and filling them with chocolate. When the rental car pulled up I went out to greet everyone. Elena didn't get out right away. Maybe she was cold. Maybe she didn't know what to expect. When she finally stepped out she looked like a frail child. She gave me a long speechless embrace.

MY COMPANIONS WERE NOT AS susceptible to the charms of Fort Saint James as I was. They thought it really was the last right turn on the road to the end of the world. I buried a piece of my heart in the snow by Stuart Lake, and on the day after Christmas we set out in the car for Jasper, Alberta.

The road took us south to Vanderhoof, then east to Prince George and on into the Rockies. We went from rolling evergreen hills to wide valleys of range country flanked by soaring peaks. Then suddenly Mount Robson, its sheer south face, stood high and massive in front of us, and I wondered how anyone could ever climb such a thing and tried to imagine what the other side might look like. This was about what Elena confessed to having thought when she looked out the airplane window on her flight to Edmonton and thought of me picking my way across the white taiga with neither roads nor houses in sight.

It was dark by the time we pulled into Jasper. We drove down the main street lined with tourist distractions—souvenir shops, outdoor sports suppliers, restaurants and pubs. A woman had told my father over the phone that we would find our hotel "on the other side of the creek from downtown." The creek was the Athabasca River. The hotel, which my father had been calling by an anonymous corporate moniker he'd read online, was the famous Jasper Park Lodge. The main structure, a copy of an original that burned in the 1950s, was an elegant polished log lodge in the rustic Arts and Crafts style of national park architecture and contained a life-size gingerbread house that cried out to be nibbled at. When Elena noticed me surreptitiously prying a jelly bean from a doorjamb, she shot me a playfully reproving glance that for an instant transported us both to a happier time. The guest rooms were sprinkled throughout a large lakeside pine grove in tens of so-called cabins—large two-story log houses containing eight or ten rooms each. They were fairly luxurious, and I was simultaneously amused and put off to see my mother at home in this unfamiliar element, calling reception to order robes and "turn down service." I was attuned to austerity and this felt decadent. I wanted back my staticky Brahms on the motel floor.

"We should have stayed in Fort Saint James," Elena said.

"Why do you say that?"

"This is too beautiful."

In Jasper, Elena was calmer. She said she regretted saying that I needn't have bothered coming back if I was coming on this trip; she had let her anger get the upper hand. She still wanted us to be married and she hoped I would learn something important from this journey—that we would both get something positive out of the experience. She thought we might find some way of living apart but still being together. What we had was too precious to just throw away. I knew that what we had was precious, but I told her it was too late for such talk and that I didn't want her to make these conciliatory gestures that sounded almost like an apology. She didn't owe me an apology. I wanted her only to recognize that we were on different paths and accept it. I almost wanted her to be angry with me, but I could see that she was exhausted with worry and sadness and didn't have the energy to put up much fight. In spite of her depression she could see beauty around her. She quietly delighted in watching elk graze in the woods as we walked, and in contemplating the thin stream of open water winding through the mostly frozen Athabasca. I was sad too, but I was also the catalyst of this disaster and was willing to accept the consequences.

The days passed. We walked and ate meals and talked. I felt free and I felt guilty at the same time. I knew I loved Elena but was convinced I had to put a cold axe to our marriage so that I could breathe this air and feel the snow stinging my cheeks. I reappropriated the whole mythology of my childhood in the woods and read it to mean that this was the most fundamental thing. I forced myself to relax in the warmth of buildings only to be agreeable for our last days together, but I knew that I was growing soft. Now I had the downtime to think of my knee, and I grew protective of it. My father wanted me to explore with him, but I didn't want to leave Elena alone, so he mostly went by himself.

Before everyone left on a Sunday, my father bought me a coach ticket back west to Prince George for early the next morning, and I rented a room in the old-fashioned Athabasca Hotel near the depot. Elena and I took a walk in the sun near the hotel and said goodbye. She wore a long coat and was bundled to the eyes. Then she sat in the car behind my father and looked at me through tears and window glass. Hers was the most beautiful face I had ever seen. It was over.

I waved when they drove off, crying to myself, until they disappeared. I walked in circles around the town for a long time. It was a beautiful day, and piercing cold. I wandered back to my hotel room and shut the door. Pink alpenglow shone on the northeastern mountains outside my window. It was the worst day of my life.

PART THREE

PRINCE GEORGE TO SLAVE LAKE

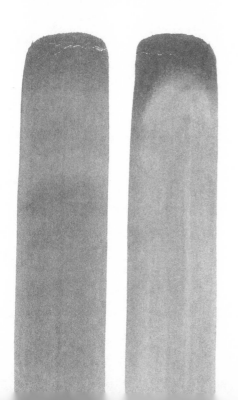

13

GREAT DIVIDE

The Prince George coach depot was bedlam. The woman at the ticket counter spoke with a marked southern accent. She was from Georgia. The effect lent something absurd to the grim northern setting. Everyone found her agreeable, even though she was consistently doling out the kind of news that ruined your day: "If you're lucky your luggage might make it tomorrow" or "The westbound bus is stuck in a blizzard between here and Edmonton."

A young woman ahead of me in line asked for a ticket to Fort Saint John.

"What's your name, dear?" said the sunny Georgia Peach.

"Greenwood," said the other woman.

"Are y'all kin ta Lee?"

"Excuse me?"

"I said, are y'all *kee*-un ta Lee?"

"You asked me that same thing last time," said the young woman, who was amused.

"Well that's just who I *thank* of when I hear the name *Grain*wood."

"I don't know who he is. I'll have to google him."

"*Hwat*?" said Georgia. "You don't know Lee *Grain*wood? He's *ree*-ul famous. Oh what's that *sawng* he sangs?" She looked at the ceiling and rattled her fingertips on the counter. Then the memory clicked and she shouted, "'God Bless the U.S.A.'" and beamed.

Every head in the station turned. The traveling woman stared blankly back at Georgia. "I wouldn't know," she said. "I'm Canadian through and through."

THE CROWDED BUS ROLLED NORTH over the Great Divide, whose greatness is understated in the northern Canadian Rockies. We went through Bear Lake and Mackenzie, where we turned around and went back to the highway to resume our journey northeastward. I had requested a flag stop at Azouzetta Lake, in the middle of Pine Pass, the northernmost and lowest road pass over the Rockies. The bus slowed down and all the other passengers looked around the cabin, wondering why. I walked down the aisle trying not to blush at all the stares. The driver climbed out in shirtsleeves and helped me take my things from the hold. She stood for a second shivering and looking at the heap of gear. "Are you sure you know what you're getting yourself into?" she said.

"I'm already into it," I said.

The bus drove off and I stood alone in the grayness feeling less than all right. I had been off the trail for a week and had done nothing to keep myself tough. "What am I doing here?" floated again near the surface of my thoughts. I stood in my empty sled to keep my feet off the ground and stripped down to my boxer shorts so I could put my long underwear back on. I packed everything onto the sled, put on my skis, hitched the sled to my waist, and drew up onto a snowbank alongside the road.

Things didn't go well on the snowbank. I sank up to my knees and was making impossibly slow progress. I moved to the other side of the road, but I had no buoyancy there either. It was snowing, and the shoulder had an inch or two of cover, but it was sandy and the going was miserable. Still, it was the only way forward. My frustration gave way quickly to tears. This was a change that had happened on the trail: the more time I spent alone and vulnerable to cold and solitude, the closer my emotions rose to the surface, and the more easily the surface broke. I pushed stubbornly ahead with my eyes locked on the ground a few steps in front of me.

It was strange to think that only the day before I had been with Elena. She could very well be back in Italy by now, strolling with Beowulf under budding linden trees where crocuses pushed through the soil. Our present realities seemed unbridgeably far apart. Yet it was not hard to imagine her, twenty-four hours earlier, making me laugh as she quipped with Voltairean mordancy about the pathology of my compulsion to immerse myself in so hostile an environment. Couldn't I just be content to know it existed? It seemed now, as the wind in the pass ripped the tears off my cheeks and sent them flying among snowflakes, that she might be right.

After a few miles of skiing in tears, I saw a point where I could access the railroad tracks and broke for it. Following the railroad had been my plan from the outset, but in my panic I had completely forgotten about it. There the going was much better. The grader used to keep the rails clear of snow left a furrow about twelve inches wide next to each rail that made a perfect track for my skis and sled. With spirits riding a little higher now, I soon made camp for the night.

The next day I skied for a few miles and then came to a narrow tunnel cut into the rock. Even if it had been wider I wouldn't have risked going through it, because there's no snow in tunnels of any length, and I couldn't see light coming from the far end. To find my way around I followed a snowmobile track down the mountain to the road and eventually linked back to the other end of the tunnel. For a couple of days my morale remained low. Sometimes the skiing was boring, at other times tiresome. Bits of wood and tar and sand in the snow, and occasionally loosened spikes, were taking their toll on my sled.

One night I stopped when the wind was blowing hard but somehow less fiercely. I took extra care pitching my tent, securing it at several points to a nearby tree for fear it might blow away. Inside I cooked dinner and noticed there was no condensation on the ceiling. I found the same in the morning. It was highly unusual; something was happening but I didn't know what. When I got out of my sleeping bag I wasn't the least bit cold. Only a few days later did I learn that a Chinook had blown down the eastern slope of the Rockies. I'd often read about the warm wind, capable of melting and sublimating a foot of snow off the western prairies in a single day, but had never imagined the befuddling effect it might have on a person who bedded down in his tent in January cold and woke up to balmy May. It had almost touched fifty degrees in Calgary.

The warm wind still wasn't enough to ruin the snowpack, and after a couple of miles of skiing that morning the woods opened into rangeland, with a farm and some horses in the distance to my south. Soon I saw a road-rail pickup fitted with flanged steel wheels coming up the tracks at a crawl. When we met, the driver stopped. He had a thick black mustache and a broad smile. He asked me through a heavy accent what I was doing and where I had come from. Prince Rupert didn't seem to register on his mental map, but for him it was sufficient to amaze that I had come from Azouzetta Lake, perhaps forty miles distant. He told his colleagues behind him over the radio that a skier was coming "all the way from Azouzetta Lake!" The sun had come out and I smiled for the first time in days.

Later that afternoon I skied through the site of an open-pit coal mine. The world of white so brilliant that I wore glacier glasses to keep from hurting my eyes was suddenly recast in the grim shades of Dickens's London. I could still hear my skis gliding over the snow, but when I looked down the snow looked more like ash. Behind me the white line of my back trail left a clean fracture in the black crust. The trees were coated in soot, as were the tracks of animals, and even the feathers of the birds that hadn't thought to fly away. The high-country winter air was now heavy and stale, making it feel as though weight were being dropped into my lungs at every breath. When I skied through a sulfur mine later the effect was even stranger. Surreal piles of fluorescent yellow powder looked like nothing that could have come out of the ground. They reminded me of my lemonade mix.

I had to cross a bridge over the Pine River. There was a road nearby, and a young man who worked for the railroad stopped his van and shouted to me to wait before crossing the trestle because a train was coming. There was a blind bend a hundred yards beyond the bridge. I waited for a long time but no train came. After twenty minutes of skiing back and forth to stay warm I decided to go across as fast as I could. My heart thumped as I zipped over the open ties, thinking of how best to get off the tracks with my sled in tow if a train should suddenly appear. Just as I was making the other side I saw the black engine come careering around the corner. It blasted its horn at me, and I shot with racing heart down the approach embankment, poling as hard as I could to reach firm ground.

I had come down gradually out of the Rockies into a land of deciduous trees, fields, and biting wind. A herd of about ten deer stood beside the tracks in the falling dark on the outskirts of Chetwynd and calmly watched me ski by. Initially I thought I would ski into town for some hot food and then set up my tent out on the edges, but when I spotted a motel that looked dirt-cheap the idea of returning in the dark to a cold tent after being in a warm restaurant lost all its appeal. The motel was uncommonly grubby, with stale cigarette ash on the kitchenette counter, cracked fixtures, and carpet that would make a cockroach cringe.

The recent history of Chetwynd, which calls itself the "Chainsaw Sculpture Capital of the World," is a condensed history of North American settler colonialism, a process that can still be seen unfolding in many northern places. In 1918, the year my living grandmother was conceived, a trading post opened on the grassy floodplain known to local Indigenous inhabitants as Little Prairie. The land was cleared for agriculture in the 1930s by European settlers from the adjacent Peace River Country. At the time neither road nor railroad connected Little Prairie to the rest of British Columbia. Coal, oil, and sulfur were discovered nearby in the following decade, and not until 1952, when my parents were children, did the province extend a road from Prince George over the Great Divide to Little Prairie. The railroad came six years later and was the brainchild of Ralph Chetwynd, British Columbia's Minister of Railways, whose biography evinces the same fast-forward quality of historical development as Little Prairie. Born in England in 1890, the second son of a baronet (and therefore not heir to his father's title), he left for Canada at eighteen and worked his way up from fruit farming to ranching to shipping, until finally the English baronet manqué had, by late middle age, become a Stetson-wearing Canadian railroad baron. When the first train arrived in Little Prairie from Vancouver in 1958 it was freighted with symbolism: lengths of pipe promised gas and oil development; the steel rails on board would be laid through the woods to the north, reaching for Fort Saint John; empty boxcars awaited loads of lumber and grain; and a transport truck secured to a flatcar was bound for nearby Dawson Creek, where it would roll onto the then fifteen-year-old Alaska Highway. The people of Little Prairie decided to rename their town in honor of Chetwynd, who had died in 1956, and on

Dominion Day (now Canada Day) of 1959 the change was commemorated with a ceremony and a parade, in which a choir of girls marched and sang:

Say goodbye to Little Prairie and the times that were so fine.
Pack our memories in a basket; put the lid on for all time.
People coming, people going, things are always changing round.
To the old folks there's a sadness as the signs are going down.
And the new folks of tomorrow, with the future looking bright,
Look ahead with hope and promise, change to Chetwynd,
from tonight.

I WALKED OUT FROM THE motel to eat and passed long lines of diesel pick-ups and work trucks idling in the night, their owners off eating or sleeping somewhere. I chose one of two Chinese restaurants in town and sat for a long time watching families enjoy each other's company. From the pay phone at the restaurant I called my brother Jon and asked him to mail a spare sled I'd left with him for safe keeping to Fort Saint John. The one I was using was lacerated and still functional but I didn't know for how long.

The next morning as I skied off a man in his mid-twenties on the street asked what I was doing. He said his name was Oleg and he was Ukrainian. He lived in Vancouver but had come to see a friend who was working in Chetwynd. He found the town insufferably dreary and was out for a morning walk, resolved to find some redeeming quality somewhere.

"Do you mind if I walk along with you for a while?"

"I'd love the company," I said, "but you might get your shoes full of snow."

He didn't mind, and he helped me to hustle my sled across the main road, which had been plowed down to the asphalt, so I could cross the sprawling railyard and exit the northeastern corner of town. Oleg was garrulous in the extreme. He told me stories of camping trips he and his family had taken in the Caucasus, bewildering my ability to follow him with inordinate amounts of detail. He told me that he dreamt of riding the Trans-Siberian Railroad. When I told him I had thought about that too, he blurted, "Maybe we could do it together!" and then blitzed off on an unrelated subject. He accompanied me to the edge of town, at the far end of the railyard. By the time we arrived there, at his fast talking but slow walking pace, it was mid-afternoon. We said a friendly goodbye, but I had heard all the talk I needed to hear for a few days and was happy to be on my own once more.

When the buzz of a lumber mill at the edge of the railyard finally passed away I had my silence back. I skied northeast past eight mileposts—Canadian railroads are still measured in miles, despite national metrication in the 1970s—and found a clearing in an unmixed stand of aspens almost as white as birch, a sure sign that I was coming into the Peace River Country, which straddles the border between northern British Columbia and Alberta. After flowing east out of the Rocky Mountain Trench (Williston Lake), the Peace River has sliced a canyon through high mountains. This gap permits the passage of warm Pacific air masses, creating a relatively temperate microclimate along this small section of the otherwise frigid eastern slope of the Rockies. It is the northernmost region in Canada where commercial-scale agriculture is possible. Ecologically, the Peace Country is a large pocket of aspen parkland, or aspen and evergreen blended with grassland—normally a transitional biome between prairie and boreal forest, although this far north surrounded on all sides by boreal forest. I felt like I was skiing through the background of a Tolstoy story. Sometimes there was a country road within hearing distance. I could see signs of farms or places where farms had once been. The landscape had little in common with the dense forests in the mountains to the west.

I came across a trail of blood running down the middle of the tracks, mingled with bits of flesh and fur. After several hundred feet the trail smeared off to the side and went into the woods over a wire fence, to which clung more hair and skin. I wondered what had happened here until I later heard a likely explanation in Fort Saint John—that a large animal, perhaps a moose, had been hit by a train and dragged for a distance before falling to the ground, where it was scavenged by a cougar who lugged it into the bush to consume at leisure.

On the second day out from Chetwynd I made twenty-one miles along the railroad. I called my contact in Fort Saint John in the evening to say I thought I could ski thirty miles the following day and be there by sunset. In the morning I was up at six. It was cold and the stars twinkled in the sky. The day began with a nineteen-mile straightaway that taxed my mind as much as my body.

There was no next rise or bend to use as an intermediate goal, because both were far out of sight and remained so until almost dusk. I'd never seen any stretch so long, straight, and narrow as that corridor through the trees. I thought of Oleg and the Trans-Siberian. The monotony was broken only by the sight of about twenty moose along the way, many that seemed more interested in me than I was in them. They would stand across my path and look at me until they had their fill, then calmly step to one side so I could pass. Finally, in the afternoon I saw a sign warning engine drivers of a steep grade ahead. A couple of miles later I was descending, by long switchbacks, the staircase of escarpments that sinks to the Pine River and then to its confluence with the Peace. Near the bottom of the grade I chanced on a moose trail that appeared to cut out one of the switchbacks. I followed it down the steep opening for a rollicking coast that earned me at least a few minutes.

Shortly after sunset I reached the rail bridge over the Arctic-bound Peace River. High above the river and 500 yards long, its surface consisted only of snow-covered railroad ties. There was no deck. Looking down between the ties I saw the slate-colored water far below, flowing year-round despite the steely cold of Peace Country winters, thanks to the dams that frequently modulate flow. North of the river I trudged the last three miles through the dark to the railyard at Taylor, an industrial satellite of Fort Saint John whose night is as lit by gas flares and the shimmerings of processing plants as it is by the stars or auroras that frequent its skies.

I called Eliza Massey Stanford, president of the local cross-country ski club, who with her husband Edward had offered to put me up while I was in town. Half an hour later the Stanfords pulled up in a massive sport utility vehicle. They apologized preemptively for owning it and said it was a necessary defense against the rigs of the twenty-something roughnecks who come to boomtowns like Fort Saint John and Fort McMurray to make fast money and vent testosterone.

They took me straight home, where we had a hot meal and shared stories. After dinner we sat in the living room sipping tea and talking by the wood-stove warmth. It was a room made to charm, filled with intriguing objects. There was a menagerie of skulls—mostly bovine—hung on the wall, a wooden airplane propeller, driftwood and pottery, antique toys and curios, art objects, and a library covering a range of subjects including a dose of the exotic.

The Stanfords were in their late forties and had come to Fort Saint John from Vancouver twelve years before. Edward spoke with an English accent but called himself Canadian. Long ago, his maternal grandfather had been the first physician in Yellowknife and had bequeathed to Edward the most extensive private collection of books on the North that I have ever seen. I would spend hours in the days to come scanning their spines along the overflow shelves in the basement, plucking out volumes almost at random to read a few paragraphs. Edward's father was the English one, and he had insisted that his sons be educated in English boarding schools, hence the persistent accent.

Edward is an Englishman—he is both wholly English and wholly Canadian in my mind—of the adventurous line, a breed for which I have long had a soft spot. I mean adventure in the old slipping-beyond-the-rose-garden-gate-and-striking-out-across-the-countryside sort of way, preferably in fusty tweeds. When he finished school his parents gave him four hundred pounds and told him to make himself scarce for a year. He landed a job on an ocean-going sailboat. The skipper proved a tyrannical madman, prompting one couple to make off in a dinghy at midnight abeam of France's Channel Islands. The rest of the crew, including Edward, jumped ship in the Canary Islands. There he lived in a cave for two and a half months, subsisting on yogurt and bread rolls. Every day he would walk to the marina to inquire after sailboats in need of crew. He finally boarded one that was crossing to the Caribbean. After traversing the Atlantic several times, he missed a train that was to take him across Costa Rica to the Pacific and decided instead to make the journey through the jungle on foot, plucking mangoes along the way and slurping the dregs of a quart of dark rum. He was then hired, along with another young man, to sail up the long California coast under a tight deadline. They took the whole thing in one-hour turns, and for the last two days, heads nodding at the helm, all they had was a tin of tuna fish and a bottle of sweet vermouth between them. When he walked off the boat in Seattle he went to find Eliza.

Eliza and Edward had been childhood friends in Vancouver, before Edward went off to school. Nowadays she is a painter and photographer. Her mother was also a painter, and her landscapes graced the walls of the room adjoining the one where we sat talking. Eliza dabbles in other media, and while I was there I watched her painstakingly add tempera to water and then add the colored water to dedicated wooden forms in the backyard at fifteen below zero. The polychromatic blocks of ice would become part of an elaborate sculpture she was making for the Fort Saint John Winter Carnival. In her twenties Eliza had supported herself by working summers as a tree planter. One day, while walking to a remote block she was responsible for replanting, she looked up to see an angry grizzly standing in front of her. Before she had time to react the bear charged, threw her to the ground, and sank its teeth into her right arm. Eliza had the presence of mind to reach for her steel shovel and assailed the bear with a steady stream of blows. She managed to pick herself up, still whacking the bear, but it was unfazed by the shovel and knocked her right back down. She got up twice more and was twice more struck to the ground. "I thought that was it, that I was going to die," she says, and with the last blow she stayed down. The grizzly waited long enough to make sure she didn't get up again, then turned and wandered off. Eliza looked up as it walked away and saw a litter of cubs skitter out of the woods behind her. Each tooth mark in her arm took three stitches to close up.

Eliza was generous and patient. Edward had to leave on business (he was an urban-planning consultant with an expertise in landscape architecture) after my first day there, and she took me all over town on the most varied errands—an interview for the local paper she had arranged, the workplace of a friend who could weld a broken ski binding, a sports store where an immigrant from a country without winter went blank when I asked him about grinding my ski bases. We went skiing on the local club trails, and one evening I was invited to speak to a group of teenage biathletes coached by one of Eliza's friends. Meanwhile I did my best to keep busy on my own, tuning my skis in the basement, taking the Stanfords' dog, Tenzing (a short-haired Golden Retriever cross), for walks, or exploring Fort Saint John on foot in the savagely cold air with the pleasing glare of sun dogs in my eyes. I made a few Italian dinners, and for one I had to personally instruct a local butcher on how to extract discs of osso buco from the shank of a hanging carcass. On another day I shoveled off the roof of the shed with the thermometer reading well below minus twenty degrees.

I talked to Elena on the phone one day when I was in Fort Saint John. She was keeping a stiff upper lip, had gone back to work after Christmas, and had even booked a place to spend her summer holidays in Italy without me. It was still very hard to imagine our lives practically going separate ways, even though I'd been trying diligently to do just that for months now. I simply told myself it was good what she was doing, which I believed, and tried not to think about it. I hoped she'd be able to go on living the kind of life she wanted and that I'd be able to follow my own chosen path. It was the last time we spoke that winter.

What I remember most about my time in Fort Saint John is good conversation and comfortable silences. On the trail I had silence aplenty but for conversation only monologue or imagined dialogue. I don't remember much of what we talked about—books, mostly, I think—but after dinner each night we retreated to the living room with tea and sometimes dessert. We would alternate talking and reading, while the Stanfords' daughter Harriet did her homework or dreamed aloud about a journey she was planning to South Africa.

One evening I went into the kitchen for a few minutes to lie in wait for some thought I wanted to catch for my diary. In the living room Harriet must have asked Eliza for some advice. I didn't hear the context, but Eliza's answer made my ears perk up. "You can't set out to find the love of your life," she said. "That will always fail, because happiness consists in so many other things too. What you have to do is lead the sort of life you want, and sooner or later you're bound to fall into step with someone. But it's not something you can be impatient about. Never alter your basic wishes to be with someone, because they will always come back, while the desire to be with a person may change or even diminish over time." I scribbled the words into my diary as soon as she had spoken them. I was sure there was something in them for me to learn.

Between me and Eliza there was an easiness that I have seldom felt in so brief a span of time, and I imagine it was somewhat like having a fond older sister. Even so, after several days of waiting for my new sled to arrive I began to fear that I might wear out my welcome. Eliza sensed my discomfort and thought I had itchy feet. I told her the real reason for my anxiety and she said, "Oh don't worry about that. I like having you around." This, and the recollection of Edward saying, in that hearty English way, "Stay as long as you like, really" the night before he left, made me feel a little better. But the sled still did not come, and in the end I called the courier service to have it rerouted to Alberta. I could survive with my battered old companion a while longer.

On the last night in Fort Saint John we were sitting in the living room after dinner as usual. "It's sad that you're going," said Eliza.

"I'm sad to be going."

Next morning she drove me out past the Beatton River, whose long sloping valley would have made for a frustrating day of travel on skis. She dropped me at the side of the road on a nearly treeless plateau above the escarpments that fell away to the valley floor. I gave her a quick hug and said thanks in the cold. Then I struck out along the edge of a field.

14

PEACE COUNTRY

Using survey maps Edward had given me, I made my way across the ever-changing landscape of gas- and oil-rich northeastern British Columbia. It was a land of fences and smooth snow-covered fields with gas flares scintillating against dusky horizons. Tired of seeing the asphalt highway, I cut south hoping to ski a parallel line running east through fields or along back roads, whichever proved more viable.

On the second day I took to seeking out shortcuts across large fields. It was laborious travel. One field might be exposed and covered in wind-packed snow able to bear my weight, while another was low and sheltered from the wind, its snow soft and waist-deep. Between the fields were sometimes thickets, and transecting them were fences dictating that everything be unpacked, lifted over, and packed once more. All this required a disciplined and awkward kind of movement that was depressingly at odds with the little spoors of mice that skittered in all directions over the surface of the snow.

The wind rose steadily, sweeping long serrate drifts into the fencerows. Sensing the onset of another Chinook, I made my way back toward the main road lest I find myself suddenly in the middle of a snow-shorn field with a hundred and twenty pounds of dead weight and miles of muddy ground to cross. I camped that night in the lee of a three-tiered stack of huge round hay bales not far from a farmer's house. He slowed his truck to scrutinize my tent as he turned into the nearby driveway but must have concluded that I was no menace and went to his door.

The Chinook rattled my tent all through the night like some atmospheric thug. Even using the lighter flap on my sleeping bag I woke up sweating. The morning brought temperatures in the low forties. I lay in bed until the sun came up, knowing today would be a day for hitchhiking.

Outside, the snow along the road was fusing into a brownish slurry. I skied through five hundred yards of it, passing a mangled coyote in the mud that made me sad, to a flat area where vehicles could stop safely. On the back of an old map I scrawled in bold letters, BROKEN SLED. PEACE RIVER, ALBERTA (PLEASE).

I got lucky. A man exiting the nearest driveway was going thirty miles in my direction. He had been born along Georgian Bay, on Lake Huron, but moved to the Peace Country with his family when he was still young enough to attend the local elementary school. He regretted the passing of the days when a man could work hard for three months in the Peace Country and not have to worry about going on the dole for the other nine. He repaired pump jacks (machines that lift oil out of low-pressure wells) for a living, had knobby well-used fingers, and vehemently opposed shale gas extraction. He also took exception to further damming of the Peace River, dismissing the controversial Site C Dam proposal as "old technology."

The man was eminently content with the land he called home, whose glories all around us he exhibited for me with a sweeping gesture of his arm, and spoke of his upcoming three-week holiday in Antigua as of a chore. Three times, he told me, he had met people in tourist destinations who had said, "You know, this place is really nice. I think there's only one place on earth that's more beautiful."

"Where's that?" he had asked.

"Northern British Columbia," all three had said.

People seemed especially fond of the Inside Passage, he admitted, and confided that he had never been there. "Imagine that! Eight hundred kilometers from my own doorstep and I've never been there!" Utterances like this one amuse anyone not from the north. It reminded me of a man I had hitched a ride with years before from Port Edward to Prince George, a journey of well over 400 miles. He greeted and asked for news from almost everyone in every store or gas station along the way with the familiarity of a small-town neighbor. Eight hundred kilometers, five hundred miles. Elsewhere that distance will take you from Toronto to Washington, D.C., or from London to northernmost Scotland.

When I stepped out of the truck my feet landed in Alberta. The asphalt and the roadsides had become only muddier, and every passing truck gave me a light spraying. Soon I was coated in a gray-brown veneer that can't have been enticing to would-be lift-givers.

Initially, the most remarkable thing about the next man to pick me up was his strange accent, which had simplified and drawn-out vowels. Instead of "OK" he said oh-*kee*, by way of assent, with an exaggerated nod of his head, after each sentence I spoke. He still used imperial units only, even though he couldn't have been more than a teenager when Canada changed to metric. His name was Michael Gross, and he raised rapeseed (for canola oil) in Hines Creek. On his dash was a small blue and yellow magnet bearing the name of an auto parts store with an address in Malta, Montana.

"I've got a cousin in Malta," I said.

"Have you?" he replied, catching me off guard with a grammatical consistency rarely observed on this continent. "What's his name?"

I told him the name but hastened to add that my cousin had only been in the town for five or six years. It turned out that Michael's wife was from Malta. "We're Hutterite," he explained, "and her family's from the colony down there." He took out a cell phone, again catching me sideways, and put a call through at once to his brother-in-law in Montana. "Malta's a small place," he said while the phone was ringing. "Eddy probably knows your cousin."

Eddy picked up the phone 900 miles to the southeast and Michael told him the story while I listened to half of the conversation.

"So you know him, do ya?"

Eddy said something.

"Oh-*kee*." Michael nodded his head. "Oh, no kiddin? Oh-*kee*, oh-*kee*. Gophers? *Kee*."

The call was over and I asked him what he'd found out. "Eddy's good buddies with your cousin, Chip. Says he likes him a lot. He comes over mornings to talk before work. They drink coffee and shoot gophers together. Said he's a real nice guy."

Michael dropped me off after about twelve miles and snapped a picture of me with his phone. "I'll send it to my brother so he can show it to your cousin." I could sense he was just as pleased with this small-world encounter as I was. "My farm's just a quarter mile up the road," he said. "If you're still out here tonight, come on over for dinner and a place to camp."

I was tempted to call it quits for the day, to hide in the ditch and wait for nightfall, and then come strolling into the farm. It wasn't because I wanted warm food and comfort but because I had a long-standing fascination with Anabaptists—the Amish, Mennonites, and Hutterites—and their mores. With Quakerism these sects are the least hypocritical species of Christian belief. But while I'd read books about the Amish and known a few Mennonites, of Hutterism I knew very little, which was why I wanted to wait in the ditch.

The Hutterite past has been one of tortuous journeys. Their origins were in the Tyrol, but persecution drove them north to Moldavia and Russia and, later, to the prairies of North America, where they own vast tracts of farmland collectively. It may be this collectivist vein, rather than the well-known techno-skepticism of the theologically cognate Amish, that sets the Hutterites apart. It is most certainly their propensity for communal land acquisition, which is viewed by many of their neighbors as a kind of antisocial hoarding, that puts them at odds, if usually only slightly, with the surrounding culture. They have earned themselves enough of a reputation to have to sometimes pursue their quest for farmland clandestinely. The Hutterites distinguish themselves visually by the penchant among their women for brightly colored homemade clothes, but they too, like their radical Protestant co-religionists, are dedicated in their own ways to the notions of simplicity and plainness. Their pacifism and the German-speaking heritage also bind them to the Amish. Among the three sects, or *Leute* (German for "peoples"), of the Hutterite faith, a brand of Low German is still in use—which probably, in conjunction with their partial rejection of Anglo-Saxon cultural hegemony, accounted for Michael's curious way of speaking. Today, Alberta has the largest number of colonies, but Hutterites can be found as far east as Minnesota and as far west as Washington State.

I stood by the side of the road for half an hour looking back toward where Michael had gone. When a truck slowed down and stopped I turned to look, but as soon as I had turned the driver hammered the accelerator. But he had second thoughts and stopped again. After a moment's hesitation he backed up. As I opened the door and climbed in, it was hard for me to stifle a laugh. The man in his sixties at the wheel was in a surly mood. He had a Jack Russell terrier that humped his arm and passed gas continually. He said he could take me the eight or ten miles to Hines Creek and "not a foot more." When he made to turn left in Hines Creek to drop me along the road that ran east to the town of Peace River, the dog objected to the unaccustomed move and sprang at the man's jugular. "You no good little son of a bitch!" shouted the man, inaugurating a torrent of sharper expletives, as he latched onto the dog's rump, wrenched it from his neck, and flung it across the cab into my lap. This nearly provoked a head-on collision. By now we had made the turn and were starting to pull over. Before the truck had stopped, I hurled the feisty animal back at the man and slipped out the door. I pulled my sled and skis from the truck bed and waved awkwardly and unnoticed as the struggle wore on inside. The truck made an illegal U-turn and drove off lurching from side to side with each renewed assault and repulse.

At the end of the day, the sun sinking low, I was picked up by a chatty man named Delwin with youngish features and white hair. He could take me all the way to McLennan, where my mail had been redirected, but first insisted on getting me a coffee and a BLT at the Tim Hortons doughnut shop in Peace River. He was disappointed that I couldn't see the river itself in the dark. When we came to McLennan, a little town of 700 inhabitants, he drove me in a loop around the main streets to show me the railroad and the post office. He turned off the engine as we rolled up to a bar and motel directly along the tracks. Although he'd never stayed there, Delwin was confident it was the cheapest place in town, and he offered to buy me a beer. When we came back outside to unload my things he gave me a business card and said, "I admire you for what you're doing. It takes ambition, and I admire ambition."

15

MCLENNAN

My sole ambition was a hot bath. I went back inside to talk to the young motel clerk who stood behind the bar fiddling with his phone. The intrusion of an aspiring guest only irritated him. He snatched the rate money and a damage deposit from my hand and dropped a key on the bar, then wrote a number on an abandoned receipt and pointed.

Upstairs there were no sheets on the bed, only a feculent mattress. In the bathroom was neither toilet paper nor soap or towel. The floors were strewn with dead flies, and the stench of stale bodily fluids wafted in from the carpeted hallway. As I stood there feeling had, I heard a drunken fight between a man and a woman in the next room.

With my hopes of a bath dashed, I went for a walk. The dark streets were covered with a thick sheet of ice. A woman zigzagged down the middle of one, looking confused. She wore only a coat, panties, and what appeared to be slippers. I went back to the hotel and called Jon from a payphone to ask if he had any news on my sled, and then retired to the bar to write.

The hotel clerk walked over and handed me my receipt. I asked him, feeling unusually bold, if he realized that my room was completely bare of furnishings. He went back to the bar and returned a minute later with a key to another room. "You'll get your deposit in the morning," he said. "But don't wake me up before eleven-thirty." The new room had a bedsheet, though it was still a long way from inspiring the confidence to bathe. I returned to the first room, piled my gear into my sled, and dragged it down the hall carpet to the new one. I slept in my sleeping bag on the sheet and had a shower on my tiptoes in the morning.

THERE WAS NOTHING AT THE post office for me yet, so I ambled over to the library with my sled in tow. After falling into conversation with the librarian, Maureen, I told her I was restless waiting for my new sled. She urged me to talk in the local school and quickly made arrangements. She even notified the newspaper of my presence. I asked her if I could help in the library, and she handed me a stack of books to sort. As I peeled off my sweater I heard her on the telephone again. When she had hung up she said it was an outfitter acquaintance of hers. He rented houses to hunters in town and would let me stay in one for a reasonable fee. "I can't let you go back to the motel," she said.

It snowed all night and on into the next morning, which I savored in the darkness listening to the radio and sipping coffee. The snow was still falling when I loaded a few props onto my sled and set out on my skis for the École Providence, the local K-7 school. Six fresh inches lay on the ground, dampening all sounds, so that shuffling along through the darkness I felt as though I were in a dream. Yellow graders and plow trucks ground back and forth doing their best to dig out, but so far they'd hardly made a dent. A man shoveling his walkway jumped when I skied up behind him out of the dark.

The school was quiet when I got there. I had beaten the students. The janitor, a woman in her fifties, welcomed me in. She told me that on account of the snow the principal and most of the students were late. Those present were running circles around the gymnasium, which she said they did every day to unwind before class. We drank coffee and ate doughnuts for an hour while she told stories of her late uncle, a trapper who had written a memoir called *Wild Cry*.

Eventually the principal, a friendly Native woman with long straight hair who took her job seriously, arrived and showed me to a room with ten students of varying ages. Most were Native or Métis, and I had been told that few of them had ever left the area, some not even to Edmonton. I wasn't sure what to say. The context was unlike the one in which I had spoken to the Fort Saint John biathletes. With them I had had a wedge of common ground. I talked for a short time and tried to involve the students with semi-rhetorical questions, as I imagined a schoolteacher might. I left them with a moral, which at the time seemed the most appropriate thing but later would seem sentimental and stupid: I am just an ordinary person—not an athlete or an adventurer—who had an idea, and by taking it on piece by piece I was now making the idea a reality. It felt pathetic, like I was giving a TED talk or teaching Sunday School. What made it most uncomfortable were the blank stares on the kids' faces. They seemed to ask only one thing: "What are you doing here?"

Back at the post office it was still no luck. "What are *you* doing?" a woman asked brusquely, when she saw my sled.

"Skiing across the country," I said.

"I work in the secondhand store across the street. When you're done here I want you to come over and tell me about it." There was no chance to say no. I dragged my load over the street, dropped the reins, and followed the woman through the door.

"Have a chair," she said when I walked in. We were surrounded by towers of used jigsaw puzzles, cassette tapes, romance novels, hardback political memoirs, and dusty glass trinkets that had evaded the dump. She took out a small notebook, fired questions, and jotted down notes from an easy chair with a price tag on it. She had never heard of New Hampshire, so she decided that I was from Prince Rupert.

Chris Jones had grown up elsewhere in Alberta but had moved to McLennan sixty-four years before, when she was married. This baffled me because she didn't look a day over sixty-four and her step still had plenty of spring. She invited me to dinner, meaning lunch, and I accepted. We went to the coffee shop in town and both of us ordered poutine with all the works—a French-Canadian invention of french fries, cheese curds, and gravy—which was the day's special. It wasn't a dish you would expect to find on a menu in rural Alberta, but McLennan and a few neighboring towns constitute one of the more important western enclaves of French Canada. Our table happened to be surrounded by members of the local clergy from all the denominations in town. Chris was amused by this and her joking revealed a full-fanged anti-clericalism. She had no use for the Catholic Church in particular and would have liked to see its authority over the local school relinquished. Her husband had died of Alzheimer's disease a couple of years before. In the hospital he was given last sacraments against his will. "He never spoke after that," she said. "I blame the Catholic Church for his death." She said she knew that the Church hadn't *really* been the cause but that she couldn't help feeling that way.

Most of her family had worked for the railroad at one time or another, but now her sons, like so many Albertans, worked in the oil industry. Both of them lived in Indonesia. She didn't know when she would see them again.

Chris described herself as politically active. She had never held office but had always participated a great deal. She didn't make her political leanings explicit but shared an anecdote about the time a friend of her husband's had decided to run for local office on the Liberal ticket. "Chris," her husband said, "we've got to vote for him."

"Well," Chris told me, "*of course* I couldn't do that. So I just told my husband I'd voted for him. He never knew the difference."

"Did he win?" I asked.

"A Liberal!" she scoffed. "In this country?"

On my way back to the library I met a young woman in the town office, which shared a building with the library, who had heard of me from Maureen the librarian. When I told her I was going to set up my tent in the woods outside town if my mail didn't come soon, she said that she and her husband had talked it over and decided to invite me to stay at their place until the parcels arrived. "We probably won't be around much, but you're more than welcome." I wrote down their phone numbers and went out to ski along the frozen slough north of town.

That evening a tall man came to my lodgings and introduced himself as the newspaper reporter. He wore a reversible quilted coat—hunter orange on one side, camouflage on the other. He was a painfully slow interviewer who didn't take notes. Everything was written out word for word and often read back to me still incorrect. He had the habit of reading aloud at writing speed what he was putting down. When asked about my diet I told him that I added butter to my meals to augment their caloric value, and then I heard him muttering as he scribbled, " ... says he adds margarine to meals to boost ..."

"No!" I interjected, perhaps overbluntly. "Not margarine. Butter!"

After the interview I heated up some food and tried to read but couldn't focus. I finally went out on the porch to look at the stars for as long as I could stand. The piercing clear cold of the night bled my mind of its residual ill humors.

In the morning I had a chance at last to talk with the outfitter who had rented me the house. Kevin McNeil had lived all over the north and could surely have told me many things I would have liked to know. He told me that McLennan was the waterfowl capital of North America, attracting toters of both guns and binoculars. It is ideally situated where boreal forest meets agricultural land, he explained in the practiced phrasing of a guide. It is rich in other kinds of wildlife too. Black bear populations are very high because nearby civilization provides an easy food source, while the bush reaching away almost without interruption to the north gives cover. It's what ecologists call an edge system. Later that day I saw a photograph of a large cougar that had recently been shot by a man on the fringes of McLennan.

Kevin and his wife, Patti, owned a fly-in lodge in the Northwest Territories and had lived in the Yukon for six years. "But the coldest winter I've ever experienced," said Kevin, "was in Yorkton, Saskatchewan. It would go down to fifty or sixty below for extended periods. There's nothing compared to Saskatchewan." He knew I would be there in a few weeks.

I showed him a map and asked about a trail I had been thinking about using north of the Athabasca River. "That's the Trans-Canada Trail," he said. "It's a nice idea, but it's practically impossible to follow in northern Alberta. You'll come to a spot and find five trails going five different ways and no marker of any kind. Sometimes it's as wide as a road, others it's narrower than your shoulders. I'd stay away. Keep to gravel roads." (The Trans-Canada Trail—since renamed the Great Trail—is not a single contiguous path, like the Appalachian or Pacific Crest Trails, but a sprawling and fragmentary network of trails, urban greenways, and sections requiring travelers to walk along asphalt highways. Its main route connects the cities of southern Canada, but a spur bends north across the prairies, touches Edmonton, and then aims northwest for the Yukon.) Kevin elaborated on the perils of following trails at random in northern Alberta. Gas and oil exploration have riddled, and continue to riddle, the bush with seismic lines and access trails that will lead the traveler only to disappointment. Many of these trails are so new that they can't be found on any maps. Some that do appear on maps are either overgrown or have never really existed, like the theoretical Trans-Canada Trail. "Stick to the stuff that's easy to follow," said Kevin. "I've spent days looking for people who have gotten turned around following cutlines right around McLennan. When you act irresponsibly like that you're putting other people's lives in danger too, especially at this time of year."

LATER, IN THE POST OFFICE, I was pleasantly surprised to find that both my food drop and my sled had arrived. It was Friday and they had come just in time, since Canada does not deliver mail on Saturday. But I had already told Susan, the woman from the town office, and her husband Luc I would spend the night with them, so there was no thought of leaving until the following day. I spent the rest of the afternoon in the library looking through obituaries, dabbling in accounts of local history, and reading about the Hutterites. In my diary I made a list of French names in the local paper: Daniel LaFrance, Rollande Dubrule, Meme Lavoie, Prosper Hebert, Mederic Laliberté.

Luc and Sue Ouellette's place was literally at the edge of town, the last house before the woods and fields began. Sue gave me the keys to her truck and I drove to Kevin's to pick up my things. When I returned I set about removing the metal fittings from my old sled to put them on the new one. Luc looked on interested from several feet away. "You'll need a seven-sixteenths wrench," he said confidently and disappeared out the front door into the cold night. He came back a minute later and handed me the wrench and a can of WD-40. The wrench was a perfect match.

As a token of my gratitude I made dinner while Sue and Luc sat at the table and hurled questions at me and told me they were inspired by my journey. Hearing this sort of thing made me uncomfortable, because I wanted to see my journey as nothing less than a necessary component of my life, like going to work in the morning or getting your car repaired, although I couldn't exactly have said why. Perhaps such admiration, if it was admiration, made me feel patronized, in the same way that being thanked for something I would have done anyway does.

Luc spoke with the warm cadence of the northern prairies and still lives in my memory as the most affable person I have ever met. All the talk of my travels reminded him of the time he had driven an eighteen-wheeler to the

Yukon and from there back down to Atlin, British Columbia. I remembered Eliza in Fort Saint John telling me I should go to Atlin. Edward Hoagland had written about it, too, in *Notes from the Century Before.* I promised myself I'd go there someday. Sue, on the other hand, had left Alberta only once, when she had taken six steps into Saskatchewan. They said my tales made them want to travel. "Goddammit, Sue," Luc said, slapping his hand down on the table in a crescendo of excitement and resolve. "We're gettin' our passports and next year we're goin' to Belize!"

We spent the next morning, which was forbidding outside, playing board games and gabbing. I knew that sooner or later I would have to go into the weather, so I called the newspaper reporter, who wanted some pictures of me skiing off, and told him I'd be leaving in a few minutes. Outside it was squalling snow, zero degrees and falling fast, as I clipped my feet into my bindings. I said goodbye to Luc and Sue, and the newsman drove down the road beside me for a minute snapping pictures from the window. I crossed the main road and got on a gravel road. About half an hour later I saw Sue's truck ahead of me in the distance. Luc got out in his shirt sleeves and took a picture. He pointed into a field. "Go down there. There's a trail on the left that'll take you to the train tracks."

16

COLD

The house looked abandoned. The cold bite of the wind brooked no second thoughts. Seeing it and turning to it were one action. In deep cold the thoughts that under other circumstances punctuate actions are absorbed into the movements themselves, resulting in a stream-of-consciousness activity. In real winter you opt for the best shelter you can reasonably obtain. The abandoned house on the wind-beaten prairie might be better than my tent. Or it might not. Poking my head inside I saw that the floor of the house was gone. I tiptoed along the spines of the few remaining joists, which were studded with nails, to keep from falling into the debris-filled cellar. I crossed the main room to explore the two smaller rooms at the back of the house. Their floors were warped and cracked and littered with scat. Snow was drifting in. My tent was better than this.

Back outside, now that I hadn't been skiing for a minute, I could feel my temperature plummeting. The wind began gnawing its way into my mind. I knew I had to act fast, so I pitched my tent in the partial wind shadow provided by the house and a broad-skirted spruce tree nearby. I worked as fast as I could, but my fingers were soon in sharp pain. The snow was shallow in the wind, so I did jumping jacks until the blood started coming to my fingers again, and then went on working until the tent was up and my sleeping bag and gear put inside. I had heard of people using this sleeping bag comfortably at seventy degrees below zero. Wanting to test its reputation, and expecting the temperature to approach forty below that night, I opted to sleep with just the thicker of the two tops, at least to start with.

In the year leading up to my journey I trained myself to sleep while shivering, but I found that such sleep was not as restful as warm sleep. The night beside the abandoned house turned out to be a night of shivering, because I couldn't muster the will to reach out of my sleeping bag to zip on the second top, and I didn't get out of bed until nine o'clock. Breaking camp was excruciating. My toes were being cut to pieces by a hundred daggers. I had to take off my boots and seek refuge inside the half-struck tent several times to rub them furiously with my hands before I got it all the way down.

Once my sled was loaded, movement was the sole directive. I had no surplus energy to sustain ideas just then. My muscles refused to work smoothly, but they did work. The day was a long and relentless shuffle through a snowy windstorm, or maybe a windy snowstorm. I broke my rhythm of brisk kicking and poling twice only long enough to stick my hand in my jacket pocket and extract an energy bar, which I stuffed in my mouth and chewed stiffly behind my face mask as I went. I do not remember anything I saw or thought.

That night I made camp in a patch of woods where the snow was thigh-deep. It was the only time I ever slept with both flaps on my sleeping bag. To the designer's credit I was too warm—but not when I crawled out in the morning. I collapsed in the snow several times while breaking camp. I simply could not stay on my feet. My extremities passed beyond pain and into the dangerous realm of insensibility. I found myself folded in two on the ground, this time weeping and crying out the names of everyone dear to me, somehow thinking they could hear me and come to my aid. The words "help" and "why" dribbled incoherently from my mouth through short, frantic breaths, mingling with tears and mucus that froze to my beard.

I somehow managed to summon all the animal force I had left and channel it into a thoughtless fury. I raced through the actions that had now become habit, successfully disallowing myself to give even a split second's attention to the pain and numbness that nearly paralyzed me. With methodical violence, I crammed everything into its place, yanked my harness around my waist and shoulders, and made off at a sprint, drawing on every last reserve. I continued this way for I don't know how long. It could have been ten minutes, or it could have been two hours. But at some point I realized I was warm and moving along comfortably. It had snowed all night and the skiing was good.

I came into the town of High Prairie at dark after another wholly unremembered day of blowing whiteness. The place bustled. The lights of trucks and snowplows blinked in all directions, and I could hear the pleasant squeaking sound of snow being squeezed out from under rubber tires that means the plows can't keep pace with the snowfall. I skied down the sidewalk past the stores and houses like I was just another person on his way home after a day's work. I found a motel and gave the clerk fifty-five dollars. That evening I ate a steak that covered most of my plate. A television hung on the wall of the hotel restaurant. The words "COLD SNAP GRIPS CANADA" cycled across the bottom of the screen. I looked out the window, grateful to be on the warm side of it, and thought about the icy expanse of prairie between me and Winnipeg, where a reporter on TV stood bracing himself in the cold for just long enough to get a good shot for the viewers.

In the morning I continued on. The temperature had come up to six degrees. When I was out on the land again a massive train came out of the east, causing the frozen ground to shudder. I moved away from the tracks and waited for it to pass. It raised a cyclone of powdery snow that enveloped me. The rhythmic wracking of the cars jostling the rail joints and the vibration that seized my body engendered in me an unfamiliar sense of what seemed to be patriotic fervor. "Whoo-hoo!" I let fly at the top of my lungs, trying to outdo the racket of the steel behemoth. "CANADA!" I shouted in a frenzy, reading the running script painted on the sides of a red Canadian Wheat Board freight car. "CANADA!"

No sooner had the train passed than I was restored to my senses. I wondered briefly about this outburst. I was almost fanatically wary of patriotism, no matter what the country. That, of all things, the brute force of industry, which I have always regarded with a measure of hostility, should stir up such feeling in me was a disturbing mystery.

The thundering of the receding train was soon replaced by a quiet but persistent buzzing. Off to my right the blinding gray atmosphere of swirling snow became suffused with electric light, making things clearer and clearer, until I could read a sign designating the High Prairie Fractionation Plant.

Into view came a row of large white bullet tanks and a tangle of transfer pipes and catwalks. It brought to mind scenes from Cold War spy movies. For a minute I was a special agent traveling on skis across the Siberian steppe and had finally discovered the top-secret plutonium enrichment facility. After two days of doing nothing at all above the consciousness threshold my mind appeared to be functioning again, if a bit muddled. It was nothing but a natural gas refinery.

The next morning the temperature had fallen again and the wind came up. Snow flew and piled into drifts that buried the train tracks. As I sprinted from aspen windbreak to aspen windbreak it felt like I was skiing above tree line. It was too cold to think of snacking. Then sleep—anxious sleep.

17

WINTER

Like northern towns whose very existence I sometimes doubt, winter is hard to imagine in summertime. When birds peep and the air pulses with cicada song and plump leaves flutter on the breeze, it takes no special awareness to see that the earth is alive and even to recognize benevolence in it. The thought of ice only brings refreshment—it's an accent on the day, like a dash of pepper on your picnic lunch. The ice cubes in the cooler are delicate things to be carefully kept from melting. It takes intense mental effort to turn the world—on which your very sense of being depends—inside out, so that those glistening little cubes that under the sun look almost like jewels become the dominant element, invading everything else, silencing the music of summer, and freezing the trees into leafless submission. Your own being will be profoundly anxious until you find some way of making heat, which your vigilance will then turn to guarding jealously. The friendly summer world has now become impossibly distant.

The purpose of winter is to reveal weaknesses in living things. Such weaknesses are identified by a restriction of the solar energy that is fed into an ecosystem, which puts everything in it under stress. Diminished sunlight and the resulting cold are the generic stressors, but more specific phenomena test individual members of an ecosystem—starvation, heavy snow loads, blowing ice particles, dehydration, and ice formation that can kill in several ways. Once weaknesses are identified, inefficiencies can be purged and excess pared away in a process of consolidating the gains of the preceding summer, so that the seasons can be seen as working together to maintain strength. Living beings that can't make do with the restricted energy input are killed without fanfare.

When on clear cold days you are skiing across a vast expanse of white emptiness and the air seems perfectly still and you almost imagine there is nothing alive on earth except for you, you can sometimes hear wind currents tangling in the upper air. They moan or make soft howling noises, and in so desolate a place they seem to cry out to have meanings attached to them. But these writhing drafts have no meaning. The rest that one poet finds in silently falling snow is, for another, winter muffling its victims' screams with a pillow.

Still, there's an irony detectable in winter that enables me to see it as something more than a single-minded eugenicist. Snow keeps things warm, for instance, by reflecting the sun's warmth, which threatens to melt it. As the snowpack ages, water molecules migrate vertically in a process called constructive metamorphism, which provides protection from cold and predation for small creatures beneath it but at the same time renders the surface sometimes dangerously unstable to large animals above. Winter's ironies multiply every time I go out skiing and look around. We think of winter as a time of restriction, but what of all the coyotes I saw one afternoon last winter as I skied out onto the lake near my home? There were seven of them. I do not see seven coyotes in seven years in other seasons. Here ice doubles the size of the world for some land animals. Winter expands the range, and the wild canids come out of hiding. But where the coyotes and wolves and foxes win confidence from the opening up of the land, the temptation to occupy the void heightens vulnerability for others. Prey animals are the most obviously vulnerable, but ice has its own dangers, and its hidden weak spots can do in even the strongest predator. Death comes in ways you might not at first expect too. Two winters ago on an exposed stretch of snowless ice I saw a frozen doe, as yet unscavenged. It seemed her hooves could get no purchase on the slippery surface, and she was immobilized beyond redeeming.

Nonhuman animals have three basic strategies for getting through winter: some migrate to warmer climates, some hibernate, and some resist.

Human beings who live in cold places react to winter's stresses with a combination of these three strategies. They make short migrations into microclimates called houses or apartments or tents or igloos that are constantly heated from the inside. Some make true migrations, whether as nomads or as snowbirds to condos in Florida. Human beings do not undergo the extreme metabolic changes of real hibernators, but most of us do spend a little more time sleeping in winter. Resistance is humankind's strong suit, although unlike other cold-adapted animals, there's minimal evidence of phylogenetic cold-resistance adaptation in humans. The closest thing is thermogenesis, or heat generation, by involuntary shivering—not a reliable long-term strategy for keeping warm the way growing a special winter coat is, as some mammals do. Three voluntary resistance strategies humans can use are eating, moving, and—to those with strong wills and the right amount of luck—altering one's perception of cold (which is not the same as altering physiological tolerance). But humans become mighty resisters of winter by what are called cultural adaptations, or simply technology. We have clothes and insulated capsules for moving from place to place and countless gadgets for generating and preserving heat. It is here that both human ingenuity and human hubris shine.

People who live in cold climates use vastly more energy at a time of year when vastly less is available. This is especially true of people in industrialized societies, who make up an overwhelming majority of the population in cold latitudes. I can think of no other animals that have the peculiar and reckless habit of deliberately challenging winter. Yet we do so with tireless zest. We heat our houses around the clock for six months of the year, often with fuel transported from hundreds or thousands of miles away. This we do even if we're absent for weeks at a time, to keep the water in our house's plumbing systems from freezing. Virtually every place frequented by humans is heated at least enough to keep frost at bay—sometimes even road surfaces, sidewalks, and city restaurant patios, where not a gesture is made to keep the warmth from dissipating immediately into the atmosphere. We are more likely to use our cars for short errands in the winter, because we don't like being outside in the cold. Plowing the roads is itself a tremendous draw on the energy economy. Huge fleets of fuel-guzzling plow trucks, graders, and front-end loaders must be maintained to push snow out of the way each time it falls. In mountainous areas, road clearing sometimes exposes workers to the risk of avalanches. Then salt and other compounds are scattered on plowed roads, from which they enter runoff and alter the chemistry of lakes, rivers, and groundwater. Those of us who live in cold places have entirely different sets of clothes for winter and summer and two sets of tires for our cars. North Americans have even gone so far as to evolve the perverse habit of putting ice in their drinks in winter as well as summer, counteracting energy spent elsewhere to ensure the warmth of their bodies.

Since plants, unlike animals, can neither move nor produce appreciable heat, they must rely exclusively on variations on the theme of resistance to survive winter. Some boreal trees use a particularly stolid model of resistance called supercooling. Hardiness alone enables them to withstand temperatures of minus forty degrees Fahrenheit or less. By a molecular sleight of hand they appear to flout the laws of physics and create the impression of taking a few steps beyond the grave. Perhaps, in another of winter's ironies, to keep themselves from dying they die a little each year. Water is said to undergo supercooling when it drops below its normal freezing temperature of thirty-two degrees Fahrenheit but does not solidify. It can persist in a liquid state at temperatures significantly below freezing, but when its molecules are affected by the slightest nucleating event they instantly orient themselves into ice crystals in a reaction known as flash-freezing. Some species of spruce, fir, and larch have evolved so the temperature of the water in their tissue can sink with the ambient air temperature to between twenty-three and eighteen degrees Fahrenheit without freezing.

When the supercooled water does freeze, it releases a burst of warmth called an exotherm (such transfers of latent heat accompany all phase changes), which brings the temperature of the wood tissue almost back up to thirty-two degrees Fahrenheit. Once all the water in the nonliving wood cells (which constitute most of a tree's mass), in the intercellular spaces, and even in the cell walls of the living wood cells has crystallized, the temperature of the tree begins to fall back into step with that of the atmosphere. At this point the vital water remaining inside the living cells hangs in a delicate supercooled balance. It is not the low temperature per se that threatens the cells but the risk of another crystallizing flash-freeze that would cause cell death. The supercooled plant cell is on the one hand protected by the extracellular ice in the rest of the tree tissue, while on the other it runs the risk of dehydration. But if the tree is in good health and the winter is not exceptionally harsh, then the adaptation enables it to come out alive in spring.

There is anecdotal evidence of cold-hardiness in humans. One hears stories in northern towns of northern people getting drunk on frigid winter nights, passing out and lying on the street for hours, and reviving the next morning to tell the tale. Such stories are usually furnished as proof that regular exposure to the cold makes one better able to survive extremes of cold. Henry Robertson Bowers, a member of Robert Falcon Scott's ill-fated 1911–1912 South Pole expedition, is said to have set out to harden himself off by taking naked slush baths in the antarctic cold every morning. As a consequence he apparently slept soundly at night while his companions shivered wakefully nearby. The usual reaction in humans who try to brave the cold the way trees do is hypothermia—a pathological condition. For adapted trees, "hypothermia" is a normal process, but it is nevertheless preceded by conditioning. A light frost in summer can do more damage to a tree than a deep winter freeze. Acclimatization, to simplify, begins when trees receive cues from the solar system about imminent seasonal change. Resistance to cold in trees, then, is indeed a built-in mechanism, but it is a built-in mechanism that needs yearly priming.

This mirrors a paradox in the nature of existence—the inextricable collaboration between free will and fate, the tension between the individual and surrounding reality. The paradox is visible in the cycle of the seasons, which are always the same, always different. A tree conditions itself to survive winter after winter until one year, for a complex constellation of reasons, it finally doesn't. We can never know how or when the end will come, but we are certain that like snowflakes every individual eventually goes down. Some race to the ground like wind-driven sleet, while others are lifted on the wind for a second, a third, a fourth chance. Some swirl and spiral, some fly along sideways for a time, and some even change shape on their transit from sky to earth. When we are seeing clearly we know this will happen, but in spite of it we try to make life beautiful, as the snowflake is beautiful, and sometimes the beauty even takes the shape of a *memento mori*, a reminder of our mortality. This is what winter is.

18

LESSER SLAVE LAKE

Was it the sun? In the morning the inside wall of my tent glowed red for the first time in a week. On the trail a fox walked in front of me. He crossed from one side to the other, occasionally letting me get closer before withdrawing to a safer distance. Later a larger creature—a coyote or a wolf—appeared across a field. He too was curious about me, but as soon as I stopped he turned and bolted into the bush. The sun shone all day. Not once was I cold or hot. It was perfect. Occasionally I had views of Lesser Slave Lake, a huge expanse of white, the far shore a blue haze.

As the sun arced over my shoulders toward the west, in the east there was a cobalt blue low on the horizon. It went to a violet-red as my eyes rolled skyward, then back to blue. The air was limpid and I could feel the steady fall of the temperature against my skin as night slowly drew the curtain. At dark I slid into the hamlet of Kinuso, surprised to find it was more than just the railroad siding I had expected. Along the tracks stood a tidy grain elevator with a new coat of gray paint that held the last shimmerings of the sunken sun. Opposite the elevator the town's main street ran perpendicular to the tracks. The side streets were dotted with cozy houses whose lights flickered on. Townspeople busied themselves shoveling and blowing and playing in the new snow. It was a *tableau vivant* of winter joy, and nothing in me could resist the temptation to make myself a part of it.

I skied up the main street, causing fewer heads to turn than I expected—I was already part of the scene—and parked my sled in front of the little grocery store. I asked the cashier if there was a place where I could get a hot meal. "The restaurant," she said and pointed to a place with Christmas lights back toward the tracks.

For once my eyes were bigger than my stomach. Feeling lethargic after eating too much, I sat and wrote and wondered why the waitress was so stinting with the coffee. The last thing I wanted to do was head back into the cold to pitch my tent. Two men who had seen my skis and sled outside started talking to me, and I decided to try to get a roof over my head for the night. It was the only time I ever hoped for hospitality from strangers. The men were a father and son, the latter in town for a visit from "the city," which I took to mean Slave Lake.

Barry, the father, invited me to spend the night at his place. He owned the local hardware store and ran a small oil well service company. He lived on a farm about ten minutes outside Kinuso. The house had a huge living room with a vaulted ceiling and a giant picture window that faced south toward the hills across the range, where he and his wife kept thirty horses. His wife seemed distant but was kind enough to give me, the unexpected visitor, a towel and some muscle-relaxing salts for a hot bath. I stayed up late watching television on an enormous screen and talking with Barry, who was dumbfounded that I had never seen *Big Bang Theory*.

In the morning he took me out for a country breakfast. The talk gravitated beyond my control toward oil and energy policy, as if he thought I were an investigative journalist with a deep-green agenda. "It's the consumers who drive demand, and yet they're the ones who constantly criticize the oil industry," Barry said, as I tucked into my eggs Benedict. Crude is a natural product, he explained. It seeps from the banks of the Athabasca River as bitumen. It is far cleaner than other things that move around in rail cars and pipelines. He was critical of energy-use habits in North America, arguing that, paradoxically, the problem of overconsumption gets worse the farther south one travels. "I am convinced that there was no obesity in southern climates before air conditioning." This sounded like something I would say in one of my crankier moments, and I laughed. North Americans, he believed, need to embrace diesel cars. Though by no means anti-American, he was critical of Americans' hypocrisy in their attitude toward Canadian environmental politics. "Can you imagine if the Canadians did to the Columbia what the Americans have done to the Colorado?"

THE DAY WAS BRIGHT AND clear again. The snow glimmered like a billion tiny crystals suffused with the soft honey light of the low winter sun. I came to the edge of Lesser Slave Lake at a place called Canyon Creek. Silence hung over summer cottages and the atmosphere was a muffled pink twilight as the moon rose ahead of me, just shy of full. I looked for a trail down to the lake and eventually found one like a bobsled chute that shot me out into the open. I set up my tent in record time. The hard wind pack on the lake ice made a natural platform, sparing me the usual preliminaries. Soon I was inside cooking on my stove and changing into my warm camp clothing. When I opened the top part of my tent flap to look at the northern sky, it was crisp and beautiful, but the opening quickly drained the heat inside so I closed it again almost at once.

A distant buzzing in the dark turned into a snowmobile. Its headlight enveloped my tent as it approached. The driver killed the light and engine, and all traces of them were neatly swallowed by the void. The machine was just a few feet from my tent.

"Hi, there," I said into the stillness.

"Hi," said a woman's voice.

"Nice night."

"Yeah. What are you doing?"

"Just eating my supper."

"You okay?"

"Yup. You?"

"Yup."

"Well," said the woman, "have a good night."

"You too."

Then a sharp *vroom*, and every trace of her was gone.

WIND IS INVISIBLE SOMETIMES IN the Alberta winter. On the lake the snow was packed. In the fields it was looser but looked the same—serene and undisturbed. The spruce trees, as well as the larches that I now noticed shooting up, stood stiff in the north wind. The trembling aspens, having no leaves, did not tremble. Nor could I perceive the wind as resistance or pressure against my body. I could feel only the heat being sucked off me and was sometimes startled by the sporadic snapping of my windbreaker when the wind changed speed or direction. In the morning I had taken out my camera to get a few pictures of the lake. I still slept with my batteries then, and to keep them warm I held them near my skin during the day. The icon on my camera display registered a full battery when I put one in, but I had been outside the tent not five seconds when it shot to a flashing red and was drained. That is how the Alberta wind carries off warmth.

Skiing on a big lake is much different from skiing on small ones, which was all I had ever done before. Owing to their constant exposure to the wind, big lakes like Lesser Slave Lake tend to hold relatively little snow. What snow they do hold is in drifts and is densely packed. The going can be bumpy, especially with a sled jerking around behind you, and when your skis don't meet with a lot of resistance from loose, heavy snow. Then there are the pressure ridges that form along cracks that can be miles long, where two plates of ice collide and one is forced upward, one downward, like subduction in miniature. The ridges can be ten feet high or more on big lakes, and when you cross them you have to be careful of open water. In places the snow had been swept off the ice where the water had frozen solid before any snow could mix with it—a mixing that blurs the ice's transparency and compromises its strength—and there were windows into the dark water below. Skiing over this jagged and drifty expanse, my shadow stretching toward the north and the shore far enough away to forget about, I imagined myself as Nansen traversing Greenland or the Arctic.

When I stopped for a snack and a hot drink from my thermos, I saw a wolf trotting out across the lake sixty yards behind me, bound for the desolate north shore. He seemed in no hurry and occasionally stopped to look curiously my way, but mostly he was unfazed by my silent presence. I followed him with my eyes for a few minutes and watched a lone raven drop out of the huge empty sky to tease him. Probably just lonely, I thought. It was easy to imagine that the wolf enjoyed the company.

I became aware at some point during the day of a penetrating soreness in every inch of my body, probably the result of eight consecutive days of hard skiing in very cold weather. I could do with a break, so I decided I would hole up for a few days in the town of Slave Lake, which is at the southeastern corner of its namesake body of water. Unfamiliar with the layout of the town, I decided to make landfall at what looked from afar to be the most promising cluster of buildings. I soon realized that the town center wasn't along the lake, as I expected it to be. The prime real estate had instead been given to the warehouses of petroleum-related service industries, truck lots, and a junkyard. For more than an hour I looped around the sandy peripheral roads looking for a town. I eventually found it and checked into a hotel. From the price of the place and the expensive-looking equipment in the pickup trucks in the parking lot, it was clear that someone was making money around here.

Over the course of the next few days the temperature again plummeted into the twenties below zero. Even though I was out in the cold for several hours each day, it was comforting to know that I had a warm room to return to. In my down time I read a truly delightful book called *The Winter of the Fisher* that took me on a poetic but informative journey through a boreal forest winter from a small animal's perspective. On imaginary snowshoes I followed stealthily in the tracks of the fisher as he drove a lynx from its den and occupied it. Lying in bed munching on graham crackers I absorbed fascinating details about the lives of old-time trappers and their interaction with the land and its denizens. I came to a deeper appreciation of the role of winter in the lives of plants, animals, and human beings, and developed a new respect and even an affinity for the clever members of the weasel family whom I'd often thought of only as bloodthirsty thieves. And why? Because farmers say they kill chickens with too much verve? The weasel must wonder why the farmer needs so many.

My mittens had come apart at the seams. I had patched them a couple of times with duct tape and seam sealant, but now they were beyond repairing. I went to Canadian Tire, a hardware store chain found across Canada, for some mittens—which would be better on really cold days than gloves—and also looked for a book of backroad maps for Saskatchewan from a series I had occasionally used to supplement my Geological Survey maps. A part of me was thrilled to discover that there was no atlas in the series for the part of Saskatchewan I was going to.

Whenever I went on errands in town I wore the pair of lightweight sneakers I'd bought in a Terrace thrift shop months before. I thought the best way to take care of my old knee injury, which hadn't given me much trouble lately, was to wear shoes that were meant for walking in the summertime sense. The uppers were mesh, and at some twenty degrees below zero my feet were cold in them in Slave Lake. Everywhere I went around town I had to run as fast as I could to stay warm. Only rarely was I ever as cold on the trail. It occurred to me in the middle of one of these sprints that civilization, with its ever-present possibility of retreat to a comfort zone, gave me the confidence to behave recklessly, to flout little measures that might seem insignificant but that if ignored in the winter wilderness could trigger a potentially deadly downward spiral.

My recklessness went far beyond wearing sneakers in the cold. For almost a year I had been sending emails back and forth to a woman named Zoë. Our correspondence had begun when she sent me a short note expressing a friendly curiosity about my planned expedition, which she had read about when she stumbled across a blog I started keeping in the run-up to my departure. Zoë herself had made an impressive expedition across Canada a few years earlier. Over three summers, she and a friend paddled a canoe from Montreal to the mouth of the Mackenzie River, on the Arctic Ocean. She was fascinated, and probably skeptical, that I proposed to make such a long journey in winter. I wrote back initially to thank her for her interest and because, as someone who had traveled over some of the same ground I planned to cover, she seemed like a useful person to know. I had a lot of questions about tools and terrain. She knew a great deal about both, and she also seemed to know people all through the boreal belt of central Canada. With every email that went back and forth, a little more about her came out, and she started to assume a shape and to take up room in my imagination. I secretly latched onto everything we appeared to have in common, no matter how trifling. Each new revelation only reinforced the black-and-white thought habit I had fallen into in the months leading up to my departure from Italy, whereby everything wild or rural was good and everything civilized or urban was bad. She had grown up near Montreal but didn't like the city, so after university she bought fifty acres of land for a pittance in the wild country north of Lake Superior, an area I knew little about but which fascinated me for its association with old-fashioned wilderness writers like Sigurd Olson and Calvin Rutstrum. She built a small cabin far from any neighbors, had a large garden in which she raised what crops the short season on the Canadian Shield (the exposed bedrock nucleus of the North American continent, which wraps around Hudson Bay like a thick horseshoe) allowed, lived without electricity or running water, and heated with a woodstove. I eventually learned that she was the same age as I was.

After a few months we were writing to each other two or three times a week. Zoë came to stand for a life that might have been. Although no clear lines were crossed, there was more affection in the exchanges than there normally is between ordinary friends. I made an effort to keep a lid on my growing fervor in the long emails I wrote to her, but it got harder and harder as Elena and I grew apart and my reasons for such discretion seemed to diminish with every day that passed. As the departure date for my journey drew nearer, I asked Zoë if she would be willing to take on the responsibility of mailing out the food drops I would prepare before setting off, since it was something she had experience with and because I wanted them mailed from inside Canada to keep costs down.

She agreed to help, and this meant that on my way west across the continent before the journey itself, I stopped to briefly meet Zoë in person and left her with my boxes of dried food and money for postage. It didn't matter that before that day I had never so much as heard her voice on the telephone, or that when I saw her, there was not the least spark of natural attraction. (She would later tell me how strange she thought it was that I shook her hand when we met, whereas she had been expecting a hug after all the words that had streamed back and forth between us.) The meeting in person was so insubstantial by comparison with the thousands of carefully written thoughts we had exchanged that it left the impression of a dream, where thoughts are organized by something other than reason and we can recognize people by something other than the appearance they present. I had an imagined Zoë in my mind who overrode the real one the minute I resumed my westward journey. I literally couldn't remember what she looked like.

Once the expedition got under way I would call her every now and then when I was in a town to tell her where to send my next box of food. These conversations were infrequent but long. After I had told Elena in no uncertain terms, for what I hoped would be the last time, in Jasper, that I wasn't going back to Italy, nothing kept me from telling Zoë how I felt—that our paths seemed to be on the verge of intersecting, that perhaps we might try being together somewhere down the line, after I had finished this journey. It was not hard to understand that she probably felt the same way. These things had been just below the surface, waiting for the least opportunity to rise. I began to articulate my feelings in a letter to which I added a few lines each night while I melted snow into water in my tent. But it was in Slave Lake, when the temperature was on its way down and I was feeling cold, that I finally said these things to Zoë, over the phone, and she said the same things back to me. When we were done I felt jittery. I never thought I would experience the initial excitement of romance again, but now here I was, getting what felt like the freshness of a second chance. It kept me awake for most of the night.

IN THE MORNING I STOPPED at the library hoping to use the internet. The woman working at the desk recognized me from the article written by the McLennan news reporter, which had been inserted in a few northern Alberta papers. She spoke with a German accent and seemed Europeanly reserved, but there was a tinge of warmth in her voice when she said, "You are a true Canadian!"

While in the library, I had hoped to read some local history, especially regarding the forest fire that had engulfed the area a year and a half before. It destroyed one-third of the buildings in Slave Lake and led to the evacuation of every single one of its seven thousand inhabitants. I was surprised, however, to find that the library was almost entirely lacking in everything but very recent fiction and children's books. This state of affairs remained a mystery until the next day, when someone told me that the library itself had gone up in the flames.

On my way back to the hotel, walking briskly along in my toque and mitts with my hood flipped up and cinched, a man shoveling snow called out to me. "Hey, how's it going?" he shouted.

"Not bad," I said, imagining from his tone that he had mistaken me for someone he knew, "and you?"

"Not too bad," he replied. "What're ya' doin'?"

I wondered what he meant. I looked down at myself and then all around me but saw nothing unusual. Then I realized it was only my walking in the cold that mystified him. Now that I thought of it, I had seen no one else outside all day.

"Must be cold," he said.

"You'd know," I said. "You're out in it too." The fact had not crossed his mind. He looked at me as though he'd had his first encounter with true genius.

The next morning I was waiting in line at the drugstore. I had skied into town and my skis were leaning on the front window outside. A man with a black beard and a large package of toilet paper under his arm turned to me and said, "You must be Anders."

"I am. How did you know that?"

"My wife's the librarian."

"You're Joe the newspaperman," I said, remembering that the woman in the library had mentioned him.

"Why don't you come around the corner to my office when you get a chance?"

After my errands I walked into the newspaper office. Joe was leaning back in his chair with his feet on the desk looking much more like a newspaperman than his McLennan counterpart had. "So you don't like northern Alberta, eh?" he said. He had just read a blog post I had written the day before. It ended, "While I wait I am contemplating my next move, dreaming of the lakes and silence of the Saskatchewan bush, ready to leave Alberta, where black gold has made the north almost as peopled as anywhere else." I told him I liked Alberta just fine. It was that winter was getting on. I was ready for a change. I wanted to get into the kind of country that skis were made for—into the beating heart of the Canadian taiga.

"You know there's a lot of work here in Alberta," he said. My environmentalist leanings shone through in my blog, and he was pulling my leg now. "You could earn a lot of money. And in your free time I could show you all sorts of nice places."

We talked for a little while longer, mostly about things he felt had been left out of the McLennan article, and he introduced me to the paper's photographer. "Do you have an hour to go out to the lake with him so we can get a few shots of you?" he said.

"Sure," I said. "I'd love to."

As we drove out to a spot on the lake north of town, the photographer asked me about the places I had lived. The list must have been long. I told him that my only intention after this journey was over was to settle down and live simply.

"Settle down? It doesn't sound to me like you know what it means to settle down," he said.

19

EDMONTON

After looking over my maps and considering what Kevin McNeil in McLennan had told me about the fragmentary nature of the Trans-Canada Trail, I decided to leap ahead by bus to Cold Lake, Alberta, on the Saskatchewan border. The prospect of skiing along the sides of paved roads wasn't appealing, and I didn't think the alternative, to ski long distances on large rivers like the Lesser Slave and Athabasca, was safe. I ran to the Slave Lake coach depot in the bitter cold to inquire about the logistics. The woman working there—who for a split second I thought might look like Zoë—told me I would have to take a coach to Edmonton, spend the night there, and then take another one north to Cold Lake in the morning. Back at the hotel, in a coincidence that would have surprised me anywhere outside Canada, I learned that one of Zoë's northern friends happened to be driving south to Edmonton by way of Slave Lake the following afternoon. She had offered to take me along, so I decided to wait for her rather than take the bus in the morning.

Theresa Driediger was strictly business at first. A serious wilderness canoeist in the summertime, she appeared in the hotel lobby in a light jacket, scooped up a full armload of my gear, and portaged it briskly out to her little hatchback. She pulled a tangle of ropes and straps out of the trunk and, working with her bare hands at twenty-two below zero, secured as much as she could to the roof, since there was little room in the car. I followed orders, pulling the lines out from under the racks and throwing them back over to her. "I'm Theresa," she said, once she'd tied off the last knot. "You must be Anders."

Theresa was easy to talk to, perhaps because at the beginning of the drive we agreed that a conversation with long silences was perfectly natural. For most of the year she worked as a psychologist, traveling every week to several remote northern Alberta communities before heading south to visit with her parents and see a few more patients in an Edmonton office. At the end of each cycle she returned to Rosthern, Saskatchewan, where she received mail and had a husband. During the summer she and her husband ran a canoe outfitting operation on the Churchill River in northern Saskatchewan. They also manufactured traditional canoe-camping gear in small lots. Their canvas tent was the preferred wilderness shelter of their late friend, Canadian paddling legend Bill Mason, and it appears in his films.

On the three-hour drive south to Edmonton the road was freakishly dark. A blizzard blew forcefully, and the little oncoming traffic was exclusively transport trucks that had a way of sneaking up and darting at us out of the frantically swirling flakes. Snow streamed fast across the road surface like fine Sahara sand in a paper-thin layer that was mesmerizing. Theresa drove as though desperate to get to Edmonton before something—the end of the world, perhaps—happened. At one point, in the middle of one of our long silences, a deer leapt from the white torrent into our side of the road. We were traveling at over seventy miles an hour. Theresa made to swerve left, when suddenly the high beams of a speeding semi appeared in the other lane. I braced myself as she coolly slithered between the truck and the deer's hindquarters without taking her foot off the gas pedal, let alone breaking. There were six inches to spare.

"That was close!" I said, once my heartbeat had been restored.

"I'm sorry. What was that?" she said pleasantly from another dimension. Later that night in Edmonton I again feared for my life when she sped through a bright-red light at a busy intersection, with the same steady foot on the accelerator, causing us to narrowly miss being smeared into oblivion by a city plow whose blade was as big as her car.

I spent the night in a guest room in Theresa's parents' house. In the morning, she drove me to the bus station on her way into the office. We gave each other a hug and went our separate ways. I bought my ticket and was glad when the man at the counter said he wouldn't charge me for my excess baggage.

Edmonton, the northernmost metropolis in Canada, is the hub on the wildly spinning wheel of the northern Alberta oil and gas complex. It is the urban gateway to the north—where northern people who have trickled down out of the bush loiter in the bus station, pacing with a disoriented look in their eyes, and sometimes vomit in the bathroom sinks. I filled my water bottles and boarded the bus, eager to be back in the bush and a more agreeable kind of north.

PART FOUR

EDMONTON TO LAC LA RONGE

20

PARADISE
BELOW ZERO

"Would you care for some parlor ice cream?" The coach was heading north-east. Snow-covered fields flickered past the window like frames projected from an old movie reel. The heater made the cabin far too warm.

"Would you care for some parlor ice cream?"

I realized the repeated question was directed at me and turned to see a Native kid extending a fork and a half-gallon tub of ice cream toward me. He was smiling broadly.

"No, thanks," I said, smiling back at him.

In Cold Lake, home to a major Canadian Forces Base and Air Weapons Range (which reaches over the border into Saskatchewan and at more than three times the size of Rhode Island is one of the largest weapons ranges in the world), I made the mistake of getting off the coach in the town center. The town was sprawled over the threshold between farmland to the south and bush to the north and east. It didn't really have a center.

I had a contact in Cold Lake who was holding a supply drop for me. In his emails he had been enthusiastic about helping me and hoped he might be able to join me for a day of skiing. I called him from the parking lot of the hotel where the bus had left me.

"Hello?" said a young woman's voice.

I asked to speak with my contact.

"Who's calling?"

I told her who I was.

"He's not here right now. Can I take a message?"

I asked if my parcel had arrived.

"I think my husband said something about that."

"Well, I'm in Cold Lake now. When will I be able to find him?"

"He should be home in a couple of hours. Where are you staying?"

"I don't know yet," I said. "Would you please tell your husband I called? I'm going to find a place to stay and will call back later."

I walked into the hotel and discovered that the prices were extortionate. "You wouldn't happen to have a special rate for people on long-distance ski expeditions, would you?" I asked, feeling shamelessly impertinent in the face of such banditry. Cold Lake is home to one of Alberta's three major oil sands deposits, and money has a way of following oil. The clerk took my question at face value and went to ask her supervisor. When the two of them came back they looked at me perplexed. The answer was no. Too bad, I thought as I walked away, because I would have enjoyed asking if they offered valet parking for my sled.

A mile down the strip I found the King's Court Motel—conveniently located right by the bus depot where I should have got off—where prices were more in keeping with my ratty budget. After a trip to the library to check my email, I got hold of my contact, who agreed to bring my supplies over. On the way back to my lodgings I stopped at the grocery store for some fresh vegetables and two cheap microwave dinners. My contact's truck pulled into the parking lot just as I was walking in. We shook hands and he carried the parcel up to the room for me. He was interested in seeing my gear, so I gave him a brief tour, but he said he wouldn't be able to join me skiing after all. He was a jet technician with the Royal Canadian Air Force and had been put on standby to fly to Yellowknife at any hour. The Russians, he explained, had been provocatively skimming Canadian and Alaskan airspace the last few days and the RCAF was on high alert. He had already been to the Northwest Territories and back twice that week.

Next morning, after putting off my inevitable return to the cold and lonely trail by having coffee and doughnuts at the local Tim Hortons, I finally mustered up the energy to leave civilization behind for a while again. Not far away a boat ramp spilled me onto Cold Lake, where the tire tracks of trucks ran away to the northeast toward fishing huts in the far distance. After six or eight miles I passed the farthest of the huts, and once the last group of three fishermen and their truck had become specks on the horizon behind me I decided to camp. Late that night I opened my tent door to look outside. Far off to my left I saw the Alberta shore, where lights illuminated the lake edge and the sky above. To my right I saw only utter darkness: Saskatchewan.

THAT NIGHT ASTRIDE THE ALBERTA-SASKATCHEWAN border, which divides Cold Lake in half, a storm came down on the ice and rapped on my tent walls, pelting them with sleet. My sleep was restless and I didn't get up until much later than usual. It had been my plan to ski in a straight line in the morning and come off the lake on the Saskatchewan side right where I wanted to be, at the mouth of the Cold River. But the blizzard raged on, and outside my tent all I could see was a swirling whiteout. Without visible contrast there were no points of reference I could leapfrog between to follow my compass bearing. I knew, however, that traveling southeast from my tent site would take me to the closest lakeshore only half a mile away. All I needed to do was get within sight of the darker blur of the shoreline, and then follow it northeast until I hit the little bay that the Cold River discharged into. It wasn't as straight a route as I had hoped for, but it was the surest.

It worked. I managed to get within sight of the shore without losing my sense of direction, and after a few hours of pushing blindly through the snow squall I found the bay I was looking for and made landfall just south of the Cold River. The snow stopped and suddenly I was in a world so utterly unlike the one I had left twenty-four hours before that it was as if I had died and awakened in an eerily serene paradise. Looking across the white expanse of the lake behind me, with its softening frame of forest at the near edges, no trace of civilization could be seen. A snowshoe hare darted noiselessly past and halted under a stand of jack pines contorted in weird human shapes and dressed in a fresh mantle of snow. Every few seconds bits of this snow tumbled off the boughs and fell without a sound.

I skied north a few hundred feet toward the river. I was extremely surprised to find it mostly ice-free in spite of the minus forty-five degree temperatures of the preceding weeks. Luckily there was a buried bridge that belonged to a summer road. I was in search of a path I'd heard about called the Boreal Trail, which runs sixty miles from west to east across Meadow Lake Provincial Park, but my old maps gave no indication which side of the river the trail started on. Within minutes I found an opening in the bush on the north side of the river that had seen some recent use by snowmobilers. Its appearance was inviting, so I chose it and soon I was glad I had. It was a narrow trail that bounced up and down through the bush, still mostly among aspens. I camped that night in fluffy snow where the aspen parkland started to morph into the spruce and fir of boreal forest.

I got off to a delayed start in the morning because I had slept in again after a late night dismantling and replacing a broken part in my stove before I could make dinner and melt snow for the following day's water needs. I wasn't concerned, because it was February now, and I knew that the sun wasn't setting until six o'clock. But I would have to start shortening my evening rituals.

Once I had broken camp I got back on the trail through the bush. It was pure boreal forest now—mostly spruce interspersed with uniform stands of jack pine or aspen. The trail was narrow, pleasantly up and down, and winding. For me this was what ski touring was meant to be. It is hard for me to imagine a better place. The snow was deep and downy, and the trail had been lightly broken.

The province of Saskatchewan takes its name from the river of the same name, the great trade route between Lake Winnipeg and the Rocky Mountains. It is a Cree word meaning "swift-flowing river." But as I slid along I speculated about other secret meanings this susurrant word might carry: "the land that rocks you in its snowy lap," "the place of white silences," or in a happy phrase from the American wilderness writer Calvin Rutstrum, "paradise below zero."

Unable to contain my enthusiasm, I started talking. The only face I could see was that of Roald Amundsen, who all day every day stared austerely at me from the tips of my skis, reminding me not to be faint-hearted. He seemed almost to scowl. I appreciated the motivation, even though the approach was old-school. But what I needed now was more cheerful company. So I decided it was time my skis had names. My left ski I dubbed Jackrabbit, after "Jackrabbit" Johannsen, one of my lesser heroes, who is credited with having introduced cross-country skiing to eastern North America. He was a spirited man who lived to be 111 years old and skied to the end. On my right foot was Fridtjof, named for Fridtjof Nansen, a major hero of mine. Although Nansen never reached the pole he aimed for as his younger contemporary Amundsen did, I've always admired him because he realized there were more important things than exploring on skis and went on to distinguish himself as a scientist and to become one of the most important humanitarians of the twentieth century.

"It's a marvelous day, isn't it boys?" I said. Jackrabbit and Fridtjof gave every indication of agreeing. They were sliding along better than they ever had. They were doing so well in fact, and seemed to be so thoroughly in their element, that I began to regret the absence of an indigenous English word for skis—*ski* being a mispronounced Norwegian loanword—and coined the term *bushsliders*. At one point the trail ran north, but a few snowmobile tracks headed east into a bog. I unhitched my sled and slid down after them to see whether the tracks continued into the bush on the far side. They didn't. Aside from these tracks in the snow, there was no trace of humanity. Everything was silent.

I forged north through deeper snow until I intersected another east-to-west trail that had recently been tracked by a snowmobile hauling a sled. I supposed I was on someone's trapline. After a couple of miles, sure enough, I came to a pile of logs stacked across the trail with steel traps stapled to them. The tracks I was following kept going eastward, but I noticed that the same driver also had a track going south from the trap pile on a narrower trail. I continued east and after another mile or two met the maker of the tracks just as he was rounding a bend coming toward me. He rode a quiet working snowmobile, not the loud muffler-shorn variety ridden by rowdies near towns. We asked each other about our respective leaving places. When I told him I had come from Prince Rupert he said, "I've never seen anyone skiing out here, let alone someone skiing from provinces away."

His name was Harley Nault. He was a middle-aged man with dark blond hair and looked focused on some task. He told me his track ended a few miles farther on. I asked him if there was a way through and he said there was if I knew where to bend southeast to avoid the Air Weapons Range, but that I would have to cover a long distance, twenty or thirty miles, breaking trail in two or three feet of snow. He said that the trail I hoped to link up with, the Boreal Trail, ran along the south side of Pierce Lake—meaning I had chosen the wrong way along the Cold River—and essentially followed the road. The best thing, in his view, would be to go back to his traps, turn south, and ski until reaching a cabin, which belonged to his brother-in-law. There I should turn east and join the little-used gravel road that weaves its way among the chain of lakes east of Pierce. The road was not often plowed and would be covered in snow.

"My truck's parked at the cabin. You want a ride down there on my snow-machine, or is that cheating?"

"I can cheat," I said.

We wasted no time loading all my gear into his utility sled with his traps and rifle. I climbed on the back of his snowmobile and we were off. After half a mile we hit a bump and one of my bushsliders went somersaulting through the air behind us. Harley stopped and I went back to secure it. A short while later we lost my duffel bag. I strapped it to my sled inside his sled and that solved the problem. We made a stop where the traps were so Harley could move them off the trail. I asked him if it had been a good season so far.

"Oh, no one traps anymore," he said. "We raise cows and outfit hunting trips. I'm just trapping wolves. There's so many of 'em now. I got fifteen this year. A lot of the guides won't even walk in the bush anymore. They're scared they'll get eaten!" He laughed. "I'd say we've gotten eighty over the last three years. And they're not killing our cows anymore." Harley lived sixteen miles to the south, in Pierceland. The wolves came out of the endless woods to the north, picked off a cow, and then retreated into the wild.

We climbed back onto the snowmobile and turned south, downhill onto the narrow tunnel-like trail I had seen before. The bush was impossibly dense. On the snowmobile it was a roller-coaster ride, with me holding onto the gear rack with one hand so I could turn sideways and keep an eye on my equipment in the sled. Bobbing up and down we went, at perhaps fifteen miles an hour, taking face shots from the branches reaching out across the trail. The odd snow-laden spruce bough served its load straight into my hood. It was an exhilarating ride for someone accustomed to a slogging pace. The fifteen-minute lift took me a distance I'd have required an hour to cover under my own power.

When we got to the cabin the sun was about to set, and Harley offered to open it up for me to stay in. He even started a fire in the stove while I unpacked, then pilfered a few snacks from his brother-in-law's pantry and rolled off in his truck, crunching snow under his tires. I had a candlelit dinner of couscous and rehydrated beef cooked on a propane range and felt like the richest man in Saskatchewan.

21

IN CREE COUNTRY

I woke up at 5:45 and went outside to look at the sky for a few minutes. It was February 5. Back in the cabin I fed the woodstove and returned to bed until 7:30. After drinking two cups of coffee, tidying up the place, and shoveling the outhouse entrance as a gesture of thanks, I didn't get off until ten. A long driveway covered in ten inches of snow, except for Harley's tire tracks, led me to a gravel road that had received two inches of snow since its last plowing. No one had been over it since. It looked like an untracked cross-country ski racing course laid down across the wilderness just for me. I moved at a steady clip all day through rolling country of white spruce, jack pine, and aspen with occasional views of large patches of pure white where the land made troughs. Under these patches lay frozen lakes. This was not the flat terrain I'd always associated with the word Saskatchewan. Sunshine beamed through the clouds, and the days were longer now. Despite my late start I made twenty-two miles and camped near a junction with another untraveled road that came from the village of Goodsoil to the south.

The next morning I continued east. It was colder. Snow fell with a quiet steadiness that made it seem like the work of an intensely focused mind. I locked into a fast pace and propelled myself over the silent land of snow by countless scissoring steps. When I reached the next junction in this broken line cut across the weirdly empty white space, twenty-seven more miles lay behind me. I was famished and exhausted.

On the third day out from the cabin I was on the road that runs north from Dorintosh to the Cree Reserve on Waterhen Lake. The road wraps around the west side of the lake and then runs eastward a few miles above its north shore. An offshoot turns south and leads to the community on the eastern edge of the lake. I expected to have a relaxed day, having come far the day before, so I slept in. When I got up the sun was brilliant and hoar frost made the air sparkle. I started skiing north through celestial spruce forests along a trail I found by chance. The sun warmed the snow and made my skis slide quickly, and I was exceedingly happy. So many moments of my journey were like this one—the purest and most innocent kind of joy. It was easy to forget at such times that many moments were pure boredom and many were hell. Everything is intensified on a winter journey.

In the afternoon, when I was near the road, a vehicle with four teenage Cree boys stopped to ask what I was doing. I told them. "What's it for, buddy?" the youngest boy in the back seat kept asking, striving to be heard. "What's it for?" The driver talked and the passenger snapped pictures of me using his phone in that unselfconscious way of millennials and veteran photojournalists. The driver, who must have been close to twenty and commanded his own style of teasing eloquence, told me I was in wolf country and was only getting farther in. He wouldn't leave the topic. "A guy was recently attacked up in Key Lake," he said with a subtle upward tick in the corner of his mouth. Finally the passenger, done with his photography, said, "Stop tryin' to scare him, eh."

I skied past the turnoff for the village of Waterhen Lake at sunset. The day had been clear, and it was long in getting dark. Eight miles lay between me and the intersection with the so-called 903 road, my objective for the day. I had decided to ski into the night because I felt good about my progress and was in a mood to improve my advantages—and because the sky was so clear. I hoped the northern lights might dance. I had seen them only once all winter, on the road near Calgary while I drove west to Vancouver, before I sailed north to Prince Rupert. At the very least I would see the stars twinkling like tiny crystals in the endless indigo atmosphere.

At about 7:30 the headlights of a truck came up behind me. The woman in the passenger's seat said she and her husband had seen me that morning, and now they had brought their snowshoes with them, in case they didn't find me along the road. They were prepared to follow my tracks into the bush to my camp and deliver warm food. They brought me a freshly made loaf of bannock, the simple fry bread of the north, with packets of peanut butter and jam, and a thermos of green tea. I asked if I could climb into the cab and visit with them while I ate. Their names were John and Pauline. John administered all public buildings on the Waterhen Lake Cree First Nation Reserve. Pauline had worked in the oil sands for years but was now at home. While I ate their food and answered their questions, Pauline sat with one foot casually resting on the front seat and turned to talk to me in the back. I couldn't see much more than their profiles in the dark. John looked straight ahead into the night, turning only occasionally, and quietly sipped at a can of Budweiser. "I'm a modern Indian," he said in a voice soft and deep. "I admire someone who can spend a night outside in the winter." He laughed at himself.

His statement made me ask if trapping was still an important part of the local economy. The question was tied in my mind to my observation that snowmobile tracks in Saskatchewan seemed to go purposefully over the land, not like the tracks I'd seen in Alberta and British Columbia, which in their aimlessness seemed to be almost exclusively recreational. John told me he had learned the rudiments of trapping from his father but had never taken it up himself. "Up north," he explained, "it's still important, but around here it's dying out with the old guys."

When talk turned to my onward route, John guessed I would be in Canoe Lake (where *canoe* rhymes with *nano*, not *anew*), the next reserve to the north, by Saturday. It was Thursday now. "We'll have to round up some Canoe Lake girls to keep you warm," he said. Another truck came along and stopped to ask if we were all right, sitting along the lonely road of a winter's night. The conversation was in Cree, which from there to Quebec is still widely spoken alongside English. John told the men in the other truck everything was fine.

After the men moved on, John gave me a simple survey of the indigenous geography of the land ahead of me: "Cree territory extends from here northeast to Beauval. Between Beauval and Pinehouse Lake is Dene country. North from Pinehouse it goes back to Cree."

It was cold when I got out of the warm truck after forty-five minutes. When the truck was gone it was darker than before. We had been sitting on a rise in the land, and under the stars that seemed to wink messages at each other across space I could see for miles over the rippling land to the north, where not a light shone. Such stillness I guessed I would never know again.

AN HOUR LATER I LOOKED for a pocket in the bush where I could pitch my tent. A truck coming north along the road from Meadow Lake braked when the driver saw the red of my back against the unbroken white of the world in his headlights. The truck stopped ahead of me and a man got out and walked my way. We stood two feet from each other, but I couldn't see his face. His voice reminded me exactly of Michael Gross's, the Hutterite man I had met in Alberta. I don't remember what he said, only that he was there, and that a few seconds later all trace of him was gone.

I slept late again. I had covered so much ground over the past few days, I joked to myself, that my internal clock still hadn't made the adjustment to central time. The sun was high and the red light it created inside my tent was bright as I lingered over a mixture of hot chocolate and coffee. This was the first time I had afforded myself the luxury of chocolate in the morning. As I savored the coming alive of the day, I heard the crunch of tires slowing down on snow. I had made camp the night before just thirty feet from the road in a clearing, but until now it had been silent. The road, after all, was just a strip of gravel laid down through the trees and muskeg. Without regular use it would vanish in a few seasons.

"Hey!" said a man's voice from the roadside.

I opened my tent door and saw a Native man of twenty-five or thirty looking at me from behind mirrored sunglasses. He was at the wheel of a red truck. "What are you doing?" he asked. "This is a weird place to sleep."

I explained that I'd traveled until late the night before and couldn't be bothered looking for a better site. I told him I was on my way to La Ronge and beyond. I told him that I had come from the West Coast.

"Whoa! You're hardcore," he said with youthful enthusiasm. "I'm going down to Meadow. If you're still out here, I'll stop and check on you later."

IT WAS ANOTHER SUNNY DAY, and the first few miles were smooth going. But then the snow turned gravelly. The plow driver had been overzealous, and the snow beside the road was too deep to pull my sled through. For ten miles there was no good way to avoid the little rocks and sand, so my skis and my sled took a rattling. Much as I hated to admit it, even snow-covered gravel roads that I might travel along for days without seeing a single car are still roads and are made with wheeled vehicles in mind. As I wished that a truck would come along and offer me a ride over this stretch, I remembered the remark of Patrick Leigh Fermor, the great walker of the Rhine and Danube, that "horsepower corrupts." But the corruption began long before the internal combustion engine, or even the wheel, when man first fashioned shoes for his bare feet.

Toward evening the young man I had seen that morning pulled up beside me on his way home from Meadow Lake. He got out of his truck like he had some business to get down to. He was still wearing his sunglasses, as well as a pair of brown Carhartt overalls and a high-visibility safety vest. I now saw that he had long black hair tied in a ponytail and a strong build. From the cab he took three bags of groceries and walked over to me. He held out the bags. "This is a gift on behalf of my people," he said in a solemn voice. The bags contained a two-liter bottle of soda, a loaf of white bread, a packet of baloney and one of hot dogs, and several pounds of fresh fruit and vegetables. I was moved. I took the gifts and thanked him, knowing as I did so that most would not withstand the inevitable freezing of the next few hours. It was sad and beautiful at the same time.

To be polite I opened the soda and took a long drink in front of him. The man told me that he came from Cole Bay, on the Canoe Lake Cree Nation Reserve. After we had talked for two minutes he turned and walked back to his truck. Before climbing in he stopped for a moment and looked at me. "By the way, Anders, if you ever write a book about this, remember one thing: *I* am the mysterious stranger."

22

MAPS AND DREAMS

Somewhere along my ski north to Canoe Lake two men stopped. They were between their forties and sixties. They came from the north. I asked them if they were from Canoe Lake. They said no, they were from Dillon. I knew, from hours poring over my maps, that Dillon was a Dene community on Peter Pond Lake, sixty miles north of Canoe Lake as the crow flies. What I didn't know was that a truck could drive straight from Dillon to Canoe Lake at this time of year, which the two men claimed to have done.

"I didn't know there was a winter road," I said.

"There's a road."

When I told them I was heading for La Ronge, they said I was going the wrong way. "The long way," I allowed, "but not the wrong way." I explained that I chose to use back roads because they usually doubled fairly well as ski trails. The men had a far-off look and the same distant way of speaking.

"Are you on your way to Meadow Lake?" I asked.

"No. We're going hunting. Wanna come with us?"

I thought about it.

"Climb in," the driver said. "Throw your stuff in the back."

"I'm tempted," I said. "When are you coming back this way?"

"Oh—" said the driver, evidently not having considered this aspect. "Tomorrow."

"Where are you going?"

He got out of the truck with a map. When he and his passenger walked over, I was surprised at the spring in their step. It seemed discordant with their battered appearance. The driver opened the map. "Down in here," he said, vaguely swirling his finger around the area between Meadow Lake and the Alberta border.

"Are you camping?" I asked.

"Maybe," said the driver. "His sister," he said, gesturing toward the other man, "lives down there. We might stay with her."

"And would she let me stay there?"

"Why not?"

"So you're coming back tomorrow?" I asked.

"Yeah. Tomorrow. Or in a few days."

"Tomorrow or in a few days?" I laughed a little.

"Whatever you want. It doesn't really matter."

I was amused. I wanted to go, but the trail was calling. Something inside me was telling me I had to move forward to some goal—that I had a plan to execute—even though I was freer of obligations, then, than I am ever likely to be again.

"I'll take you to La Ronge," said the driver suddenly, a change of plan that seemed not to faze his fellow traveller. La Ronge was 185 miles in the opposite direction.

"But I thought you were going hunting."

"Yeah. But we can go to La Ronge."

In the end, I explained that I preferred to ski to La Ronge, that I didn't need to be there as quickly as a car would take me. Yet it was something else that held me back from accepting their invitation—something that puts most North Americans in races against clocks and across maps, something that makes us feel anxious if we double back on ground we've already been over. Almost as soon as they had gone, I wondered if this would be one of the regrets of my journey.

It was not the hunting I regretted. It was for a chance to learn something—and these two seemed like they could teach me—about the non-necessity of the relationship between planning and efficacy that I wished I had gone with them. Early in my journey I had read a book by British anthropologist Hugh Brody called *Maps and Dreams*. Brody, tasked with making land-use maps for the government, tells the story of a pair of hunting expeditions he took with a group of Dene in northeastern British Columbia, the Beaver people, not far from Fort Saint John. He describes his inability to nail down the details of when they were to leave and where they were to go. He finds an almost willful refusal even to consider making a plan. Any mention of time is approximate at best. Even when Brody and his companions are on the hunt and part ways in the bush in the remote and limitless terrain of northern British Columbia, they reject the idea of a set rendezvous, feeling that things will work out, that they will find their way back to each other at the right time. And according to Brody, they always seem to converge on the same point within a few minutes of each other. Everything works almost perfectly, perhaps more smoothly even than it might have had a strict plan been followed, with watches, maps, and meeting places. The trips are as successful as they need to be. No one is lost. There is no sense of time wasted. I badly wanted to discover something about whatever mechanism was hiding here.

Of course, there is a cultural leap between the Beaver Dene in the 1970s, when Brody's book was written, and the Buffalo River Dene of northern Saskatchewan in 2013, but I suspect there is a common denominator, in the same way that the clock governs alike the life of a Russian, a Spaniard, or an American.

I told an Italian friend the story of these two men. I mentioned that this was the biggest regret of my winter journey and wondered aloud why I hadn't gone with them.

"You didn't trust them," he said.

"But that's just the point," I replied. "I did trust them." I had no idea what they were doing, but I felt it would have worked out fine. The problem was that I could not cut the line that is forever drawing me to the imaginary future horizon.

23

CANOE LAKE

That night I followed a trail into the woods on the merest hunch. Someone had told me there was a cabin within a few miles of there, and my wishful thinking suggested that this trail would lead me to it. I tramped a short distance through the deep snow, and by the time night began to fall I had found no cabin. I settled for a clearing in a stand of jack pines and pitched my tent with the door facing north, as I always did. It didn't matter tonight, because by the time I had finished my dinner of frozen baloney sandwiches, it had started to snow and there was no starlight in the north. I was woken at intervals by the sound of tiny avalanches sliding down the outer walls of my tent as the snow grew deeper.

It snowed all night and into the morning. I had put a few baloney sandwiches in plastic bags and kept them in my sleeping bag overnight so I could eat them for breakfast. In the morning I found them squashed and crumbly, but at least not frozen. Having already poured out the soda the night before, I ate as much of the rest of the mysterious stranger's food as I could for breakfast, kept what would reasonably fit among my gear, and burned all the waste before hitting the trail.

Back on the road, I skied for about half a mile in blizzard conditions. A truck pulled up, heading north, with a big friendly-looking man of thirty behind the wheel. He was going to Canoe Lake and wore a blue-and-black-checked flannel coat, glasses, and a baseball cap. I asked him for a ride.

Philip Cardinal had moved north from Regina and now lived in Cole Bay. He sat casually in the driver's seat in cotton sweatpants and untied sneakers with bright orange laces, the way he might lounge in an armchair at home and play video games. He seemed only relatively interested in the dangerous road ahead and drove fast and loose—unconsciously, I thought, the way you might walk or drink a glass of water—holding a single finger lightly on the steering wheel. I heard the muffled whistling of tires spinning fast over dry snow. Half the time the wheels on the truck were probably sliding rather than gripping as they spun, in spite of our seventy miles an hour. Philip had been south to Meadow Lake that Saturday morning to pick up a cabinet, only to discover on arriving that somebody else had already picked it up. The distance was sixty miles down and sixty back. He didn't mind. He liked to drive.

He mentioned wolves but thought I was right not to be overly concerned. "I've only seen one wolf since I came up here," he said. "Right off the side of the road, a black wolf, just standing there." His right hand started fussing near his hip. "You know," he said, taking an iPhone out of his pocket, "I think I have a picture of it." Both hands and both eyes were now focused on the phone as the truck careered into the blinding snow squall nearing eighty miles an hour, yawing under us like a tiny airplane accelerating for takeoff. He shuffled madly through his pictures muttering to himself, "I don't know where it is. I bet those crazy girls erased it. Man, I'm tellin ya'. Crazy Canoe Lake girls."

Philip never did find the picture. He dropped me off, after a short ride, a few miles shy of the turnoff for Jans Bay—another of several small communities on the Canoe Lake Reserve—and I skied into the blizzard again. I looked back and saw Philip wearing a perplexed expression as he watched me go.

An hour later, a little car came slipping through the deepening snow from the east and stopped. The passenger, a woman, had heard about a man skiing down the road and resolved to stop and interrogate me if she saw me, which she now proceeded to do. I responded cordially to the familiar script of questions. An absent-looking man in a worn-out bomber jacket leaned forward to the passenger window from the back of the car. (Northern Natives, I had noticed by now, often make sensible use of all the seats in the car.) "Where can I donate?" he asked gravely.

"Excuse me?"

"Where can I donate?"

I explained that I wasn't doing this for a cause but that if he wanted he could donate to the Canadian Parks and Wilderness Society in the name of my expedition. It wasn't just something I was saying. I really had set up a fundraiser with the organization in the early planning days of my expedition. But my comment provoked only a confused stare, and I instantly felt embarrassed for having made it.

"Take this," he said. He pressed a five-dollar bill into my hand. I looked at him, unsure of what to do, but before I could tell him to keep his money he had sunk again into the back seat of the car to stare blankly into the gray void of falling snow outside.

Later that afternoon, a Royal Canadian Mounted Police officer on patrol in his truck stopped to talk. He was clean-cut, in his thirties, and had a friendly face. "Of all the places to end up on a trip across the country," he said, "you end up in Canoe Narrows." He said "canoe" like I would have. Wishing to take advantage of someone who was obviously not from here to ask about distances, I asked him how far it was to Beauval, the first town of any size that I would come to in Saskatchewan (756 inhabitants). He told me it was about sixteen miles to Beauval Forks, where I could find a bar with a few motel rooms if I wanted. I asked him the time. It was 3:40. I decided I would ski hard for as long as it took, despite the raging blizzard, and hopefully sleep in a warm bed.

Over the next hours, as darkness approached and eventually settled, the storm became more fierce. It was a furious and whipping night. I crossed a country of bogs studded with low black spruce so spindly and sparse they did almost nothing to break the wind. I stopped to "mug up"—as old-time northern travelers termed breaking for a restorative warm drink along the trail—and a car full of women slowed to a halt beside me in the now six-inch-deep snow covering the road. It hardly seemed wise for them to be out here in their Buick sedan. The woman in the passenger's seat was elderly and had no English.

The driver translated everything I said for her. "What's your journey?" the old woman asked through her interpreter. I wondered whether the poetic nuance was deliberate but limited myself to a prosaic answer.

I asked the women about the motel and bar the Mountie had mentioned. "Yes. It's called Amy's. You're real close." I was glad for the confirmation but knew I was still a long way off. A driver's "real close" means next to nothing to a traveler on foot. I had another ten miles to travel through some of the harshest weather I have ever seen. As the car drove off, I snickered to myself at the thought that these women were all I had seen of the crazy girls of Canoe Lake I'd heard so much about.

The home stretch was a sprint. I knew now that I was going to get out of the weather, even if it meant pleading to sleep under a pool table in the bar, so I gave it everything I had, paying no mind to the sweat that streamed dangerously out of my body. Drifts piled up so fast around me that I could actually see them mounting. I despaired a little for the human race that two vehicles passed without even slowing down to ask if I was all right. I tried to justify them on the basis that they were probably afraid of breaking their momentum and not getting started again in the deep snow. Finally I reached a junction of two abandoned roads. I could barely read the sign in the darkness and blowing snow: LA LOCHE, BUFFALO NARROWS, ÎLE-À-LA-CROSSE pointing left. BEAUVAL, right.

I turned right and in a few more miles skied into a lighted parking lot with a row of trucks in front of a bar with a metal door and no windows. It felt strange to stop, to bend down, to take my skis off. My legs wanted to keep on marching. I hobbled into the entrance vestibule. Behind a locked cage was a bank machine. You had to stick your hands through a hole to put in your PIN number and take your cash. Inside the second door the place was dimly lit. I walked over to the bar and asked about a room. The young girls working knew the rate but little else. They were there to pour drinks and sell liquor off-license from the back window of the bunker-like edifice. Eventually they found a key, handed it to me without a word, and I walked off to find the room myself.

Once my things were inside and spread out to dry, I lit my camp stove and cooked macaroni and cheese mixed through with the last of the baloney, which I had pried from the frozen bread.

24

THE COSSACK

I took the next day to rest, reorganize, and dry some of my sweat-soaked clothes. A few hundred yards down the road from the motel was a so-called gas bar, the reserve's one-stop place of commerce—grocery store, restaurant, fueling station—and the only other building around. The place looked new. It was clean, freshly painted, and had bright fluorescent lights. In the restaurant were eight or ten tables with an open service window to the kitchen, where orders were placed over a counter. The menu was written on paper and taped to the wall above the window. On the day I was there, a grooved plastic letter board with a set of changeable letters and numbers had just arrived, and two women were busy at a table transferring the old paper menu onto the new sign. I was writing at the next table. One of the women went to the kitchen for a few minutes, and when she came back the other was fretting over something. "We're all out of Cs," she said.

The first woman, without skipping a beat, said, "Well, take some Os and cut 'em in half! *Indians* don't get stuck."

I learned the next morning, February 11, 2013, that a pope was retiring for the first time in modern history. When I checked out of the motel the young woman who gave me back my deposit was insolent, as if she were angry with me for not having trashed the room. The only customers in the bar at that hour were a group of teenagers sitting in a dark corner.

"Hey," said one of them aggressively, "you're not an Indian. You're in the wrong bar."

"Sorry, buddy," said one of his friends. "He's drunk."

So my mood was not of the best when I slid off on the snowmobile track toward the town of Beauval. The snow was soiled by road dirt kneaded into it by snowmobile treads, and the bright sun behind a thin layer of overcast made a jarring light. A couple of hours into the day I passed near the town of Beauval not far from the roadside. I saw a car pull over and stop a hundred yards in front of me. It was a black sedan, and the driver appeared to be waiting for me. When I came closer he got out and stood watching my approach. He wore a leather jacket and was smoking a cigarette. I skied up to him, even though he looked like he might be a creep. He shook his head slowly and smiled when our eyes met. "I know exactly what you're up to," he said confidently. "I saw you from the road and I knew it. 'This guy's in it for the long haul,' I said. I've done a lot of this sort of thing myself."

I was skeptical. Standing there by the side of the road in his jeans with a cigarette in hand, he hardly looked the part. "I used to mush dogs all through this country," he said. "Come on. Let's load your stuff into the car. We'll go back to my place, pull out some maps. You can regroup and I'll help you put together a route." His directness was somehow captivating and my instincts said he was probably harmless. I didn't hesitate in stuffing my gear into the back of his car, and off we drove with the creaky trunk hatch flopping at each bump in the road.

We drove four miles back west to Don Skopyk's cabin, which he and his sons built from ninety pine logs they felled nearby. The cabin had electric lights but was otherwise primitive. Don lived alone and you could tell. His house rules demanded strict parsimony, which he called cheapness. "The toilet's in here," he said, showing me the bathroom, "but if you just have to take a leak, don't flush it. Or better yet, go outside. If you do have to flush, just pour the water from here into the toilet." He indicated a five-gallon bucket under the sink drain. "And make sure you remember to put the bucket back under the sink, because I disconnected the drain pipe. Also, if you decide you need a shower—which you don't—take the bucket with you and try to catch as much of the water as you can." The kitchen consisted of a woodstove. A few pots, pans, and utensils hung on the wall behind it.

Don kept a supply of dry firewood inside the house. He rationed it carefully and was forever studying ways to burn less while still keeping the house tolerably warm. He asked me if I knew any tricks. The floors were littered with books and photographs and contraptions for exercising. There was a large flat-screen TV that had never been hooked up, and everywhere were boxes of rare coins that supplemented Don's pension as a retired high-school teacher. Near the boxes were scribbled lists of customer orders and addresses all over Canada and the United States.

He had grown up in Prince Albert, 190 miles southeast of Beauval. As a teenager, exploring the wilderness north of his home and gazing wistfully at maps of the lakes that dot Saskatchewan's north by the thousands, it became his ambition "to know the trails of the north better than any other white man." He moved north and married a Native woman from Beauval who bore him two sons, but the marriage didn't last. He had a working grasp of Dene and Cree and had spent years exploring the north by dogsled, canoe, and bush plane. Over the last ten years, however, Don had spent little time in the wild. He had taken to spending several months a year traveling in Europe, mostly in Ukraine and Russia, where his forebears came from. He signed his correspondence "The Cossack" and could speak Russian. When he saw me skiing along the side of the road, at the edge of the bush, it had reawakened something in him. He seemed to want to connect again to a world he had once been immersed in.

Don was excited as he climbed up to his sleeping loft and, after digging through a few layers of cumulus, pulled out a four-foot-long cardboard box. He threw it down to me and descended the ladder. The box was open at one end and was stuffed full of crumpled pieces of old paper. We stood in front of the stove and Don began pulling out balls of paper and tossing them on the floor. "Not this. Not this either," he said, discarding sheet after sheet. They were topographical maps, tens of them. To the untrained eye they would all have looked the same. Each one covered a couple of hundred square miles of townless, lake-strewn granite earth, but before even seeing the names on each map Don could understand almost instantly what it showed.

He eventually found the maps he wanted, got down on his knees, and flattened them out on the floor. His eyes lit up and his voice brightened as his fingers ran over them, skimming easily from lake to lake. The maps were old and yellowed, but the basic shape of the land would be the same. With a pencil, he marked the locations of cabins. He told me the local names of bodies of water, which differed sometimes from the names used by mapmakers, and gave explanations of Cree place names.

After this initial survey of the maps, we tentatively decided that I would go to Pinehouse Lake to start. Don said he would be more than willing to drive me there. He had taught in Pinehouse, a Cree-Métis community on the large lake's northwestern shore, for a time and had nothing but good to say about it. "Even if they make an easy ski trail, you shouldn't be skiing along roads. Saskatchewan is meant to be traveled on its lakes. We'll get you up to Pinehouse and send you on your way to La Ronge over the ice."

Don still had to finish the errands he'd been on when he found me, so we got in the car and went back to the store at Beauval Forks. I told him about the kid who had said I was in the wrong bar that morning. "I'd like to see him try that one on me," he said. At the store we ran into an old friend of Don's he had not seen for some time. His name was Eli George and he lived in the bush near Primeau Lake, thirty miles east of Patuanak (pronounced *patch*-nak) on the Churchill River. The first few words of the conversation were in Dene. Don learned that one of Eli's brothers was dead. Eli looked frail with age and said he was on his way to the hospital somewhere farther south. Don told him what I was doing and asked whether a certain trail I might use still existed. Eli looked doubtful. "People don't use the trails no more," he said. "When they stop using the trails, the roads start growing in." Another old man lingered around the store asking everyone who came through if they were driving north to Buffalo Narrows. He had heard on the radio that a friend there had died and he wanted a lift to the funeral. As we drove off Don said, "Eli isn't as old as he looks. The Dene age fast."

On the drive home we made a loop down to the shore of Lac La Plonge. Don pointed at houses and told me who lived in them. Several of the people he described were sick or dead, mostly from hard living it seemed, and Don had no qualms about telling me which sons of bitches he thought were better off dead anyway. He had a colorful lexicon of demise: this one was schmucked by a snowplow, that one shit the bed. Death was simply part of the picture, no matter when it came.

The sky was clear as we started home in the evening. The first sliver after the new moon was visible. "Look," said Don. "You can see the arms of the new moon holding the old moon. It's a sign of fair weather."

Back at the cabin we had spaghetti and tomato sauce for supper, washed down with shots of vodka Don had brought home from Russia. When I mentioned all the teasing I'd heard about Canoe Lake women, Don told a story. "Years ago," he said, "I was driving my dogs from Canoe Lake to Keeley Lake. In Canoe I asked if there was a packed trail to Keeley. 'Oh sure there is,' said the locals. 'There's a guy out there comes to see his girlfriend in Canoe Lake just about every day.' So," said Don, "I drove the dogs into Keeley and put up at the lodge. I got talking to the woman who kept the place. 'How was the trail?' she asked. 'Oh, it's a friggin' highway!' I said. 'Apparently there's a fellow goes back and forth between Keeley and Canoe just about every day to see his girlfriend and keeps the trail wide open.' 'Well,' said the lady, 'my husband goes about *halfway* to Canoe every day to check his traps.' 'No,' I insisted. 'This guy goes *all the way*.' The woman turned pale as a ghost before I realized what I'd said."

In the morning, the sun burned through a picture window that faced southeast. The radio had been left on low all night, tuned to Saskatchewan's First Nations broadcaster, and I woke to strains of Dwight Yoakam and Buck Owens singing "The Streets of Bakersfield." I did my stretches and then sat in my long johns on an upright log before the open stove, taking up all I could of its warmth. For breakfast we had fried eggs, toast, and moose-meat sausage that had simmered on the stove all night. We chewed in silence and looked out on the day.

"So it's late fall," Don said, after sipping his coffee, "and two trappers head out to spend the winter in the bush. When spring finally comes around and the river ice breaks up, only one of them appears at the Hudson's Bay post with a load of furs to sell. 'Where's your partner?' asks the agent. 'My partner?' the trapper calmly replies. 'I had to shoot him.' 'Shoot him?' says the agent, backing away from the counter in horror. 'What did you do that for?' 'He lost his mind,' says the surviving trapper, counting his money. 'He started hanging the little pan on the hook where we always put the big one.'"

I let Don wash up while I packed my things.

25

PINEHOUSE

It was late morning when I had the car loaded. Don walked out of the house carrying only a rifle in one hand and something white in the other. He raised it like a flag to reveal a pair of briefs. "Always gotta bring extra underwear to Pinehouse. Last time I was there it was supposed to be for three hours, and I ended up staying three days."

He pitched the rifle and briefs onto the back seat, got in the car, and backed out of the driveway. He nodded distractedly toward the coin dish in the center console. "See if I've got any bullets in there, will you?"

"There's a couple," I said.

"Good. You never know when they might come in handy."

Before leaving town we stopped at the post office, where Don mailed a heavy box of coins to a man in Quebec while I filled his car with gas.

When we were under way Don told me that the road to Pinehouse was straightforward: "Thirty miles east and thirty north." Then he said, "Sorry, I'm still on the miles." There's no population between the two points, and the road was lonely. At one point, on the northbound stretch, we took a break on the side of the road where there was a weather-worn map of northern Saskatchewan on a billboard that seemed out of place. Far to the north of the line of small settlements shown strung out along the Churchill River, there was an isolated dot at Key Lake.

Until the 1990s Key Lake was home to a high-grade uranium mine and is still the site of the largest uranium-processing facility on earth. It is economically important even in Pinehouse, 130 miles to its south. It must have been the thought of uranium that prompted a leap to nuclear waste and the selection by Canada's Nuclear Waste Management Organization of the Precambrian shield outside Pinehouse as a possible dumpsite for spent nuclear fuel. Don told me about rumors of payouts being used to win the support of power brokers in Pinehouse. Similar claims have been made about Patuanak, another proposed site. It was sad to see this part of the world, which appears hardly touched by industrial modernity, and to know that such ideas have been put on the table. Regardless of one's views on nuclear energy, it seems the height of folly to propose storing high-level radioactive waste underneath one of the most intricate and extensive hydrological systems on earth. The Canadian Shield, still rebounding from the weight of its last glaciation (which ended only about as long ago as the invention of agriculture), to this day can still flip the pitch of a watershed, like players in the marble game Labyrinth who tilt the board on its perpendicular axes to steer the marble home. Thanks to intense grassroots resistance, which was in full swing at the time I was there, neither community was being considered any longer.

Don drove slowly and surveyed the roadsides, commenting on the animal tracks he saw. At one point he braked to a crawl. "I'm trying to figure out what that track is. It looks like a wolf, but it's perfectly straight. It must be a lynx. There's lots of rabbits in through here." Canada lynx, which are about twice the size of large house cats, subsist almost entirely on snowshoe hares (commonly called "rabbits" throughout North America), so much so that populations of the two species can be seen to rise and fall drastically in cycles lasting about ten years. Hare populations can go from as high as 6000 per square mile to as low as 31 per square mile in a matter of a couple of seasons. In such years lynx will produce small litters, forego breeding altogether, or suffer devastating rates of infant mortality. Lynxes hunt by stalking and then bounding after their prey on snowshoe-like paws that keep them afloat in the snow.

Six miles south of Pinehouse we saw a set of clumsy human footprints going into the bush off the right side of the road. Don suspected someone had killed something. A few yards farther on was a truck backed away from the road and a man standing in the bed keeping watch. Don stopped, rolled down the window, and greeted the man in Cree. He asked if he had shot a moose. At first the man tried to dodge the question, but he eventually admitted that he had, explaining that his hunting companion had wounded it the day before and they were just getting it out of the bush now. Don and the man seemed to recognize each other but evidently didn't know each other well. Nevertheless, Don felt compelled to tell him that he so enjoyed coming to Pinehouse that he had brought an extra pair of underwear with him. The man nodded and smiled uncomfortably. Don wished him luck, and we drove on.

It was a brilliant sunny afternoon as we crested the hill above the village of Pinehouse and were afforded a sweeping view of the lake that gives the village its name. For a small place of about a thousand residents, the village teemed with life. People were outside walking, talking, and pulling their children on sleds.

We pulled up in front of the town offices and there was a man in his forties standing outside with his arms crossed, legs wide, and a stern look on his face. "That's Ken" said Don to me in the privacy of the car. "A real racist asshole." We got out of the car and Don walked over to shake the man's hand. Ken shook Don's hand and gave him a questioning look.

"Don't you recognize me?" asked Don. "Don Skopyk."

"Ah," said Ken, "you've lost some hair and have a little more . . . " and he tapped Don's modest paunch with the back of his hand. Ken chuckled and didn't seem so bad.

Inside the town office there was a large script painted on the wall describing how Pinehouse sees itself. Although the village was once demeaned as "The Drinking Capital of Northern Saskatchewan," the statement explained, community leaders have become convinced that the key to thriving Native and Métis communities is self-determination, finding and defining their own reasons for being, and pursuing those reasons on their own terms. External governance of remote communities had failed.

Don and I had not been inside the building for two minutes when we were whisked off to the kitchen and fed meatball soup, fried bannock, chocolate cake with cherry sauce, and hot coffee. I had the strong impression that they (and I couldn't say exactly who *they* were) had somehow known we were coming. There was a hidden force at work that generated a collective spontaneity. Four women busied themselves in the kitchen, and townspeople of both sexes flowed in like tidewater—lent a hand, just visited, or lingered to eat something—then flowed back out. Everything fell into place with no shade of a plan.

Later in the day I would see things unfolding the same way at the school. I asked Don about this mysterious harmony when we were alone for a moment. His look said, "Why do you think I love this place?"

We ate our lunch in the gymnasium off the kitchen, whose walls were painted large with scenes of traditional life along the Missinipi, or Churchill River, of which Pinehouse Lake is a pooling. I was introduced to a man of about fifty with a thin black mustache. Glen McCallum was the head of social development for Pinehouse and seemed to draw a lot of water in the community. He told me about a group that had driven their snowmobiles across country to La Ronge two weeks before and suggested I follow the same route. "Just stay clear of my trapline while you're out there," he admonished with a serious look on his face.

I was about to ask how I would know I was on his trapline when a quiet man on my left said, "Glen, the only trapline you got's for catchin' mice where ya spill yer crumbs." Glen struggled briefly to uphold the ruse, but his composure broke into a laugh and he let it fall.

Don told the story of the pair we had seen taking a moose out of the bush that morning.

"Were they on my trapline?" Glen asked. "Was it one of my moose?"

"Mighta been," said Don. "It had a mousetrap clamped to its ear."

A phone call came in for Glen, and a moment after answering he turned to me and said, "Anders, what's your last name?"

"Morley," I said.

Glen spoke back into the phone. "He's skiing across Canada," he said, "and is leaving Pinehouse for La Ronge tomorrow." My plan had been to leave that afternoon. Glen hung up the phone and explained that he had been talking to the Missinipi Broadcasting Corporation, Northern Saskatchewan's radio network—which broadcasts from La Ronge in English, Cree, and Dene—and that I had better finish my cake and report to his office for a telephone interview with a man called Abel Charles in five minutes. I shoveled the cake into my mouth, gulped my coffee, and asked for directions to Glen's office, since he had already disappeared.

Abel Charles told me the interview would be recorded and aired during the following hour with a Cree translation. Most of the interview questions had to do with my reception along the route of my journey. I told him about eating bannock and drinking tea with John and Pauline near Waterhen Lake, figuring that they or someone they knew would probably be listening. I couldn't imagine my prattle was worth translating, but as a lover of language it touched me to know that my words would play some tiny part in keeping alive a language that, while spoken in healthier numbers than any other indigenous language in Canada, is at risk of loss.

The two people Don had talked most about during the preceding twenty-four hours both worked for Minahik Waskahigan High School, where Don had once taught. When we found Curtis Chandler he was teaching a science lesson, and Don poked his head into his classroom. Curtis must have heard we were around, because when he finished his point he introduced us, although he had never met me, and invited me to talk to his students about my trip. I worried about being able to hold their adolescent attention, but I found them engaged, friendly, and keen to ask questions. A few students even began debating the merits of different routes I might take eastward from Pinehouse. Male and female students spoke confidently with each other of bays, lakes, and islands where they hunted or fished with their fathers.

After class, Curtis, who also drove dog sleds, pulled some topographical maps out of a box at the back of the room and went over the route again with me, confirming what Don had said but bringing to bear more recent experience on the portage trails that connect the lakes on the Canadian Shield.

"The biggest problem you're going to have to deal with is slush," explained Curtis, "especially on the smaller lakes like Johnson and Neale." He pointed them out on the map.

Then he turned serious. "Another thing you have to be careful of is wolves."

"Really?" I said. "You think they're a serious concern for a grown man?"

"When they pack up they can be pretty dangerous around here. There have been a few attacks, and even one death at Key Lake a few years ago. Now, the wolf who killed that guy was not healthy. It was sick with mange. But still, if you do see aggressive wolves, you're going to want to get up a tree as fast as you can, and high. When they jump they can reach up to about eight feet."

Don caught sight of something through the window and, as soon as Curtis had finished talking, gestured for me to follow him outside. A group of children from the adjacent middle school was sliding ashore from the lake on skis. At the back of the line a man of about sixty with a graying Van Gogh beard and glacier glasses came along on snowshoes. He wore a heavy buffalo-plaid shirt and green knickers. This was Earl Stobbe, a mushing companion from Don's younger days and a legend in Don's mind. He came up a rise and stopped in the sun.

"I tried to call you yesterday," said Don, "but you never answered. I said to myself, 'I know he's sitting right by the goddamn phone, but he's not gonna pick up.'"

"What's your number?"

Don said his number.

"I did see that. Thought you were a salesman."

"This here's Anders," Don said. "He's skiing across Canada."

"That's something else," said Earl, trying to sound impressed. "But I'm afraid you won't find me on skis." Don had told me Earl was a purist. Skis belonged in Europe and Asia, where they were invented. Saskatchewan was for snowshoes, dogsleds, canoes.

After Earl had sent his students home for the day we went to his house, which was even messier than Don's, and ate a frozen pizza heated up in the oven. "I just love watching this guy eat," said Don, as I snapped slices off the tray. "Reminds you of the old days, doesn't it, Earl?" Earl smiled. He wasn't much of a talker.

Don and Earl caught up on their news for a few minutes, and then Don announced, somewhat surprisingly, that he'd be heading home. There was a hockey game in town that night and Earl was planning to go. "You're welcome to come with me," he said. We all dressed to go outside, where Earl and I took our leave of Don in the dark street and then walked around the corner and up the hill toward the village center.

The game was in a semi-enclosed plywood rink that was naturally frozen. The local youth team was playing against the small community of Dillon, the town on Peter Pond Lake where the hunters I had met a few days before had come from. We came in just before the start of the third period, and Dillon was losing badly. They were giving it everything they had and it was a mildly heart-rending spectacle. But Pinehouse was simply the bigger village.

I recognized one of the referees as Glen McCallum. When he saw me, he skated across the ice and leaned over the boards to ask me if I had had a chance to look at maps with someone. Then he told me that I could sleep that night in the high school. I could use the home economics room as my kitchen and the locker as my bathroom. In one hand he held the whistle that hung around his neck on a lanyard, a token of authority. I said I was being taken care of like an old family friend, which visibly pleased him.

"For years," said Earl, once the game was underway again, "the kids up here have wanted hockey teams, but there was no one, certainly not myself, who knew the first thing about hockey, or putting a team together." Earl had grown up in Uranium City, on Lake Athabasca in far northern Saskatchewan. It delighted me that he talked about hockey as a southern game. "But now we've got some teachers from Ontario," he said, "and they've got their team." He watched a play or two. "I'm not sure they're any good though."

It didn't matter. "The kids here are so nice," Earl said. "You know, I left to go teach down south for a couple of years. You'd say something to the kids and they'd just ignore you, or they'd look at you like they wanted to say 'Fuck off.' Then I came back here to visit and all the kids are saying hi to me. They'd come up and hug me, saying they missed my unmatched socks." (Earl's inability to choose two socks of the same color was a running joke in town.) "So I said, 'What the hell? Better come back to Pinehouse.' And here I am."

After the game I said goodnight to Earl and went to the school to make supper in the home economics room. Afterward I sat down at a computer in the school library, where I had spread out my sleeping bag on a couch, and wrote an email to Zoë. Then I scrolled through my other mail. So many of the messages in my inbox had to do with the planning of this very journey, but now the things I'd looked forward to were behind me, and it was hard to imagine them ever having been ahead of me, to imagine a reality shaped differently from the one I inhabited now. I spent an hour or more deleting every single email in my inbox except for the ones that came from Elena, reaching back ten years.

In the morning I made pancakes from a mix I found in a cupboard in the home economics room. A teacher I hadn't met yet walked in, looked at my stack of pancakes, and said, "I knew a guy who was a champion marathoner when he was your age. He used to eat like that. Now he weighs four hundred pounds, easy. Eats every day at a restaurant in Winnipeg called The Fat Man. Careful." Then he walked out of the room.

Next a soft-spoken local man with a mustache and round glasses came in. He had a pageboy haircut that gave him the look of a medieval sage. He told me that long-distance canoe paddlers going up or down the Churchill River frequently came through the area in the summer. He obviously considered me their winter equivalent. "Hardly any of them come into town though," he said. "It's really not a long detour for them. We'd like to have them come visit with us, drink some tea, spend the night. But they just want to keep moving." He was thanking me for giving Pinehouse an opportunity to be hospitable.

26

THE PEARL NECKLACE

I skied southeast across Pinehouse Lake, rounded a point, slid past an island over a small pressure ridge, and kept my eyes peeled for a large angled boulder and a buried pickup truck that I was told marked the entrance to the first portage trail. Pinehouse Lake. Bar Lake. Johnson Lake. Neale Lake. Besnard Lake. The lakes of northern Saskatchewan are strung together by well-trod trails the width of a canoe. They are low, cozy tunnels through dense bush or sunken traces across windblown tracts of muskeg. To travel by them requires a leap of faith, for there is no way, besides hearsay, to verify their existence from afar. Yet miles and miles of travel are staked on their presence. Along the most frequented historical routes they are marked with dashed lines on topographical maps, but there is often no way of knowing when they were last used. And trails, when disused, disappear. But if you give your trust to the lakes of the north and the hidden trails that connect them, you will find a network as seamless as any modern highway system. To travel this region is a lesson in the power of trust and cooperation.

THE VOYAGEURS WHO TRAVELED THIS country in the olden days used lob trees to mark the positions of trail breaks on the often monotonous horizons of the taiga. A tall tree would be stripped of its lower branches, leaving an awkward tuft at the crown that stood out from the surrounding trees, even from the far side of a miles-wide lake. I had no such markers to guide me. Most of the time old snowmobile tracks were good guides, but in one instance, on Bar Lake, it seemed to me that they were heading off course from the slight dip in the tree line that often marks the point where two bodies of water come closest together, which is also usually a carrying place for canoes. I left the track and made for the point, breaking trail through a half mile of heavy snow. I was vindicated when I got to the trail. The snowmobile tracks reached the same point but had swung south a couple of extra miles before turning around and coming back to hit the link.

At one point I found a pile of fishing nets. I had been told I might see commercial fishermen out on the remote lakes, if I saw anyone. I decided to stop for lunch in hopes that the fisherman might come around. He did not. Only a little mouse shot out of a tunnel in the snow and scribbled back and forth over the surface before going back under, where he was safe from at least his aerial predators.

When I came to the mid-size Besnard Lake, I skied a few miles down its length and then spotted a summer cottage hidden among the trees on an island. Night was beginning to fall, so I crossed over to it. The snow in the bush around the house was especially deep, well above my hips, and I was exhausted lugging my sled up the slope from the lake. The door was unlocked. Inside, the cottage was rustic but well-appointed, with a woodstove, a pair of sofas, some books and board games, and even an indoor pit latrine. There was a bin of firewood behind the stove, and within an hour I had the place warm. I cooked my supper and melted a day's worth of water on top of the stove. Then I sat back in an armchair in front of the fire to watch the flames and write in my diary.

After a restful night on the couch I packed up my things, refilled the firewood bin from a pile buried in the snow, and left a note thanking the owners of the cottage. The following summer I received a friendly email from the owner of the cabin, who chided me playfully for having left the firewood bin not quite as full as he had left it. He told me he was glad his cottage had been of use and that his decision to follow the old northern tradition of not locking doors was a principled one.

I left my island paradise in a nasty wind under overcast skies. Traveling again, I saw a moving black dot in the bleak distance. It came closer and revealed itself as a snowmobile. It approached me and I could see that it was towing an empty orange sled that looked like mine but was perhaps five times as voluminous and covered in grime and bloodstains. The driver was a silent Native fisherman who wore furs. He was bulky but his skin was tight and weather-beaten. His eyes were as drawn as Inuit eyes. He slowed down only long enough to tell me that I was on the right track for La Ronge and motored on in the direction I had just come from.

Not far from a narrows where the two basins of Besnard Lake are almost pinched off from each other, the snowmobile track splintered in several directions. Most of the tracks seemed to veer south, but the one or two tracks that made landfall on the closer northern side of the narrows seemed to make more sense to me. Had I refreshed my memory by looking at the old map Don had loaned me, I would have seen that the telltale dotted line marking the portage trail cut across the peninsula on the south side. Skiing through the narrows itself was out of the question. The narrows of a lake is always a place of strong currents, and the fast flow of water can erode the underside of the ice, so that even if a transport truck can drive over other parts of the lake, the ice above the narrows may not be thick enough to support a single person.

I crossed the spit of land that came down from the north and slid back down onto the ice. There was no track here. Giving the narrows as wide a berth as I thought necessary, I rounded toward the southeast, where I needed to go. But I didn't make the arc wide enough. My skis started to lose their glide and got heavier and heavier. The snow still looked bright white, but when I looked behind me I saw my trail had become the gray color of slush. I had no desire to break trail through deep snow for miles with my skis dragging this way, so I kept bending to the right until I made landfall on the south side of the narrows, where I took off my skis and scraped off all the ice.

There was a road that ran south down the point. I knew there were a couple of ways to get through the bush and over the lakes to La Ronge from here, so I opted for a change of plan. The slush was an ominous sign. I skied south and a couple of miles down the point came to a narrow neck, where two bays almost touched, and here I saw where the snowmobiles from Pinehouse had crossed. It seemed so obvious in hindsight. I wished I had trusted the tracks when I had first seen them, but the skiing was so fast on the unused road that I was reluctant to break my newfound momentum. I continued south seven miles to a trail that turned east into the bush, where a snowmobile track had broken a way. If I was lucky this trail might take me through to Sikachu Lake, which was the first of another chain of lakes connected by the Montreal River that would take me to La Ronge. I turned east and made camp in a clearing.

Next day I continued my march down the lonely trail, up and down little hills and around wide bends under dreary skies. In the late afternoon I came to the end of the snowmobile track. My heart sank. I was still more than fifteen miles from Sikachu Lake, where I could next count on finding a broken trail. The snow was two feet deep. I tried proceeding but made only 500 yards in more than half an hour of hard pulling. It would take days to get through. I knew I had to backtrack.

A mile or two behind me I had seen a packed spur heading south off the main trail. It didn't appear on my map, but I figured it would wrap southwest around an unnamed lake that did appear and eventually link back to the road I traveled south on the day before. And maybe I'd save a few miles. I decided to chance it.

It was snowing now and for the first time it annoyed me. What if I didn't make it back to the road and a foot of snow fell on my trail? It would take me three times as long to get out as it had to get in. I wished I was traveling on snowshoes, or at least on bigger skis. Since taking to the Saskatchewan lakes I had been working out a pet theory about why snowshoes—disparagingly called "misery slippers" by skiers who love speed—had never evolved in North America into the sleek sliders I was traveling on, as they did in Eurasia. I figured the snow was too deep and too fluffy, and the population density was too low for enough trails to be kept open for them to be feasible as a reliable means of long-distance transportation. With snowshoes a traveler can break his own trail and create a wide and level pathway for the load he is hauling in all but the deepest snow.

The snowmobile trail held out until dark, and I set up my tent next to it in the middle of a frozen swamp. I suspected I was close to the lake on my map. Sure enough, in the morning, after a few minutes of skiing I reached the lake. But what I found was disheartening. The snowmobiler had driven a hundred yards out on the lake, looped around, and driven back up the trail as easily as he had come down it. All it had cost him was a few dollars in gas and perhaps a chill. For me it had been hours of wasted time and exertion. So I spent the whole day backtracking. I traveled hard, having set myself the objective of getting all the way back to the southbound road before camping again, no matter what. Fortunately the snow had not lasted. The sun was out and I found myself in good spirits. I had been traveling for nearly three months, after all, and this was my first major navigational setback. It was bound to happen sometime.

By the time I got back to the road, the sun was well into the western sky but still an hour or two from setting. It was warm, and for the first time all winter I took off my skis and sat down on my sled load for a daytime rest. It was February 15. I basked in the rays of the sun and looked out over the muskeg and the crooked line of black spruce trees behind it. The silence was total. When the temperature began to fall with the sinking sun, I clipped my skis back on and began traveling south at a sprinting pace. It felt like I had covered half a day's march in an hour and a half when, to my surprise, I heard a vehicle in the distance behind me. I turned to see a gray truck coming south.

When the driver stopped and rolled down his window, I asked, "You're not by any chance going to Sikachu, are you?"

"Sikachu? We're going to La Ronge, but we can take you to Sikachu. It's only a few miles out of the way."

I hefted my gear into the bed and climbed into the back seat of the cab next to a scrawny white man in the far corner. Two Native men were in the front seat with a high-powered rifle between them. All three men were thoroughly drunk and sipping cans of Budweiser. Dwight Yoakam sang on the stereo. A beer was held out to me, but I politely declined it.

The trio delighted more than a sober crowd would have in my stories from the trail and said they were proud that I had been treated so well by the people of Saskatchewan, but in their drunken state they couldn't quite follow much of what I said. The man next to me in the back, who laughed a lot to himself, asked if I was worried about wolves and whether I carried a gun. His question prompted the man in the passenger's seat, who had a pleasant sing-song accent, to launch into a mystical defense of "brother wolf." "The wolf," he almost whispered, "he's a kindred spirit to mankind. You won't see 'em when you're in the bush, but he sees you. Oh yes, he sees you for sure. Him an' all his brothers are surroundin' ya, at all times, but you won't never see 'em." He wagged has finger to reinforce *never*. "They're invisible. They're protectin' you, ya know? Watchin' over you, eh. They keep you safe from the other animals. They guard you from the spirits that might wanna bring harm unto you." He wore a subtle ironic grin that could have made him a killing in westerns had he been born fifty years earlier.

The man in the back looked like he was suffocating as he folded in half, possessed by laughter without noise. Meanwhile I pictured myself being hunted by a bloodthirsty herd of caribou, only to be saved from death by slow rumination by the sympathetic intervention of a pack of wolves.

27

ORDEAL BY ICE

We rolled into the tiny reserve settlement of Sikachu—two rows of six or eight rough cabins running down to a lake of the same name. Dogs yelped as I unloaded my sled in the fading twilight, said thank you while the three men from the truck made conversation with an acquaintance there, and pushed down the snow-covered road that ended in the lake. My muscles warm from having been in the heated truck, I kept a fast pace until I was across the main body of the lake and around a point.

I chose a spot near the shore that looked sheltered from the wind and set about tamping down the snow for my tent. When I took my skis off and my feet post-holed through the snow, I noticed that my prints were gray, the tell-tale color of slush. I wasn't happy, but it was dark now and I had no desire to move my camp if I could avoid it. I was sure the horizontal distribution of my weight inside the tent would keep me from sinking down into the slush layer.

As I was putting the finishing touches on my camp, I noticed a tiny light in the distance to the south. It was rocking slightly and reminded me of a lantern on a ship at sea. It appeared to be moving very slowly my way. I went about my business, but when the light got close I turned to see a person on foot. I said hello, and a man walked up to me. He was wrinkled and ancient, with a heavy load of fishnets on his back and shoulders. He carried the lantern in one hand

and on his feet were the longest snowshoes I have ever seen, at least four feet from tip to tail. They bent sharply upward at the tips, which rose several inches out of the snow. The babiches—the rawhide strips holding the wooden frame together—were as thin as fancy round shoelaces and woven almost as tightly as a basket. When the man spoke his English was very broken. He had seen my headlamp, he said, and assumed I was a snowmobiler stuck in the slush. I turned my lamp off so as not to dazzle his eyes. His light was dim to begin with. He looked at the sky for a moment, then said, "Almost home now," and gently bade me goodnight. He slipped off to the west swiftly and silently.

It looked like it would be a calm night, but once I was in my sleeping bag a ferocious wind blew down and rattled my tent without mercy until morning. I slept very little. All my life I had loved sleeping in tents. I had honestly preferred a tent on the ground to a bed, and considered it second only to sleeping under the stars. The sound of cloth, even nylon cloth, rippling at irregular intervals in the breeze had been like a lullaby to me for as long as I could remember. But lately it had begun to irritate me. It constantly deprived me of my coveted sleep and unsettled my mind with threats of ugly weather.

Snow started falling again during the night, and in the morning I lay in bed hoping the storm would pass. I took my time over breakfast and finally accepted that the storm had no intention of letting up. I had already notified contacts in La Ronge that they should expect me that afternoon. My phone never worked when the sky was full of swirling snowflakes, and so I had no way of getting hold of them now to let them know I might be delayed. Since I didn't want to become the objective of a search party, my only choice was to move.

I opened the door of my tent a few inches to see whether any trace of the packed trail I had been following was left. There was only the faintest sign. What made me doubt my eyes was that a few hundred yards to the south I could see as through a veil the old man from the night before. Bent under the weight of his heavy gear, he forced his way into the storm to check the nets he had set beneath the ice or to set new ones. I jumped up and threw my things together as quickly as I could. By the time I was ready to go, the old man had disappeared into the white blur.

The first part of the day involved crossing a wide body of ice to the north shore of the Montreal River. Here I could still see some faint ridges in the snow where the edges of the snowmobile track had been. Although the wind was strong, I soon warmed up enough to take off my sweater. For the next few miles the track clung to the north shore of the river. The trail wove into the bush and back out again, every so often sliding down onto the ice, a pattern that repeated itself over and over. Since the wind came from the north the trail here was well protected and the track was still intact. My mood was almost cheerful with the memory of the old Cree fisherman still fresh and inspiring. As the blizzard stormed around me, I couldn't help but feel like the trail revealing itself ahead of me was a kind of lifeline. All I had to do was not lose sight of it, and it would lead me safely to friends and warm shelter in La Ronge.

East from the narrow stretch of the Montreal River lies Egg Lake. Before the eastbound traveler comes to the main body of this mid-size lake there is a large bay that must be crossed to a long peninsula transected by a short portage trail. I skied out onto the bay, following what was left of the track, in the strengthening wind and driven snow. Very soon I had lost sight of the shore behind me, and my own tracks were being obliterated by the wind almost as quickly as I laid them. I forged on and soon realized that I had lost the lead track too. The dimples I had taken for remnants of it were nothing more than natural irregularities on the surface of the snow. Looking around me, I now noticed the same divets to my left, to my right, in front of me—everywhere. But which one was my track, my lifeline, I couldn't decide.

I took out my map to review the orientation of the bay, holding it firmly against my thigh to keep it from sailing off. Then I looked at my compass and aimed in the general direction of the trail break marked on the map, trying to bear a little to the west so as not to accidentally run along the now invisible peninsula south of the trail, which would involve a long ski around to the main body of the lake and bring me considerably south of where I needed to be. I stuffed the wildly flapping paper map back into my pocket and skied on.

But soon I was overcome with a feeling of total disorientation. Reason began to slip. I was in the middle of a lake with what seemed like a hostile vortex whipping around me, making such a loud and terrible noise I could hardly have heard my own voice. I was getting scared. I wished I had stayed in my tent that morning, and wondered how long this could last.

It kept on. As I grew tenser and tenser the storm seemed to turn more and more aggressive. I plodded on but still could not lose the haunting feeling I was wandering off course, or perhaps traveling in circles. Only slowly did I realize that my skis were dragging and my poles were getting heavier each time I lifted them. I looked down and saw water coming up around my boots. I swore and asked no one in particular why this had to happen now.

Several times I stopped to scrape the ice from the bottom of my skis, but the farther I advanced, the worse the slush got. It felt like I had weights tied to my feet, and I had to move my grip halfway down my poles to lift them out of the snow with the cantaloupe-size globs of ice that had built up on the baskets. In a fury, I whacked them hard together in hopes of freeing them up. The right pole snapped in two, and I watched the bottom half fall to the ground.

"God damn it!" I shouted.

I stuffed the broken piece into my deep jacket pocket almost without stopping and plowed forward as hard as I could. Tears streamed slowly down my face now. I was terrified and angry. I was furious. I didn't know who with. With myself? With fate? With Elena? With God?

I didn't care any more about the ice that was weighing me down. It had become trivial. I didn't care that I had only one pole to push with. I didn't even care which direction the shore was. The storm didn't care about me, and I didn't give a damn about it. I exploded into a maniacal tirade of profanity. "God damn you! Is this all you've got? Do you think you're going to kill me? Fuck you! Gimme your best shot, you cowardly little son of a bitch!" The storm seemed to intensify as I stumbled along. I was weeping uncontrollably now and short of breath. "Who are you? Who the hell are you?" I screamed. "Is that God up there? I thought you were supposed to love us! I guess that means you don't exist. Fuck you! And fuck your little storm!" I raged on explosively for several minutes. Never in my life have I been so angry. Never have I felt so intensely that death was dancing—dancing and laughing—only an arm's length away in the white veil. I felt for an intense few moments as if someone, or something, was making a concerted effort to kill me—perhaps to punish me—and I knew I wasn't going to succumb without a fight.

Then quite suddenly my emotions were sapped, my tears ran dry, and an exhausted clarity came back. I realized no one was trying to kill me. I understood as I never had that nature was simply there, unfeeling and uncaring, with no conscious force behind it. It couldn't care less whether I lived or died. "What am I doing here?" came to my lips once more, and for several minutes I breathlessly repeated the question with each weary stride. With the ability to think restored, I told myself the bay was never more than a mile or two across. The chances I had skied far enough south to have entered the main body of Egg Lake were slim. My compass wouldn't lie, and if I only had the patience to look at it every few yards and proceed slowly and steadily, I should eventually make land not far from where I wanted to be.

Eventually I reached the shoreline and, guessing, turned right. The visibility was still impossible, so I hugged the line of dense spruce trees as closely as I could out of fear that I might miss the trailbreak or, worse, lose sight of the shore and not have the strength left to come out the back end of panic a second time. I knew the portage trail I wanted would be no wider than three or four feet.

When I saw the break I felt a pulse of blood race through my whole body. I turned into the shelter of the trees and felt immediately relieved to have the tormenting sound of the wind out of my ears. Knowing that on the far side of the peninsula there was a five-mile open lake crossing with the wind coming unobstructed out of the north, I took my time. The woods formed a tight corridor that made me feel protected, although it took only a few minutes to get through them. I stopped several yards short of the far side, still hidden from the wind. First I found a birch sapling that would serve as a good pole and sawed it down to size. Then I sipped on a hot drink and took out my map and compass to take a bearing. Out on the lake the storm blew undiminished. I could see where the old snowmobile track went down off the shore, but as soon as it left the wind shadow it disappeared.

I started getting cold and knew I had to move again. There was no way I was stopping for the night in this hell, and anyway the trail opening was too small to set up a tent in. It was about four o'clock. I looked over the lake before pushing down the chute out of the bush. To the east the wind was beginning to force a small gap in the snow-spitting cloud cover, but here the storm went on. I buckled my sled harness, took my poles in hand, and pushed out onto the lake. Within seconds I was having a hard time keeping sight of the track again. Before I could panic, though, my ears picked up on something uncanny. I thought I heard a faint buzz under the howling wind, faint as the sound of fluorescent lights. I thought it must be an aural hallucination, but it seemed to be getting gradually louder. I looked around for the source but saw none. Then I saw a soft flicker of light through the flying snow to the east. It looked like it was being jerked up and down. My heart raced again as I started to realize that it was a westbound snowmobile being tossed by the wind as it rode over the large drifts. I pointed for its headlight in anticipation of meeting whoever was driving it.

The man on the machine appeared. When he took off his helmet he looked as if he were staring at a ghost. I think I told him how happy I was to see him and probably babbled a string of confused and ecstatic sentences. The man's name was Regan Chell and he lived in La Ronge but had a cabin on the Montreal River—the only dwelling I had seen since Sikachu. I asked him if his track went back to La Ronge. He said it did.

"I'd better get following it before this wind wipes it out."

"You should be okay. The weather's clearing on the other side."

I looked at the eastern sky and already the clouds were being pushed southwest. The visibilty had suddenly improved. The wind was still blowing, but it had gone from being the bully to being the kid who was pushing the bully out of the playground.

"Is the trail to Bigstone Lake easy to see?" I asked. Bigstone was the last lake I had to cross before coming to La Ronge.

"Yes," said Regan. "And when you get to Bigstone, just look for the big antenna. That's La Ronge. If it's dark it's got a red light on it. You can follow that right over the lake to town." He must have understood I was badly shaken up because he said, "You'll be all right. I'm going back to town tonight and I'll keep an eye out for you."

The north wind blew so hard that it had pushed the last of the clouds out of the way by the time I hit my stride. It was as if a curtain had been whisked open by the sharp tug of a hidden stagehand. Now the late afternoon sunlight saturated the atmosphere. The sky was a vibrant, even blue, and the view to the far side of the lake was so clear it looked like I could touch it. If I kept a fast pace and didn't wander off course, I could put the five miles behind me before dark. Then I wasn't sure how far I would have to go to La Ronge, but I decided I would call my contacts from the other side to let them know I was all right. The wind hit me and I leaned forward into space. There were moments when it felt like I, the only thing different on this vast expanse of sameness, could be lifted off the planet and sent unremembered into orbit. I skied as fast as I could. Even Regan's recent back trail was drifting over quickly. I used it as a directional guide and not necessarily as a ski track. On the open lake the wind pack made an efficient surface for sliding over. Even if there had been slush below the surface, the crust easily bore my weight. The sunlight on the snow was blinding and I was glad I had my glacier glasses. Long streaming drifts spread out for miles on all sides. The wind kept up so forcefully out of the north—along the five-mile expanse of lake in that direction—that I imagined Boreas somewhere up there with cheeks inflated, like you see him on old maps, blowing his lungs out.

When after an hour or two I approached a point on the eastern shore, I saw a small dog jumping around in the snow. It appeared to be playing but I couldn't see any other sign of life. Then a human form slid out from the cover of the trees. The fluidity of the movement immediately betrayed a skier. I had traveled hundreds of miles, and this was the first skier I had seen on the trail. Whoever it was, he or she was skiing toward me now, with the little black and white dog running along behind. We approached each other in the snowmobile track and then came up alongside as if we were going to pass. The other skier was a man of about forty, and standing beside me, he said, "If this were a movie, I'd say 'You're going the wrong way!' and keep on skiing."

"I'm going the wrong way?" I said. I gave the man a brief account of the preceding hours and assured him that he didn't want to go where I had just come from.

"I'm Dave, by the way," he said suddenly.

"Figured you might be," I said. "I'm Anders."

Dave Fast and I had written back and forth a few times and now we pulled off our mitts to shake hands. He turned around and we headed toward land. We skied onto the rolling trail as the last of the sunlight was fading, but before its warmth had gone completely, Dave stopped and took out a thermos of tea. He offered me a cup. While I sipped he held out an apple and said, "How goes the scurvy?" I devoured the apple, core and all, and then did the same with a small piece of chocolate.

The temperature fell off drastically as we skied the remaining three miles to Dave's car in the dark. The dog, Sherlock, ran along behind, giving me pangs for Beowulf back in Italy. He had often run behind me in the Alps, skittering on the tails of my skis to try to avoid sinking in the snow. Regan drove past on his snowmobile, as promised, when we were crossing Bigstone Lake. At the car I had to take apart all my hauling gear to make it fit inside. I could hardly feel my fingers by the time I was done, and I was cold down to my bones.

28

LA RONGE

Dave's wife, Crystal, welcomed me casually while we unloaded my gear, leaving my skis and sled out in the front yard. I carried my duffel and food box into the guest room and stripped down to my long johns.

"Ready to eat?" asked Crystal when I reemerged. "I've got some big steaks."

My stomach rumbled and I salivated perceptibly. When we sat down at the table I was still bushed and didn't add much to the conversation. Along with the steaks we had mashed potatoes, Swiss chard, and a green salad. I imagined the vitamins suddenly teeming in all my cells. The steaks were so big they hung over the edges of the large plates, and Dave or Crystal said that I could take any scraps they didn't finish. "I feel like John Candy taking on the Old '96er in *The Great Outdoors*," I said. Dave's ears perked up. "I thought you'd appreciate that," I added, "given your opening line this afternoon." When he'd met me on the lake and confessed to wanting to say, "You're going the wrong way!" he was quoting another John Candy movie.

"So you did pick up on that," said Dave. The ice was broken, and the conversation flowed freely until bedtime.

The next day was a holiday. At breakfast Dave announced, "I don't know what you guys are doing today, but I plan to remain in zombie mode." It sounded like an excellent idea to me. I spent the day reading and writing and slowly stretching out my muscles. After another hearty dinner Dave and I stood in the kitchen listening to Stan Rogers and talked admiringly about the winter-adaptedness of Norwegians. Dave's grandfather had emigrated to Canada from Norway. His neighbors in central Saskatchewan were sometimes stranded for days when blizzards erased the roads, so he would strap on his skis, make for the nearest town, and carry home supplies on his back. We also discovered a common predilection for Nansen over Amundsen—a matter on which all ski explorers must take a stance—and I learned that Dave knew a great deal about the history of polar exploration. But, although he was an accomplished wilderness traveler, he concluded, "I turned forty last week and I no longer feel any need to try and emulate these guys." At thirty-four I was skiing quickly toward the same conclusion.

Crystal had contacted the local CBC radio station to tell them of my arrival. They assigned me a slot on the Saskatchewan morning program from Regina, *The Morning Edition*. I was instructed to call in a few minutes before my interview time, and while I waited I listened to the preceding segment, which considered the emerging trend of people writing their own obituaries. Once my interview was under way the host asked, "So are you headed back out there today?" The temperature had been falling steadily since my arrival in La Ronge. It now stood at forty-five degrees below zero. "You know," I said, "if I get a chance to write up my obituary before lunchtime, I might think about it. Otherwise I think I'll stay put until tomorrow."

"Nice one," said Crystal, when I hung up the phone.

I offered to make osso buco again for dinner that evening. To look for the cut of meat I needed, in the afternoon Crystal drove me across town to Robertson Trading, a La Ronge landmark. From the car we literally ran inside through the icy air. The place was a journey back in time to the Old North. Robertson's is a combined grocery and hardware store, outfitter, and fur-trading post. In the aisles at the front of the store I found everything from canned goods and fuel to sleeping bags and skeins of nylon lanyard for stringing snowshoes. Mounted moose heads and prize pickerel hung on the walls, and a ledge running the width of the store was lined with stuffed beavers and every member of the weasel family from ermines to wolverines. Canoes, vintage traps, and intricately beaded leather garments and footwear hung from the ceiling and walls. New steel traps were piled high on the floor, for sale in boxes of ten. Behind them, at the back of the store, was the trading counter, where a woman with a ledger was taking in furs from a couple of gritty trappers. On either side of the counter were heaps of raw pelts for sale—hundreds of them.

I asked the butcher if he had the crosscut beef shanks I was looking for, but he did not. So we went to the more ordinary supermarket but had no luck there either. I decided on some scraps of beef chuck as a passable substitute, bought a few other supplies, and went home to make dinner. Afterward Dave took me downstairs to his shop to fix my broken pole with a wooden dowel, a piece of fiberglass cloth, and some resin. He rolled a short length of wax paper around the pole, a handy trick that would guarantee a smooth cure, and left it till morning.

29

LAC LA RONGE

Dave and Crystal's house was not more than a hundred yards from Lac La Ronge, which at 546 square miles is the fifth largest lake in Saskatchewan. The lake lies on the edge of the Canadian Shield, and on a map the long islands of Precambrian rock that streak its northern half look like welts that appeared on earth after repeated swatting by an angry grizzly. Hundreds of snowmobile tracks from town went out on the ice and then funneled their way into two or three major arteries as they reached farther abroad. My direction was predominantly east, under a line of glacier-scoured islands, toward Nipekamew Bay in the southeastern corner of the lake. When I was a mile out on the ice, a bush plane approaching from the north buzzed as low as a kite and dipped a wing at me.

I skied far out onto the lake in the clear afternoon light. The wind was only a breath, but in such an exposed place it didn't take much to be penetrating. Near sunset the temperature fell sharply. I made camp several hundred yards shy of a giant pressure ridge. I thought of old stories I'd read of horses falling into lakes through the open leads of the cracks that cause these ridges to form. I imagined the innocent animals, who on their own would have known better than to be out in such places, flailing in the frigid water while their masters looked helplessly on, wishing they hadn't tempted fate. The sun had sunk past the horizon while I was pitching my tent, and with the wind I had one of the coldest moments of the winter. If someone had come up to me and said, "Let's go home now," I would have gone.

But only more wind came. Before I left La Ronge, Dave and Crystal made me a gift of earplugs. I wasn't sure what to make of them until they said, "We never sleep in a nylon tent without them. We've had enough sleepless nights out on the lakes to learn that." When I crawled into my sleeping bag after a quick stretch, I put the plugs in my ears and slept straight through until morning.

It was at about this time that I started to become conscious, as I lay in bed at night, that I was chronically stiff and sore. The sensation penetrated to the core of my body. I felt as if I had aged twenty years. I supposed all these nights sleeping on the cold ground, and long days clenching my fingers around ski poles, would revisit me as pains in old age. It was the first time I had thought of the potential long-term effects of a journey like this one on my everyday life. For all my immersion in the natural world, what I was doing seemed for a moment to fly in the face of health and the sensible dictates of the natural order.

There is an unmooring from time and space that comes with traveling over wide monotonous expanses. I spent two nights and parts of three days on Lac La Ronge and have few localizable memories of it. I only know the numbers because I wrote them in my diary. A thin black thread of land on the southern horizon and the sun rolling overhead kept me generally oriented, without demanding that I think about it, and for the rest I just leaned into the direction of dawn for ten uninterrupted hours at a time. The world I could see consisted of exactly two elements that kissed each other in a perfect seam along a horizontal line—blue sky and white snow. There were two tent sites, but in memory they have merged into one, the terminus of a straight line from the west I'd left behind me. Looking back I could see the line retreat toward a golden horizon but vanish into the flatness long before it got there. Near the end of the second day, not far from the southern end of Long Island, I bent away from my eastward line to head south through loose snow toward Nipekamew Bay. The diary reports that progress slowed in the absence of a hard snowpack. I made camp earlier than I had the night before to avoid the bite of the twilight wind.

In the morning I resumed my landward march. A whiteout was blowing in from the west and slowly erasing the islands that had been visible behind me. I fought to beat it to the shore, but fortunately it veered northeast, while I went southeast and was passed by. I reached the opening of the bay, plotted a bearing to where the portage was marked on my map, and sighted it on the black horizon. A distinctive cluster of trees to the east served as my shifty stand-in for a lob tree. I concentrated intensely and kept my eyes locked on the trees, relearning their shifting appearance as I slowly closed the three-mile gap between us. I had taken my bearing from a guessed-at starting point out on the lake, and it was gratifying when I made land within yards of the shrouded entrance to the portage trail. Before skiing into it I took a last look at Lac La Ronge and whispered a goodbye to Dave, Crystal, and Sherlock.

The trail was beleaguered with trees that had fallen across it and come to rest barely high enough for snowmobiles to pass under. I remembered a resolution I had made in Telkwa Pass in early December that I would spend the rest of my life helping to keep trails open. I pondered the duties of the wilderness traveler: to keep the roads from growing in, to keep alive the ancient paths that work in harmony with the natural world. Now was as good a time as any to begin. I took out the pull saw that Nick had given me two months before and set to work cleaning up the trail as I moved along—a little here, a little there. My meager effort retouched some infinitesimal part of a line stretching from me to Nick and Mika in Telkwa and to Don's Dene friend Eli George in Primeau Lake. The line touched Regan Chell on the Montreal River, the Cree of Canoe Lake, the Dene hunters from Dillon, and all the voyageurs who had ever trodden these trails.

I exited the bush onto a lonesome road marked by the passage of a single vehicle, which had stopped there and retreated. The road had not been plowed after the last few snowfalls and was ripe for ski tracks. It ran twenty-two miles south to just below the shore of Wapawekka Lake, where it intersected another gravel road that ran east toward the Manitoba line. I skied for a couple of hours and made camp in a grove of jack pines. In the morning I awoke early and found the day relatively mild, so for the first time all winter I built a fire and sat outside my tent drinking coffee and eating breakfast. My clothes took on the heavy scent of pine smoke as the sun shone down on me, and the sight and sound of the crowns of the trees swaying in the wind soothed me and transported me to my boyhood bedroom, where I used to watch the trees dance outside my window.

I didn't start skiing until after midday, and the bright sun was invigorating when I did. I stopped several times to bask in its rays and mug-up with hot chocolate. I skied the rest of the twenty-two miles along the Wapawekka Road by well before sunset, then turned east onto another road and skied half a mile. The snow was gritty with sand on the new road, and I decided to quit for the day while I was still in good spirits. I set up my tent awash in sunlight, cooked supper, and spent the evening reading Arthur Karras's novel about the Saskatchewan trapping life, *North to Cree Lake*, with a thermos full of coffee and cocoa.

In the morning I was up early, inspired by the "rugged lives of the trappers" I'd read about the night before. But back at the road my spirits started to wane. The sun was warm and promised spring. Traveling east, there was less and less snow on the road and more and more mud. I tried skiing in the deep snow on the roadsides, but the sun made it unmanageably sticky. With every step forward a new inch of it clung to my skins, until it got to be six inches thick and I could hardly lift my legs. I tried skiing without the skins but had no traction to move my sled. By now the road was almost all mud, with shrinking isthmuses of white between hungrily colonizing dark patches. I took off my skis, secured them to my load, and walked down the road, dragging my sled in the mud. After three and a half miles I decided this was no good at all. I unclipped my harness and sat down on my sled to wait.

After an hour a Jeep came creeping from the direction of La Ronge, and the two men inside offered me a ride. I loaded my things. Inside I asked them where they were going, wondering about their slow pace. "Just out for a drive," the passenger said. The driver slurped a can of soda through a straw. There was a gun on the console between them. The vehicle inched forward at a steady fifteen miles an hour while the men scanned the sides of the road. "Seen any moose?" one asked.

AT THE JUNCTION WITH THE Hansen Lake Road, the main route between Prince Albert and Flin Flon, I climbed down from the Jeep onto a paved surface that had not only lost all its snow but had also been dried by the sun. It seemed years since I'd seen asphalt. My last clear memory of it was crossing a road in Chetwynd, British Columbia. I stood for a minute and had a snack. When I had brought all my gear to the eastbound side of the road I put out my thumb for a lift. The temperature was forty degrees.

A lift came in just a few minutes. Leon Dorion was on his way from La Ronge to his home in Pelican Narrows, and that evening planned to travel by snowmobile from there to his cabin, forty miles north of the Churchill River. He said he had glimpsed me heading into the bush to make camp the day before on his way to La Ronge. Leon coordinated operations for crews fighting bushfires. He had started out as a firefighter himself and worked his way up. He said fighting fires in northern Saskatchewan was straighforward because there was water available everywhere. Every fire season provided plenty of work. "In the spring," he explained, "kids here are bored after being cooped up all winter, and setting a fire's a great way to bring an airshow to town." Leon said this without a hint of frustration. For him fire meant business. "Last year was wet and we didn't get enough fires. But they're calling for a hot and dry summer this year. I think we're setting up for a pretty good season."

We picked up a second hitchhiker, whom Leon recognized as a fellow Pelican Narrows resident. Pelican Narrows, he told me when I asked, had 2500 inhabitants. The hitchhiker was long-haired and spoke softly in the same mystical-poetic tones as the man near Sikachu who had sung of brother wolf. He and Leon switched freely between Cree and English. He didn't have any particular plans in mind, because when I stepped out at the turnoff for Pelican Narrows he said, "I'll get out and walk along with you for a while." I told him he was welcome to, but that I would be waiting for another ride rather than walking, since the conditions for skiing were still not good. He decided against staying but helped me to unload. Before leaving, he took out an unopened packet of chewing gum and pressed it into my hand with both of his. "Here's a booster for you," he said, looking deep in my eyes. Then the sound of a vehicle caught his ear, and without so much as looking at each other he and Leon stepped boldly into the middle of the highway and spread out their arms, like bandits or hijackers, to block the approaching van. They told the driver he should take me to Flin Flon. The driver said he would have but that he too was headed north to the reserves.

30

TRAILS

While waiting for a ride and looking at the unadorned strip of asphalt stretching out across the wild land, I thought about humans and the ways that we move through our environments. When you come out of the wilderness the contrast is stark—thousands of square miles of spruce trees, lakes, and snow, then suddenly a ribbon of pavement with motorized steel capsules rolling on it at unearthly speeds.

I sometimes find myself envying the simple ways of nomads. In such moments I fancy theirs a life with only the sparest technologies and liberatingly devoid of the accoutrements that clutter up ours—devoid, most of all, of the invasive infrastructures and the superspecialized technologies required to make them serviceable. Isn't it the highways, the sprawling buildings, the power lines, the dams, the officially sanctioned networks of all kinds, the harbors, and the airports that, while purporting to make our lives better, actually render them more hectic and enable us to exploit and eventually destroy the earth more efficiently? There's a crass but telling pun in the fact that these infrastructures give us such easy access to resources that we are collectively and individually becoming less resourceful.

The argument may be made that the establishment of one-size-fits-all infrastructures levels the playing field, making it possible for us human beings to standardize the pragmatic aspects of our everyday experience and so to make our lives more convenient, more quickly and seamlessly transferable, and of course more marketable. But is life a game to be played, and if it is, are we humans its only players and thus the ones who decide the rules? I don't think it's only a romantic preference for the retention of some vestige of mystery in the inner workings of material reality that makes us suspicious of an existence organized on the model of an assembly line. Mystery is a moving target and will always be somewhere. You don't need to be a romantic to take a moral cue from the observation that diversity and flexibility seem inherent in everything that is healthy and beautiful.

A hundred muddled thoughts in this vein bounce around my head whenever I go out walking. I began to see on my northern journey that it's not infrastructures themselves that are problematic but the motives underlying them. The simple and unassuming portage trails connecting the lakes of the north are infrastructures. Without them it would be impossible for humans to travel very far in so wild a country. The canoes of the First Peoples here were practicable for long-distance travel only in conjunction with these trails. Anthropology can no doubt identify analogous adaptations in every society that has ever existed. Good infrastructures and the technologies associated with them find a way of striking a virtuous balance between the concrete reality of place and the abstract reality of invention.

Trails are good infrastructure and so fundamental that even animals use them. Anyone who walks in the woods will easily notice these so-called game trails as soon as their eyes begin to shed their anthropocentric lenses. In the wintertime, deer and moose create yards—which are essentially circumscribed networks of paths—so that they can move about and access browse without each having to break its own trail. I had begun to learn on my journey that I too needed some kind of trail in the snow to cover any great distance on my skis with my heavy load behind me. This much should have come as no surprise, for I have been a user of trails all my life. The mythical ideal of self-sufficiency that had grown in my consciousness during my years in Europe, in reaction to a sense of claustrophobia, began not only to fade but to look downright dangerous. I started to realize that there was only a short step between the idealization of independence and misanthropy.

But I still believed in the value of simplicity and lightness. Perhaps one of the virtues underlying a simple kind of infrastructure, like a trail, is its impermanence, or rather its ability to impinge on the physical universe only when it is needed and then to fade into a near invisibility. These are really two separate things. In one sense, a trail has a lightness to it such that if it is not used for a time, it will grow over—or be snowed in, in the case of some winter trails—and be swallowed up by the landscape. In the other sense, even when a trail is still used regularly, in the intervals between uses, whether those intervals last hours or days or weeks, it has a way of blending into the background, so that life around it can go on without distraction. But so many of our infrastructures, when they are unused and eventually abandoned, persist as scars that clutter the landscape and perhaps, by their presence in our mindscape, detract from our ability to think in closer harmony with our natural environment.

It is precisely its ability to promote such harmony that may be another motivating virtue of an infrastructure like a trail. Portage trails foster harmony insofar as they respond to the locomotive needs of the land's inhabitants by bringing out the potential of the lakes to act as passageways without bringing harm to the lakes themselves. There is also a harmony that arises out of the creation and use of a winter trail, whether it is traveled over on snowshoes, skis, dogsleds, or even a snowmobile. Rather than move snow out of the way like some nuisance, as we do in plowing roads, the traveler on a winter trail adapts to float on top of it and, in the case of skis, even takes advantage of snow's slipperiness to move faster. In a sense, the migratory paths of birds, whales, and caribou are a kind of natural, built-in infrastructure. The same might be said of the earth's valleys, mountain passes, rivers, and chains of lakes. The only technology—or better, technique—required to make them usable is the ingenuity of the user, whose virtues are transience, mobility, flexibility, and the fact that the mind needs no storage space. Perhaps grace, a species of intelligence, is the ability to recognize the most appropriate way of moving, or not moving, in any set of circumstances, paired with the skill requisite to act accordingly.

Trails are simple and demanding, in the best sense of both words. They are like good books: no electricity or data connection is needed, only a pair of reading eyes or listening ears, but they require that you use your mind.

Trails too keep the mind switched on, and to work well the mind must always be engaged. But they leave it freer than pure wayfinding—a necessary but exhausting activity—does. This may explain why trail-walking and contemplation so often go together. Trails guide you but still leave you with a sense of freedom that roads do not. The trail in use is thus an eloquent manifestation of the tension between free will and fate that drives history.

The blend of challenge and simplicity results from the fact that we don't outsource the processing of information that goes on between user and infrastructure to an intermediary that asks us to sacrifice part of our intelligence. In a thought habit entirely unlike the one we rely on to drive along a highway, interpreting a trail calls upon the mental faculties of attention, memory, concentration, curiosity, and sometimes even imagination. Trails give our intelligence the benefit of the doubt; most roads assume that the people driving along them are idiots. It is the translation and manipulation of the world through high-level thinking that makes us human. Trails make us use our brains to combine information we gather from our environment and use it to arrive at conclusions—conclusions that then carry us forward, and not just anywhere, but to some place we need to go.

The paragon of lightness and litheness in human infrastructure is language. It is the purest distillation of the kind of intelligence that is also found in trails, and comparing trails with language can help us to appreciate some of their brilliance. Using language, human beings can transmit precise and complicated messages across time and space without reliance on any matter outside their own anatomy in a way that to other animals must seem miraculous. After they have done this they can be silent, but language goes on working. Trails are more like writing, a derivative of language, operating by simple markings left on the landscape that sometimes lead followers easily along and other times make tricky allusions, either because circumstances demand it or just to keep us on our toes. "There's no bridge here," says the walker to himself. "Does this mean I ford the river, or is there some other way across upstream or down?" Read more closely and you'll eventually find out. Roads, on the other hand, are like simplified editions of serious books; you get the message instantly but will always feel you've missed out on something. The singular charm of the Australian songlines probably lies in the fact that the cues for following a trail are contained in language itself—in the euphonious and mnemonic form of song. In this system, individual members of an Aboriginal community were responsible for memorizing pieces of long descriptive songs that contained information about how to travel safely across a stretch of their territory. When members of distant communities were passing through an unknown area they had to seek out the guardian of the song for the tract they needed, have it sung to them, and commit it to memory. Songlines share in the lightness of language in a way no other trails have managed.

Anything that is passed from person to person is amenable to refinement, and this opens up trails, which are dynamic systems, to the possibility of constant improvement. Trails are traditions in the basic etymological sense of "things handed down" (from Latin *tradĕre*, "to hand over"). They are diachronically crowdsourced. To blaze, to break, and finally to follow a trail is to join in a conversation across time among strangers you may never meet otherwise. Anyone can lay down a route across space and then wait to see if it takes. Chances are that individual contributions will become only a small part of something much bigger than themselves.

When I skied out onto Lac La Ronge from the west there were literally hundreds of snowmobile tracks coming from every point on the shore within town limits. As I went farther out on the lake, two or three tracks would merge into a single track, and then two or three of these doubled or tripled tracks would merge again, until finally hundreds of individual tracks had converged into three cardinal directions deemed most useful by a collective intelligence. Useless deviations are abandoned and dependable solutions are reinforced. When trails meet obstacles they find ways around them, as anyone knows who has ever come across a tree fallen on a trail before a sawyer has found it. For all this to work properly, however, there needs to be a right to roam—like the *allemannsrett* ("everyman's right") in Scandinavian tradition, more recently codified, that protects public access to rural land as long as it is not disruptive or profit-motivated. Such a right should be as sacrosanct as the right to air and water! There is after all no necessary connection between private property and the right to exclude. In Italy, where the sense of personal property is arguably even stronger than it is in North America, trails nevertheless wiggle their way into every nook and cranny of the peninsula, driving little wedges of no-man's-land between property lines and sometimes squeezing between a country house and its outbuildings with no sense of the owner's rights having been violated by the trespass. Trails require first that we trust each other, and once they become established they propagate trust. When this mechanism is allowed to work freely, trails become timeless edifices of culture, like epic poems that animate the landscape. But when people give up on trails, as Eli George from Primeau River said, the roads start growing in.

Of course no one can seriously deny the indispensability of roads today, but every higher technology or infrastructure should take what it can of value from its precursor, and there's a lot to be learned from trails about making good roads. Dutch traffic engineer Hans Monderman developed the concept of "shared space," which effectively fused the wisdom of trails with urban planning by removing signage and hard edges from city streets in order to compel direct communication among travelers. As a result, traffic flowed better and accident numbers went down. With a degree of intimacy that roads simply cannot achieve, however, trails flesh out the notion that we humans do well to understand the earth as an extension of our own identities. Trails prove this connection by bringing feet, mind, and earth together in a collaboration whose productive simplicity is hard to surpass. Like our special relationship with dogs and horses, trails affirm simultaneously our humanity and our inseverable link with the rest of the natural world. Finally, trails go places where roads simply cannot. I remember trying to explain to the cab driver in Terrace that there were at least two ways to Smithers, by road along the river or by trail across the mountains.

We say that a person must find his or her path to come into the fullness of being. Just as a trail without a traveler will vanish into the wilderness, a traveler without a trail will vanish into the wilderness. The traveler and the trail need each other. There is something lean and beautiful in this connection. Direction and impetus meet as the trail and the traveler, and both direction without impetus and impetus without direction are rather hopeless things.

PART FIVE

LAC LA RONGE TO WINNIPEG

31

THE SUNLESS CITY

A large van came south along the road from the reserves and halted at the junction. The driver rolled down his window and said, as though he'd been expecting to find me waiting, "You'd better come across the highway and load up your stuff." I thanked him and started to move, but when he saw the coast was clear he swung the van across the road and climbed out to help. I pulled myself inside and made my way through the crowded van to the back, where there was one seat left. The driver and I were the only males in the van. The women had come from Sandy Bay, as far north of Pelican Narrows as Pelican Narrows is of the Hansen Lake Road, and were on their way to Flin Flon to buy groceries. The trip takes nearly three and a half hours, but they had less than an hour to go when I joined them. The woman next to me talked ceaselessly while the rest of us sat in silence.

"Isn't this something?" she said once the van was moving again. "When we stopped in Pelican I said to all the girls, 'Maybe we'll pick up a hitchhiker out on the highway,' and here you are." She told me and whoever else was listening about the time they'd given a lift to a young man who was canoeing across the country. "He kinda looked like you, you know. You're not the same guy, are you?"

"No," I said.

"Anyways. We tied his canoe to the roof and he got in with his dog. I tell you, it stank in here! We tried to talk to him but he wasn't too interested. We asked him if he missed his girlfriend or wife. He said he didn't need female companionship. He had his dog, and dogs were better than women."

As we drove east in the spring-like afternoon, I looked out the window and imagined being left alone anywhere out there. The idea didn't scare me. I thought back to that first moment, when the cab driver from Terrace had dropped me off at the mouth of the Copper River. I had seen the endless wilderness stretching out in front of me and felt uncontrollably disquieted. That feeling was alien to me now—not because I had become a master of bushcraft, but because I had learned that most of the time you could survive by simply putting one foot in front of the other and not stopping until you got to a safe place, and that the energy available to drive this mind-numbing process was nearly endless once you knew how to tap it. What was becoming equally alien, however, was whatever impulse had pushed me to strike out into the winter in the first place. Looking back, I wonder if this is the way a life takes its shape—with a thesis and an antithesis fighting back and forth inside each one of us, until a synthesis finally emerges that is able to hold the center. I loved cold and solitude, but I also loved this warm vanload of people.

Somewhere along the way we crossed the Sturgeon Weir River, a key piece of the historic northern fur-trade route. Voyageurs traveling up its eighty-one-mile length—modest for a river of continental importance—from the Saskatchewan River could reach the Churchill River system from here by a single 300-yard portage. From there only one more carrying place lay between them and a downstream paddle all the way to the Arctic Ocean. The river was open, almost completely free of ice. I could hardly believe my eyes. Water in its liquid state seemed unnatural to me now. The closer we got to the Manitoba border and the town of Flin Flon, the more often I saw signs of snowmobile tracks along the side of the road. Before long there was almost a parallel snowmobile highway. Part of me felt guilty for being in a van and wanted to be let out so I could start skiing again, but inertia held sway. The trees shrank or disappeared as we moved east. Bulging slabs of granite broke out from the snowfields—it was the Canadian Shield. My neighbor looked left out the window and said with a sigh, "Ah, Flin Flon, the town with the giant smokestack." I saw the smelter chimney looming over the land like the barrel of an enormous rifle that had been stuck upright in the snow.

The van stopped first in the adjacent town of Creighton, Saskatchewan, named for the prospector who discovered the mother lode veining these rocks and gave Flin Flon its curious name. The story goes that Tom Creighton was camped near present-day Flin Flon in 1914 while prospecting for gold. He stumbled on a discarded copy of a 1905 novel called *The Sunless City* near his campsite and read it. The book's protagonist was another prospector named Josiah Flintabbaty Flonatin, known in the novel by the nickname Flin Flon. The book tells the story of Flin Flon's exploration of the depths of a reportedly bottomless lake in a submarine. He discovers that it is not bottomless at all but is in fact home to a strange city made of gold and other metals. The book was an apt find for Creighton, who struck one of the largest deposits of base minerals on the planet, and he decided to name the settlement above it in honor of the story's hero.

In Creighton, the women piled out of the van and walked up the steps of the liquor store. Only the talker, the driver, and I stayed behind. In two minutes they came back out and loaded large bags of spirits into the vehicle. A total change had come over them. They were cheerful now and nearly as talkative as my neighbor had been all along.

A short drive across town and over the inconspicuous Saskatchewan-Manitoba border brought us into Flin Flon. The women got out at the grocery store and the driver asked me where I wanted to be left. I had arranged to stay with someone while in town, but I'd arrived earlier than planned and didn't want to show up unannounced. I asked him if he knew of a cheap hotel and he took me downtown to the Royal. He helped me carry my gear into the lobby, then said goodbye and went to play the slot machines next door. I took a room and carried my things upstairs as quickly as I could, eager to go for a walk around town before it got dark.

Flin Flon looks just as you would expect a mining town to look, in the same way that, say, Butte, Montana, does. There are metal and brick shacks and boxy houses that look like they were thrown together in a hurry, which they probably were. Even though it had been there for close to a hundred years, the clock is always ticking for a resource town. The old aboveground sewer system crisscrosses the town's core on trestles like the ones that once supported the tracks for minecarts. Putting anything underground in bedrock entails a lot of work, and Flin Flon's present-day sewage disposal system differs from the historic one only in the details. Main Street is a flash of the 1970s, anchored by the Royal Hotel with its vertical neon sign harking back to a still earlier decade. The backdrop comprises the soaring two-tone smokestack of the smelter and the inevitable headframe (the structure over a mine shaft that supports the system of pulleys linking the surface to the subterranean world), property of Hudbay Minerals, the town's major employer. I walked to the end of the strip, toward the stack and the mineshaft, and looked over the desolate expanse, whose effect was softened by the presence of snow. Trees don't grow around the Flin Flon mine.

Before setting out on my trip I had managed to get in touch with a local skier named Dave Price. The morning after my arrival I called to let him know I was in town. He came over to pick me up, and for the rest of my stay Dave was my almost ever-present guide. Born and raised in Wales, he had lived in Flin Flon since 1970. He came as an exploration geologist and worked full-time until his forced retirement in the late 1990s. I soon learned, though, that he was a frenetically active sort, and retirement appeared to have had no effect on his pace and enthusiasm. In addition to his continued work as a geological consultant, he was vice president of the local ski club, active participant in the civic and cultural life of Flin Flon, and a skilled and devoted practitioner of his hobbies.

Dave took me for a drive around the perimeter of town so I could have a sense of the place. He showed me a few of the older tracts of the aboveground sewage system that snaked around the exposed bedrock flanks of the hump atop which Flin Flon sits. The iconic smokestack, he explained, quit spewing its toxic smelting by-products in 2010. It was the sulfur dioxide in the fumes that had made much of the land downwind barren. It acidified what soil there was and killed plant life—nearly all of it. Now Dave was one of two coordinators of the Green Project. Inspired by an initiative in Sudbury, Ontario, another major mining center that experienced the same vegetal kill-off, a few dedicated Flin Flonners hatched a plan to reclaim the soil around town by simply amending it with crushed limestone. Its alkalinity is enough to counterbalance the acid effects of the mine's pollution. Every summer Dave and a group of volunteers organize teams of youngsters to carry buckets of stone out onto the barrens and empty them in rows. They have achieved speedy results. Dave has carefully documented their progress with before-and-after photographs, and the winning out of the green patches over the gray is a persuasive testament to the project's value.

Dave also showed me the statue of Flintabbaty Flonatin, known to locals as Flinty, the town's fictional namesake. The statue is of a plump man in a green jacket and gray hat, marching forward with a prospector's cheerful look of greed. He looks like a character from an old comic book, which is no surprise because the statue was designed by Al Capp, creator of *Li'l Abner* comics. Dave sat on a board responsible for the commissioning of a new Flinty monument for the twenty-first century. The contract had recently been awarded to a firm in Calgary and was worth a whopping $100,000. The new statue would show Flinty cruising in his submarine. It seemed a tremendous extravagance, especially as one hears fears expressed around town that Flin Flon might shrivel up and die, as resource-dependent towns across Canada still sometimes do.

We returned to Dave's house for lunch. He opened a cabinet and invited me to choose from among a large collection of Campbell's soup cans. I had clam chowder with a chunk of orange cheddar cheese and a few slices of bread that Dave defrosted in the microwave. His library reflected a wide-ranging curiosity reaching well beyond science. In towns I was always drawn to people's books, since the trail seldom afforded the comfort to read more than a few pages a day.

As my eyes moved along the spines, Dave pulled down an old photo album from the shelf. It was a selection of his own photographs, mostly of a journey through Switzerland and Italy that he took with his sister in the 1960s. The early color pictures were beautiful. Even those depicting the most mundane things were composed and executed with such an eye for spatial relationships, color, and subject as to make them genuine art. He also showed me photographs of trips he made later, as a geologist, to Antarctica and northern Norway. I complimented him on his pictures, but his reaction was so modest that I wondered whether he knew he had a gift for photography.

In the afternoon he showed me a little more of town on our way to the newspaper office, where he had scheduled me for an interview. While I waited to speak to the sports writer, I was engaged by another woman in the office who had come to Flin Flon from Cape Breton, in Nova Scotia, and claimed that her new home reminded her of the old one. Maybe it was the sense of lurking economic demise. She asked me so many questions that I began to think she was the reporter, but then the real reporter showed up and asked me the same questions all over again. Afterward I walked down Main Street to another appointment with the editor of a glossy magazine called *North Roots*, which had adopted the precise mission of celebrating life in Manitoba and eastern Saskatchewan north of the fifty-third parallel. The editor's name was Frank Fieber. We had been in touch a few months before, and he'd asked me to drop by if I came through town.

The *North Roots* office was unassumingly located, as such places are, in a shared building on a side street downtown. The interior walls were hung with the covers of old issues showing famous northerners and scenes of northern life—bulging white rivers, wolves, bush pilots, the northern lights. The framed covers were interspersed with traditional artifacts like moccasins and furs. Frank had shelves full of books and files on all things northern and showed me pictures and diagrams of old Cree snowshoes, just like the ones I'd seen on the fisherman at Sikachu Lake. We talked for three hours, and Frank talked as much as I did, telling stories of people like Will Steger—the dog-powered polar explorer from Minnesota who passed through the area in the winter of 1984–85 on a little-known preliminary leg of his record-breaking North Pole expedition of the following year—and Bobby Clarke, who is only the most famous NHL player to have come from Flin Flon.

For much of the time I felt like I was talking to a psychotherapist. Frank showed me photographs of Ragnar Jonsson, the legendary trapper of Nueltin Lake, in far northern Manitoba, and even had the audacity to compare me with him. "No, really," he insisted, when I scoffed. "Sure, Ragnar's decision was a lot more extreme than yours, but guys like you and him go out there for a reason. There's something you have to figure out. It's not like he just wanted to be a trapper or you just wanted to go for a long ski." Being mentioned in the same breath as Ragnar Jonsson made me feel like a poser. Jonsson lived alone in a tent and almost entirely off the land in a truly roadless country. He is known to have gone for as long as two years without speaking to another human being, and he ran what is thought, at three hundred miles, to be the longest trapline in the history of Canadian fur harvesting. He would make a round of it every couple of weeks, sleeping in miniature tipis along the way. He was the epitome of ruggedness. He must also have been singularly misanthropic, or mentally deranged.

As for me, during normal life I also enjoyed solitude, but since being on the trail I had come to relish almost any human contact I could come by. Although for sleeping I'll often choose the open ground over a bed, over the course of my northern winter so far I had spent plenty of comfortable nights indoors with no qualms, and I had never gone more than a week without seeing another person. And what, I wondered, was the mysterious reason that Frank was talking about? I was still firmly convinced that the reason I had set out on this journey was a vague sense of homesickness and claustrophobia that needed soothing. I knew, of course, that the journey and its reasons had evolved, but I insisted that its first cause was simple. But Frank insisted there was something more to it from the start—and he seemed to think that deep down I knew what he was talking about.

"To me it sounds like you've done what you need to do. You're tired. It was about the walking. Walking heals people. Sometimes what the mind needs is hard physical exertion. You might think it's just your legs moving forward, but it's your mind too." It had the comfortable ring of so much nonsense that happens to be true. At the time I thought I would ski southeast over the lakes to Grand Rapids, Manitoba, on the northwestern shore of Lake Winnipeg, and call it quits there. It would take maybe another two weeks. It was February 26. "Go to Lake Winnipeg, or wherever, if you need to. Right now it's about enjoying yourself," Frank said. "Your work is done." When he said it, I assumed he was referring to my having set some distance between myself and Elena, and perhaps he was. Perhaps his absolution from the hardships of the trail served some greater purpose, but he neglected to mention that when my legs stopped marching my mind would still have a long way to go.

That evening Dave invited some friends over, and we sat around the living room sipping Scotch and sharing stories. No one was plumbing my soul. The talk was of adventure and easy things. Rick Hall was a neighbor and an avid skier and paddler with a good grasp of the surrounding land. He was tall and lanky and wore glasses. He looked young but was old enough to be a retired schoolteacher. His smile was contagious and his enthusiasm for what I had done was ridiculous but flattering. I tried to tell him I hadn't done anything especially impressive, except condition myself never to stop moving when it was cold, and that I was only a traveler, not the sort of adventurer who had to cover every mile under his own power, make the summit at all costs, and never sleep indoors. But he would hear none of it. We looked at maps and talked over alternative routes. I showed him my plan for crossing the lakes to Grand Rapids, and he voiced serious doubts. He suggested I talk to someone from the Cormorant or Moose Lake area to ensure that they and Cedar Lake, the large and labyrinthine body of water behind the Grand Rapids Dam, were passable. "I'm pretty sure you'll find too much slush to be able to travel," he said.

MY PLATE WAS JUST AS full the next day. In the morning I talked to the tenth-grade students at the local school, where a woman told me that she was related to Roald Amundsen. I could see no family resemblance with the man on my ski tips. The students weren't nearly as interested as their counterparts in Pinehouse had been, but they were polite. They didn't ask about trails or the weather, as the Pinehouse students had, but about how I managed to take showers and relieve myself. It was the difference between being in a place and being of it.

Dave arranged another informal get-together at the ski club that evening. I briefly showed the features of my kit, which only these people could find interesting, and then the club president, Duane Davis, a talkative and jovial character, suggested we make some hot chocolate and sit around and "bullshit" for an hour or two. The club members told me about the successes of their youth team, which had just returned from a national Nordic skiing competition in Canmore, Alberta.

Dave had set an exact time for my departure at least forty-eight hours in advance of the event itself. I was to be at the north end of Ross Lake, just under the great rock of Flin Flon, at nine o'clock sharp the next morning. But before that he'd squeezed me into a live interview on the local radio station. I showed up a few minutes early and walked into the studio to meet a big man in his late twenties wearing a T-shirt and a three-day beard. His name was Raphael but on air he called himself the Hungarian Heartthrob, exhibiting an admirable ability to laugh at himself. The Heartthrob quizzed me for a few minutes while a rock song played on the radio and suddenly we were live.

It was immediately apparent that Raphael had found his calling. He was a skilled talker and had in spades the quickness and spontaneity that I envy in those to whom words come easily.

"So is this just an elaborate way to do yourself in?" he asked on the air. He was the third person now to have made this remark. "I mean, I'll be honest. If I were out there, I'd be dead in a few hours. Okay, maybe a little longer today. It's a beautiful sunny morning out there right now. And that brings us to the weather, folks. Thanks for coming by to talk to us, and the very best of luck on your trip." Raphael ran through the weather and put another song on. A muscle-bound man with hair halfway down his back and skin-tight jeans who looked like a roadie for Aerosmith unexpectedly ran into the studio with a large camera. He ordered me and Raphael to strike poses and smile wide, snapped a picture, and vanished as instantly as he had come. I wondered what, in Flin Flon, could keep him going at such a pace.

Dave took me back to his house for breakfast before whisking me over to Ross Lake for my official seeing-off. At the lake I found the sports reporter for the newspaper, a ski club member named Larry, Frank Fieber, Duane Davis, and one or two others. Larry, a tall man of sixty-five who didn't look nearly that old, wanted to ski the first mile or two with me. We pushed off while Dave and Frank snapped pictures of me sliding away against the backdrop of the great Flin Flon chimney. Larry was on narrow racing skis and was able to move much faster than I was along the beaten track. He literally skied circles around me and probably wondered how anyone could get it in his head to spend a winter this way. Bundled up against the stiff wind and pulling no load, he was amazed at how quickly I peeled layers off. We came to a road south of town near a landing strip groomed for ski planes, and here again were Dave and Frank with their cameras. They took a few final shots. Then I said thank you and goodbye to all three men and forged south toward Schist Lake.

32

ON THE SHIELD

It was brisk and brilliant in the morning. As the hours passed, the day became magnificent. I felt alive to be moving alone through the bush again. The snowmobile trails I now traveled along could not have been more perfect. I kicked along with the peace of mind to enjoy my surroundings. I didn't have to worry about breaking a trail, and I had excellent maps supplemented with straightforward explanations from Rick Hall. I skied up and down the giant bedrock outcrops of the Precambrian shield in a land full now not only of spruce but also of birch. In the first two days out from Flin Flon, the area's major population center, the only people I saw were two speeding snowmobilers who broke the silence for all of sixty seconds.

At one point I came around a bend and suddenly found myself on a long, steep descent. I hadn't seen a downhill slope in months and was caught off guard. I went into a snowplow to try to slow down, but the hundred pounds of my sled bore down hard against the stiff rods that linked into my harness. I noticed sections of exposed rock on the trail ahead and pulled my skis together to avoid striking them with my metal edges. The trail turned this way and that, and the sled flared wildly out to the sides, threatening to take me into the trees. I had skied down far hairier descents for almost as long as I'd been able to walk, but rarely had I felt so out of control.

As I came hurtling around the last bend I saw a series of foot-high wash-board ripples running across the trail ahead of me. At each crest I slammed my weight down into the troughs so as not to become airborne, but over my sled's caprices I had no say, and it jumped and jerked behind me. Then *bam, bam, bam*, it came slapping down, making me cringe at the thought of the cold brittle plastic each time I heard it. I schussed out onto the lake at the bottom of the run and stopped. The silence sealed out the chaos of a second before with guillotine swiftness. "Whew!" I had to shout in affirmation of my exis-tence. I took a moment to acknowledge to myself, before surveying the dam-age, that it had been exhilarating. I turned around and saw that a few pieces of my kit were missing, but the sled itself looked fine. I took off my harness and skied back up the hill with my heart still racing to collect the pieces that littered the way down.

Much of the day was spent traversing the fingers of land that stretch down into Schist Lake and the lakes within lakes that freckle those fingers. Late in the afternoon I spied a cabin near the southern end of Schieder's Bay. Per-haps because it sat within easy reach across the ice from the road at Bakers Narrows, it was locked, but the lawn gave a protected spot for my tent and had a fire ring with a fine view toward the sunset. I built a fire and ate my supper in an Adirondack chair that someone had neglected to take in from the weather.

In the morning I crossed Athapapuskow Lake—abbreviated locally to Athapap—in two large and exposed sections. The wind blew hard and a few times I feared a repeat of the Egg Lake debacle, but fortunately I was able to keep sight of the trail, and the ice was solid.

My third day out from Flin Flon was overland travel, and I started to see people on snowmobiles. Snowmobilers, whether or not they are aware of it, are the archenemies of backcountry skiers, most of whom look down their noses at motorsports, particularly when they're brought into wild places. Snowmobilers are thought of as soft and lazy, despite their virile posturing, for their apparent aversion to strenuous activity. I certainly held this view of them. But over the course of my winter in the bush my opinion evolved. While I still firmly held that there should be vast areas kept wholly free of motorized vehicles, I had to admit that snowmobilers have a closer bond to the northern winter than people sitting at home in front of a TV with the fur-nace raging. Part of the problem for many of us who do not like snowmobiles is that we fail to see them as potential allies in a war against the encroach- ment of the wheel on winter's spaces. Most people, even in places where they don't have to, think of snowmobiles as merely recreational, which they usu- ally are south of a certain latitude. But in places where snow cover is consis- tent, snowmobiles and snow coaches have the potential to represent a more efficient alternative to wheeled traffic in the wintertime. It is hard to fathom the amount of time and fuel wasted on clearing snow across the world's snowbelt, snow that could be more easily compressed and slid over, as it was in many places before the advent of cars. Yet most towns—and I remembered the refreshing exception of Fort Saint James—ban snowmobiles from public roads and central areas, while plow trucks sling their gray slurry at stumbling sidewalk pedestrians who would be better off on skis.

My change of heart toward snowmobilers had partly to do with the friendly encounters I had with them in northern Manitoba. Eight or nine miles south of Athapapuskow Lake, I came to the Goose River, which was open and flowing fast, and crossed a bridge that was maintained by the local snowmobile club. On the far side of the river I found a warming hut, a wel- come surprise and courtesy of the club. No one was in it, but a fire was smol- dering in the stove. I added a log and sat down to have lunch. Before leaving I left a note in the guest book, as other travelers had done, saying where I had come from. Then I walked out onto the ice along the river's edge and filled up my water bottles, something I had last been able to do west of Telkwa Pass in British Columbia.

Looking down at my feet as I shuffled along a few hours later, I saw that the inside edge of my left ski had blown out. It must have been forced out during my out-of-control descent above Schist Lake. I could still travel on it, but it would need fixing soon since it protected the seam that held the top and the bottom of the ski together.

While I was in Flin Flon I had talked on the phone with Zoë. She had worked in Flin Flon once and was thinking of coming north to see some old friends. If I was comfortable with the idea, she was interested in joining me for a few days on the trail. I knew she was an experienced outdoorswoman and I was eager to see her, so I said I thought it was a great idea. Our original plan was for her to meet me later that week near Cormorant Lake, a few days' journey to the southeast, where a box of provisions was waiting. I knew Zoë was due to be driving up from Winnipeg to Flin Flon the next day. If I moved fast enough, I might be able to intercept her at the road in Wanless and hitch a ride back to Flin Flon for some epoxy to fix my ski. It was a pragmatic move but also a pretext for seeing her a couple of days early.

With this in mind, I picked up my pace. I still had a long way to go if I hoped to reach the road by the following afternoon. Just as dark was setting in, two snowmobilers sped past me and then hit their brakes a hundred feet down the trail. They dismounted and pulled their helmets off. "I want to shake your hand," said the man, walking briskly toward me in his own tracks. They introduced themselves as Curtis and Colleen Cook. They had seen my entry in the log at the Goose River hut and were impressed. Curtis told me he was president of the snowmobile club in Swan River, about 180 miles south, and said that if I happened to come down that way I should contact him. "We've got some great trails. The Porcupine Mountains are a beautiful part of the province."

"We'll give you a place to stay too," said Colleen.

"If you're down there," Curtis added, "drop us a line. I mean it. The name's Cook, Curtis Cook. Ask anyone in Swan River and they'll point you in the right direction."

"Aren't you cold?" asked Colleen, as they prepared to go.

"Not at all," I said. "I was going to ask you the same thing."

We wished each other good night with a warmth that only those who have traveled in lonely places of a winter's night can comprehend, and traveled on at our different paces.

THAT NIGHT WAS THE LAST that I was alone on the trail, but at the time the thought didn't occur to me. I was restless and vaguely lonely, and the prospect of company on the trail excited me, so much the better if it was the company of a woman I had a romantic interest in. Looking back on that night, I imagine into place a melancholy that should have been there, because something rich and necessary—no matter how hard—was coming to an end.

I traveled well alone and enjoyed my own company most of the time. I could play by my own rules and move at my own pace, which had become decidedly brisk. Now there would be Zoë on the trail for a few days, and after that my father planned to drive up and meet me. He had been eager since my departure to spend the last few days on the trail with me, whenever that would be. After Frank in Flon Flon gave me the leave I apparently needed to wind down the journey, some vital energy fell out of the enterprise in a way that was beyond my conscious control. I knew I would quit in another ten days or two weeks, so I called my father and told him to start driving northwest soon. I didn't wonder, then, whether my new companions would be able to keep up, or whether I would be able to tolerate a lax pace and the unaccustomed sound of other voices. I didn't consider the fact that if I traveled too slowly I would get cold. Such sensible thoughts barely skimmed my mind.

The night was like any other night, except that for the first time since early December I didn't have to melt snow for water. It was March 2. I pitched my tent in the dark following the usual long preliminaries and crawled partway into it with a sigh of relief, flipping over to sit on my rear end with my feet held high, then clapping them against each other to knock off the snow before pulling them into the tent too. I thought for a split second about the slight pain that sometimes still gripped my knee when I suspended my legs this way. I drank hot chocolate with my dinner and then read and jotted notes in my diary for a few minutes before brushing my teeth, doing a few cold stretches, and finally slipping into my sleeping bag for what, whenever the moment came around, was the best part of the day—sweet and hard-earned sleep.

Move, eat, sleep: this was the way of the trail.

33

ZOË

I got up before sunrise, packed my things, and began skiing hard. Somewhere along the way I called Zoë and told her to look out for me in Wanless. I skied south and then east between Atik Lake and Rocky Lake on the wide trails that curled through one of the world's great boreal wildernesses. My nostrils flared as I inspired the pure air in breaths deep and fast and cold. I was in space but out of time, suspended in a state of focus that was shot through with aromas of fir and pine. I reached Wanless feeling invigorated and walked into the gas station store, where I saw from a clock on the wall that it was before one o'clock. I had covered eighteen miles by lunchtime and had no desire to stop.

Flin Flon is a nine-hour drive north of Winnipeg, so it was still early for Zoë to be coming through. I dragged my sled out to the roadside, slid it onto the top of the snowbank, and stuck my skis upright in the snow in hopes that she would see my equipment and know I was inside. I went back into the store and poured myself a cup of coffee. Noticing a swivel armchair in a room off to the side, I asked if I could have a seat while I waited.

"Help yourself," said the girl working the counter.

I took two steps down into a grimy room that served the dual function of chainsaw repair shop and can-recycling depot. Saw chains of varying lengths hung from nails in the walls beside bars painted with the trade names Jonsered and Husqvarna. The workbench was cluttered with motors and stained with spilt oil. A woodstove burned in the corner with its door open, and I moved the armchair nearer to watch the flames while I sipped my coffee. People came in periodically to leave garbage bags full of beer cans. Some of them noticed my skis outside and said they had heard me on the radio with the Hungarian Heartthrob. After finishing my coffee, I bought a copy of the *Winnipeg Free Press* and read it cover to cover. Then I fell asleep.

I had been excited about seeing Zoë, especially since finding out I'd see her a day early, but I was nervous at the same time, and every time the door creaked some part of me hoped it wouldn't be her. From the chair where I dozed I finally heard the front door open slowly. The door was out of sight, but I somehow knew it must be her. A few seconds later a woman appeared in the entrance to the room. I was certain it was Zoë only because it had to be. There was something strange though. She didn't look like the Zoë who had taken up residence in my imagination in recent months. For the unfamiliar person standing in front of me, looking at me with a huge smile, I felt nothing. Nevertheless I was standing up, and we were walking toward each other. Suddenly she was kissing me and I was kissing her back. I felt no tingle but kissed her all the same, with the same terrifying thought one has just before waking from a bad dream in which you've made a major decision that will alter the course of your life for the worse but there's nothing you can do about it; you've passed a point of no return. But when our mouths parted I realized this wasn't a dream. She spoke, and it was her voice—the same sweet voice I had heard on the telephone, disembodied. Maybe, I thought, these things evolve.

I don't know if Zoë sensed any of this. The kiss did not last long, and in a minute we went outside together to load my things into her small car. We somehow managed to fit them alongside her gear, and then drove sixty miles back north to Flin Flon. It turned out that the friend she was visiting in town was someone I had met at Dave Price's house the week before. Her name was Heather and she had invited us both to stay at her place. When we arrived I telephoned Dave to let him know I was back in town, and he came over with an annotated scrapbook he had already put together documenting my visit.

Rick Hall, who lived two doors down, also came over, and when I told him about my ski he jumped at the opportunity to fix it himself.

After Zoë and I helped cobble together a supper from whatever was available for Heather and ourselves, we walked over to Rick's house with my damaged ski. In his shop he sanded smooth the groove that the edge had come out of, filled it with epoxy, and clamped the edge into place. He said it would need twenty-four hours to cure. So we would be in Flin Flon another night.

On the way back to Heather's, Zoë and I stopped in the street, which was soft and firm the way snow becomes when it's been driven over. We held hands and looked up at the sky. It was a clear night and I could see thousands of stars distinctly. It took years of traveling at unimaginable speeds for light to traverse the spaces between them. The light was blue and looked cold—not like the light of a flame. The sky was an enormous arc, vaulting up from the bright-white ground studded with dark houses that looked small and square, like cardboard boxes tossed on the snow. Our mouths came together again.

Inside it was not very long before we fell asleep.

WHILE I WAS IN FLIN Flon I talked on the phone with Art Fenner, who was holding my final box of provisions on Cormorant Lake, a remote settlement between The Pas and Lake Winnipeg. Art ran a trapline on the land between Cormorant Lake and Moose Lake. I asked him about slush, and he said it was a certainty. He advised me to steer clear of the lakes, saying there would be no packed trail to speak of. It was the nail in the coffin of an all-but-dead plan.

Another consideration was my father. I had to be some place where there was a road when he arrived. I finally accepted that my journey was ending, and from now on I would be winding down in preparation for a return to everyday life. I would enjoy the country I was in and not worry about aiming for far-off places. With Zoë I would spend a few days exploring the Rocky Lake area, north of The Pas, and after she had gone I would head south to wander around the Porcupine Hills that Curtis and Colleen, the snowmobilers from Swan River, had recommended. My father would prefer the relief there to the flatness farther north.

In the morning Zoë and I drove back to Wanless and left her car near the gas station. The day was advanced by the time we started skiing west toward Rocky Lake. It was the first time all winter that I had skied west by design.

Zoë had come with old wooden skis, no skins, and a utility sled she pulled with yellow nylon rope, but she was able to move everything at a good pace. When we were a few miles into the bush we took a narrow path that led downhill onto the lake. On the mild descent, Zoë's sled sped out on its ropes to one side and caught a tree, jerking her to the ground with what looked like painful suddenness. She stood up laughing and dragged the sled from behind the tree. We skied across a bay to where there was shelter from the wind and made camp.

It felt good to be in the bush again, but something had changed. The atmosphere was too easy, and the spur to move, now that I was consciously traveling backward and had much else on my mind, had gone away. It was warm now too and comfortable enough to linger outside and watch the sunset.

That evening, as I was lighting my stove, a metal piece inside the burner broke again. The only replacement part I had was faulty, and my attempt to jury-rig it nearly set the tent on fire. It was late by the time I gave up, and we settled for a supper of beef jerky, dried fruit, and energy bars. After supper we went straight to sleep.

THE BROKEN STOVE ON OUR first night out turned out not to be such a bad thing. It forced us outside into the now pleasant air to build campfires at every mealtime. The flip side was that where there is a campfire there is a temptation to sit by it.

We moved our camp the second day to a spot farther west on the lake. A ten-foot rock face with a large white stain on it made a good heat reflector, and a slight overhang offered protection from inclement weather. We collected heaps of firewood, and while Zoë built the fire I went about pitching the tent in a sunny spot and unloading food. I had never seen anyone make a fire so quickly. Zoë could go from a match to a fully cooked meal as fast as most people could with a gas range. The fact that we had fire and two cook pots also meant that meals could be more elaborate than they had been when I was alone. Zoë was shocked at the one-pot gruel I was in the habit of eating to make efficient use of my water. "Aren't you going to rinse that pot out before making hot chocolate in it?" she once asked.

"Rinse it out? Why?"

"Because it has chunks of tuna fish in it."

"So?"

"You're not serious?"

"It's not a horrible combination."

"It's disgusting."

THE WEATHER TURNED SPLENDID. The sun cast its warmth on Rocky Lake and daytime highs approached fifty degrees. We decided to savor the weather by leaving our camp where it was and skiing off without sleds to explore the shores of Rocky and Atik Lakes. I had almost forgotten how much sheer fun it could be to just ski.

There's a closeness to living beside someone in a narrow tent that accelerates acquaintance. I once picked up a hitchhiker in Minneapolis while driving west to Oregon in early May. By nightfall we were in western North Dakota and were both tired. We drove out onto the prairie and pitched his one-person tent in the grass. Eight inches of snow fell during the night, pressing against the tent walls while we slept, and when we woke up in the morning we were spooning. By that afternoon we felt like brothers as we stripped naked and plunged into the frigid Yellowstone River, then warmed ourselves passing a bottle of whiskey with shivering hands. When we put our arms around each other and said goodbye in Livingston a few hours later it was as if a chapter of life had been compressed into thirty hours. With Zoë it was like that too, but what those hours should have shown me was that she could never be to me what Elena was. Instead I would refuse for months to release my grip on an illusion I'd so jealously cultivated.

When we came out of the bush after a few days I still had a day before my father was due to arrive. We decided to drive to Cormorant Lake to retrieve my last box of food from Art Fenner. We took the road northeast from The Pas along Clearwater Lake to the tiny Native community of Cormorant, where we found Art in shirtsleeves on a four-wheeler plowing his driveway in neat rows. His wife, Helen, welcomed us at the door, where cooking smells wafted from the kitchen.

"You must be hungry," she said.

"Always," I answered.

Helen laid out a moose stew, wild rice casserole, warm bannock, and fried pickerel cheeks, a delicacy on the northern lakes. The news was that Art and Helen had recently been granted treaty status. It was a recognition by the Canadian government that they were entitled to the benefits promised their ancestors in perpetuity when they ceded control of their territory to the Crown. "We're Treaty Indians now, after years of being considered Métis," Art vaunted, not without sarcasm. "Finally I can hunt without a license." The Métis, a distinct people of mixed European-Native ancestry, are not entitled to the treaty rights of other First Nations in Canada.

The irony was that at the very moment their treaty status came through, the Manitoba Métis Federation—representing the core historical population of the Red River Valley in the south of the province—had just won a major legal victory. The Supreme Court ruled that Canada had not fulfilled its obligations under the Manitoba Act of 1870 to set apart land for the children of the Métis as a condition of their joining Confederation. Although the ruling was largely symbolic, in the news there was talk of millions of dollars in compensation and even of new land grants to Manitoba's Métis population. But despite having lived their whole lives as Métis under the law, Art and Helen, who were now about sixty, would reap none of these benefits with their changed status.

Zoë would be going back south and I had decided I would meet my father in Swan River, which was on her way home. He wasn't due until the next day, however, and neither of us was in a mood to pitch a tent by the side of the road. We needed somewhere to stay, and preferably closer to Swan River. I remembered Curtis and Colleen Cook's offer and found their number in a phonebook in The Pas. Weighing the disagreeable alternative, I tossed shame to the four winds and dialed the number despite the late notice. I hoped they would remember who I was.

"Hello," said a bright male voice.

"Hi. Is this Curtis?"

"Yes, it is. Who's calling?"

"Hi, Curtis. It's Anders Morley. I don't know if . . . "

"Anders! Hi there. I'm so glad you called. What can I do for you?"

"Well, Curtis, I'm in The Pas right now with a friend and we're on our way south. I've decided to do the last leg of my trip in the Porcupines. My dad's coming into Swan River tomorrow and—I hate to impose at the last minute like this—but I was wondering if I could take you up on your offer to spend the night at your place."

"Sure, Anders. We'd love to have you!" Then I heard him project his voice away from the telephone and say, "Hey, Colleen. Anders and a friend are going to come spend the night tomorrow."

I grimaced with embarrassment. "Um, Curtis?" I said. "Actually, I was wondering if we could come tonight."

I waited for the uncomfortable silence, but it never came. "Oh, tonight! That's fine. I'm sorry. I wasn't listening. So when do you expect to be here?" He said that getting to his house from the highway was a little tricky. "I'll just drive out there and wait for you," he said.

Zoë laughed as I fretted aloud over my bad manners for the whole drive south from The Pas to Mafeking. "What are you so anxious about?" she said.

"Ill breeding," I said.

"What are you talking about?"

"I'm talking about the fact that we've just shamelessly foisted ourselves upon two perfect strangers at nine o'clock at night."

When we reached the turnoff for Bowsman, a black truck sat out on the highway and flashed its lights as we came into view. The window rolled down and I saw Curtis wearing a grin. "Follow me," he shouted with a sweeping wave. It was ten o'clock on a winter night, and all across the prairie people were sleeping in warm beds. The Manitoba license plate says "Friendly Manitoba," and it couldn't be more true.

34

DAD

I gave my father instructions over the phone the next morning to meet me at Curtis's office in Swan River, and in two hours I found him there looking dazed. He and Curtis hit it off immediately. In minutes they were trading stories like old chums. My father held forth with a colorful account of the effects of the energy shots he had picked up at gas stations along the way. "You know," he said, "they call it Five-Hour Energy, but starting in about Indiana I conducted a series of experiments on myself, and I think that— if you take them under the right conditions—you can get up to eight hours out of one dose, especially when used in conjunction with caffeine. Then, of course, you can take them back to back. I believe the label advises against it, but I'm telling you, have you ever driven through a blizzard in Fargo? You *need* the second bottle. It may be possible to take even more, but I have yet to ascertain the exact limit."

Curtis told the story of a time he and three friends had gone through the ice in the middle of a lake on four-wheelers, losing them in sixty feet of water. They were able to climb out of the frigid water and walk twelve miles out of the bush with no harm done to themselves. Later they managed to winch their four-wheelers up from the bottom of the lake using two beams set crosswise over the hole.

Zoë briefly met my father, who wasn't sure what to make of the situation (and so made nothing of it out loud), and then left to make her way south. It was agreed that I would see her again soon. Curtis spread out a map of the Porcupine Hills on his desk. The aspen-covered highlands just northwest of Swan River were laced with snowmobile trails maintained by Curtis's club. He explained the merits of each trail and suggested a few ways of tying them together to make loops. He also pointed out the warming huts that dotted the trails. The thought of sleeping in these simple cabins with woodstoves appealed to me as I grew soft from too much company and too much ease. Curtis told us we could leave my father's truck at his place, and he would drive us from there across town to the trailhead. We went back to the Cooks' to pack my father's gear into a backpack, and after a cup of tea Curtis drove us to a place called Antler Corner.

It was starting to get cold again. We set off at a fast pace to stay warm. Sunset was approaching quickly, and our only plan was to put a mile or two between us and the road before making camp. For me it was just another night, and once I warmed up I could have skied for hours, but my father was used to sleeping inside and at most poking around the New Hampshire woods on weekends. He was clearly eager to camp as early as possible, and I grew frustrated with what seemed like an unwillingness to hold out for an acceptable site. This had long been a struggle between us: he called it my indecision; I called it his impatience. I eventually gave in, and we camped at the edge of an old clear-cut near the crest of a hill, but I was irritable. I said I thought the spot was too exposed to the cold wind, but I wasn't ready to argue about it.

Rather than try to forget about our disagreement, I insisted on building a fire in a trench behind the tent, saying that it would be too windy elsewhere. My fire made so much smoke that I crawled out of the hole coughing and spilled half my supper down the inside of my jacket, with no one but myself to blame. Fortunately I had already given my father his. I went to bed nauseated from the smoke and woke up the next morning feeling like I had a hangover.

I set off at my usual clip and felt myself becoming impatient again with my father's plodding gait. Eventually I calmed down as I fell into a hard rhythm and felt the bracing cold again. I reminded myself that my father had been sitting in a car for three days and that he had always preferred to go at a slow and even pace. I felt badly about having made him take to the trail right away and realized I should have given him a day to rest and adjust to his surroundings. But I was sick of waiting around, no matter who I was waiting for. It had nothing to do with him. I wanted to tick the days off the calendar and move on to whatever was next.

My mood had improved considerably by the time we reached the first cabin. It was a sunny afternoon and there was a sweeping view to the east, where we could see a patchwork of fields and woods stretching to Lake Winnipegosis. We decided to stop for the day. We built a fire in the stove and rolled our sleeping bags out on the old school-bus seats that lined the walls. With no tent site to prepare and no tent to set up, we had time to enjoy the late afternoon hours reading, talking, and drinking tea.

Before sunset a man on a snowmobile drove up and came into the cabin. He was in his forties, quiet, and limited his conversation to essentials. My father asked him about the view and he pointed out two or three highlights before driving off. A few hours later, after we had eaten and my father was reading in his sleeping bag while I looked at maps, I heard an engine in the distance. I looked outside and soon recognized the man from earlier. This time there were two snowmobiles, and his wife and children were with him.

"Dad," I said. "Get up. We've got visitors."

When they came in they were carrying a cooler. "We brought you some hot food," said the man. They were all silent as they unloaded foil containers of meat, rice, potatoes, and cake. Once everything was laid out they made awkward conversation for a minute or two, hardly long enough for us to thank them, and drove away into the night again. Thinking ahead to breakfast, I put the food in my plastic tote to keep it from mice. My father was taken aback. He normally falls asleep as soon as he makes contact with a horizontal surface, but lying in the dark that night every few minutes he would say, "I can't believe they came all the way out here in the middle of the night," or "Maybe your mother and I should retire to Manitoba," until fatigue finally got the better of him.

Our plan the next day was to go ten or twelve miles deeper into the Porcupines to another cabin. I didn't have topographical maps for the area, only the flat snowmobile-club plan, but it looked like another easy day. After a mile or two of gradual descent we were at the bottom of a climb as steep as any I had seen since the first week of winter. To make matters worse, I had started feeling sick that morning. When we started up the hill I turned feverish, almost deliriously so. Not wanting to disappoint my father, who had come halfway across the continent to join me, I did my best to push through it. I trudged up the half-mile-long hill with my heavy sled trying to pull me back down, stopping every hundred feet or so thinking I was going to vomit. At the top, with my father out of sight behind me, I took out my first-aid kit and looked for a packet of acetaminophen I knew I had somewhere. I wasn't sure it was the indicated treatment for whatever I had, but I took it anyway and the effects were almost instantaneous. In a few minutes I was strong again and was skiing along like I always had, feeling only a little light-headed.

My father is a doctor, and a family joke says that we were never allowed to be sick. "Suck it up," has always been one of his favorite lines. But when we got to the tiny cabin at twilight my dad looked at me and told me to lie down on the floor and rest. He built a fire in the rusty stove and put supper on. I looked up at him through glassy eyes and felt like I was seeing him as I seemed to remember seeing him when I was a helpless child. Among the paper left in the cabin for tinder, he found a copy of the *Winnipeg Free Press* from a year before, almost to the day. He read it out loud to me. A record-breaking mid-March heat wave had brought temperatures of over sixty-eight degrees. He held out the page so I could see a photograph showing Winnipeggers in swimsuits splashing in the water. Meanwhile the temperature had been steadily falling since we had taken to the trail forty-eight hours earlier. The thermometer outside the cabin read minus ten degrees.

We had a restful night. I felt better in the morning and told my dad he could start skiing if he was ready. I would catch up with him. We planned to return to the cabin we had spent the second night in. Curtis and Colleen were going to come out on their snowmobiles for a party to celebrate the end of my travels. Once I started skiing I realized that my father had his trail legs now. It took me an hour to catch him. When I did, we skied along at the same pace until we reached the top of the big hill we had come up the day before. I remembered my wild ride down the hill outside Flin Flon. This hill was twice as steep in parts and half a mile long. Had I been without a sled, I wouldn't have thought twice before speeding down it, but the load at my back changed everything. The narrow tree-lined corridor became a dangerous proposition. We put our heads together and hatched several schemes for getting down with our gear in one piece and without too much effort.

First, we attached a length of nylon cord to the back of my sled. My father held the cord in one hand behind the sled while we both went into a snow-plow, but my dad was unstable under his top-heavy pack and couldn't use his poles and hold the thin, slippery cord at the same time. Next we tried the same method with sidestepping, but I couldn't get into a sideways position with the stiff poles attached to my harness, and my father had the same problem gripping the cord as before. Our last idea was for him to tie himself to the sled and sit down and drag as a deadweight behind it, but even with the extra weight the speed was still hard to control, and the rope painfully pinched his arm.

Finally I gave up. "I'm just going to ski straight down it," I said. "I don't care. We're going home tomorrow." My father thought it was a bad idea, but before he could dissuade me I pushed off. I built speed fast into the initial straightaway. I started feeling confident as I approached a blind corner and flashed around it. Suddenly I saw a herd of deer standing in the middle of the trail about 200 feet in front of me. "Get out of the way!" I yelled, waving my poles above my head. "Move!" The deer froze and seemed to consult with one another for a split second before breaking apart and dashing into the woods, but not before my father, who had pushed off right after me in a spasm of solidary zeal, took my yelling as a signal to stop immediately. He fell onto his side to break his fast descent, and now at the bottom of the hill I turned to see him racing down the trail on his side with his skis flailing in the air above him. "Friggin' deer!" he shouted after the last stragglers leaping into the aspens. We were both in hysterics when he ground to a halt. He lay in the snow for a minute shaking his head and then held out the end of his ski pole for me to pull him up.

AT THE CABIN WE TOOK a few celebratory pictures and set about warming and tidying it up for our visitors. Shortly before sunset we heard the growling of snowmobiles. Besides Curtis and Colleen, Curtis's parents, Colleen's brother, and a neighbor they'd picked up along the way joined the party. Curtis and Colleen unloaded containers of food from their sleds. They hurried the steaming aluminum trays in from the cold and plopped them down on the hot woodstove. "It's nice and warm in here," everyone was saying as they peeled off more layers than a skier would ever need to wear. Soon the back-woods cabin was filled with laughter and talk.

Curtis was still busy taking cutlery from bags and peeling tin foil off the trays warming on the stove. I watched him stealthily pull something from one of the bags and hide it behind his back, then step gingerly across the room wearing a Manitoban smile. "Hey, Dave," he said to grab my father's attention. "I've got a little surprise for you." I wondered how he could be so excited about giving a gift to someone he hardly knew. "Now I know you're a big Chardonnay guy," he said, "so I brought you something real special from my collection." From behind his back he drew his finest bottle of Chardonnay and neatly flipped it around, resting it in the palm of his other hand for my father to scrutinize the label. "You're gonna *love* this one," Curtis said.

Meanwhile my mind was working hard, trying to reconstruct the sequence of events that could have led to this bizarre outcome. I had only ever known my father to touch white wine under duress. He claims that even a whiff of it gives him a hangover. He drinks almost exclusively Cabernet Sauvignon and is, of his own admission, hardly a connoisseur. I thought, where on earth could Curtis have got the idea my dad was a "Chardonnay guy?"

The only possibility was that the topic of wine had somehow come up at Curtis's office after my father had arrived and I stepped outside to see Zoë off. Other than those few minutes, Curtis and my father had never been together in my absence. Now I could almost hear my dad joking that what he needed was a glass of wine to offset the stimulant effects of all the Five-Hour Energy shots he'd imbibed. Curtis, in order to advance the conversation, must have mentioned that he happened to be a wine lover himself and asked my dad whether he was particularly fond of any one wine variety. "Do you like Pinot Grigio, Sauvignon Blanc, Chardonnay?" he might have said, just to get the ball rolling. Again I imagined my dad's voice: "Chardonnay? Oh yeah! I love Chardonnay. Something about the floral bouquet. The semidry, semisweet *je ne sais quoi.*" He would have been indulging in a trademark rhetorical habit of his that my brother Dave has long described disapprovingly as "staking minor conversational gains on major practical risks." But now the chickens had finally come home to roost. I intensely wished Dave could be there to see it unfolding.

My father probably had no memory of his earlier conversation, and I could sense the desperation behind his smile as he showered profuse thanks on Curtis and Colleen. But in seconds he had worked out an ingenious strategy.

He swept up five of the plastic goblets that the Cooks had brought for the occasion and set them out in a row. He pulled the cork and announced, "I think this calls for a toast!"

"It does indeed!" shouted Colleen from the far side of the cabin.

"Glass of Chardonnay, Colleen?" my father asked, his voice rich with hope.

"No, thank you, Dave," she replied. She stuffed her hand into a backpack and unsheathed a bottle of Cabernet Sauvignon. "I'm a Cabernet drinker myself. Anything white kills me."

My father was almost sweating, and he knew that I knew it. He redoubled his efforts. "Chardonnay anyone? I feel terrible keeping this whole beautiful bottle to myself. Anders?" he tried, looking to me for succor.

"No, thanks," I said. "I think I'll stick to red tonight."

BY THE TIME WE STEPPED outside to see our new friends off, it was well after midnight and the temperature had fallen below zero. Standing in the bitter cold, our breath mingling with snowmobile exhaust in the blinding head-lights, I was glad we would be in front of the stove again in a few minutes and not driving twelve miles through the stinging air back to town. We said a loud goodbye over the rumbling engines. The Manitobans revved their machines a few times in anticipation and then roared off together down the trail. In sec-onds their lights had been smothered by the bush, and within a minute it was as quiet as if they had never been there.

"Wow, Anders," said my father.

We went back inside to tidy up and rearrange the bus seats for bed. My father crawled into his sleeping bag and I stayed up a few minutes longer to run through my never-absent stretching routine. Just before turning in, I stepped outside again to look at the sky. For the first time all winter I heard a chorus of wolves howling. I stuck my head inside to tell my father, and he listened from his sleeping bag. The howling got louder and seemed to come from nearby. I stood outside listening and gazing at the stars for as long as I could. When it was too cold I went in, slipped into my sleeping bag, and drifted off with wolfsong in my ears.

THE MORNING WAS LIKE JANUARY. It was unpleasant to step out into the air, but I was happy my father would have a chance to feel something of what my winter had been. It was a ten-mile ski back to the road, and I had every intention of going hard. The edge had sprung back out of my right ski, probably during the reckless descent of the day before, but this time it didn't matter. In a few hours Fridtjof and Jackrabbit would be hung up for the season.

Outside I told my father to start skiing while I loaded up, so his muscles wouldn't get cold. I packed my sled quickly, flying through the motions that I had refined to second nature over the past four months. I turned to look at the cabin and out over the land, then skied off at as fast a pace as I thought I could sustain for ten miles.

I caught up with my father but had to leave him behind because my fingers felt like they had daggers in them, and moving my whole body was the only way I could get them warm. I was explosively eager to be back to the road and finished. The idea of sleeping somewhere warm for as many nights as I wanted, for the rest of my days, impelled me forward. Soon I beat the cold, but I pushed on. My father was never far behind me. We stopped once for sixty seconds for a drink and a snack.

I skied out of the bush at noon. When I reached the roadside a truck drove by. I unhitched my sled, took my skis off, and put some extra clothes on. Exhausted, I sat down on my duffel bag to call Curtis. Then I lifted my eyes to see the truck that had just driven past coming slowly back up the road. I recognized the driver. I'd met him at David Price's house in Flin Flon. His name was Bill Fulford, and by now he had his window down.

"Hi, Bill," I said. "Small world." We were 230 miles south of where I'd last seen him.

He said he was on his way to a meeting in central Manitoba. "Wasn't expecting to see you down this way, but when I drove past I thought, how many people are you going to see skiing out of the bush with a red jacket and an orange sled behind them?"

"It's great to see a familiar face," I said.

"It's good to see you too."

There was nothing more to say. Bill rolled up his window and had turned south again when my father came out of the bush.

"Who was that?" my father asked.

I watched the truck until it disappeared behind a bend. "Just someone I met up north."

35

THAW

On the drive south to Winnipeg the prairie wind threatened to hide the road ahead under migrating snowdrifts. When we arrived in the city, the same wind somehow felt colder on the streets than it had on the trail. We checked into a hotel where the young man at the desk, seeing our weather-beaten appearance, asked what we had been up to. "My son just skied from British Columbia to Manitoba," said my father. It wasn't quite the truth, but I wasn't going to split hairs.

"Oh my god! You're like Don Starkell," said the young man. I must have made a strange face because he said, "Do you know who that is?" I knew who Don Starkell was and had also read *Paddle to the Amazon*. The Winnipeg canoeist, who had died several months before I began my journey, was loved and loathed in equal parts by Canadians for his spirit of adventure and for his callous recklessness. My own spirit of adventure paled beside Starkell's, and it was doubtful that the young man behind the desk had any insight into whatever recklessness was in me. I told him I was flattered by the comparison but that my journey wasn't as impressive as it sounded.

The last ten days on the trail, apart from the moments of tenderness and laughter with my father, were a low ebb that in the months to come only went lower. For all my high hopes, things with Zoë proved to be nothing more than a short exothermic burst on my way down. That things don't always go the way we expect them to is the end realization of every good story I know. The discovery can be liberating if we let it be, because it shows us that even when things take a bad turn, or a series of bad turns, a downward spiral is not inevitable.

"What am I doing here?" I had asked myself from the moment my feet hit the snow until the end of the journey. For years afterward I thought that if I couldn't give a clear answer to this question in connection with a journey I had planned myself then it could mean only one thing—that I shouldn't have been there. This reaction was linked to a sense of regret about becoming involved with Zoë while I was on the trail, which I thought had made the journey into at best a wasted opportunity.

The real problem was that I never seriously listened for an answer to the question, "What am I doing here?" I couldn't handle the open-endedness of it. I had all but made up my mind by the time I landed in Prince Rupert that, in addition to my earlier reasons for coming, I was on this journey to end my marriage. But the journey, as if it had its own sense of integrity, would not be duped into playing along. So the question bombarded my consciousness every time my confidence in my own ability to control things was shaken.

I can see now that Frank Fieber, the journalist in Flin Flon, was right: the journey did have a mysterious purpose. No matter how much I loved skiing and the trail life, I didn't just go on a journey through a northern Canadian winter for the fun of it, the way I might have taken a summer off and hiked the Appalachian Trail. Proof enough of this, for me, rests in the fact that, although my love of cross-country skiing and trail living have if anything only grown since 2013, I would never think of making a trip like the one described in these pages again.

So what was I doing out there in the winter? The short answer is one a wise fool might give: I was out there to go through winter. Of course, this is exactly why every living thing pushes to make it to the end of fall each year—so that it can go through winter. Winter is the inevitable obstacle facing anyone who wants to reach spring. The curious thing is that, even as I was daily assailed with the literal season, I seemed to think that metaphorically I could pass straight from fall to spring, like a bear crawling into its den to hibernate.

As a journey meant to fulfill certain expectations then, the journey failed. I did not come close to skiing across Canada, as I had originally intended to do. I didn't even achieve my amended ambition of skiing until the spring equinox. I left the trail five days before it, and not because I'd run out of snow. I could have skied for another month had I kept pushing southeast.

Insofar as we learn from our failures, however, the journey was, after years, a success. It was a success in the way that winter is always a success. Winter's reason for being is to give things an opportunity to make themselves strong enough to resist its ability to kill them. What winter aimed at in me was the illusion of a one-dimensional self. Looking back, the impression I have is that at age thirty-two I had forgotten things I had once known about myself. I suddenly remembered my halcyon childhood but forgot all the solid stepping-stones that led me from there to a happy adulthood in the city on the cusp of middle age. No one had forced me into the life I found myself living. At university I had learned to love the inside of libraries as much as I loved the great outdoors. I had eventually gone to Europe because those library hours had generated an interest in the Old World. Once in Europe, I decided to stay because I had met a woman the likes of whom I knew I would never meet again, and because there was much about life in Europe that I loved. And so on. But as I raced to accommodate all these new facets of my developing adult self, I let the needs of the earlier self—which I imagined living across the ocean—fall by the wayside. Seeing the *National Geographic* photograph of Andrew Skurka picking his was across an icy Alaska river in 2011 suddenly woke me up to this neglect. In a fit of panic I reversed the current, channeling all my energy into creating a journey that would boldly articulate the tenets of the forgotten first mythology. But I was repeating the very mistake I had set out to correct. Several years passed before I came out of the crisis, as if emerging from winter into spring, by reappropriating all the truths I had learned along the way. The result is a composite adult self.

TO STAY ALIVE IN THE wilderness in winter you have to move as fast as possible. When you are lost in the wilderness of human living, on the other hand, you must move slowly and deliberately to find your way again. It seems to follow that spending a winter traveling across northern Canada is a bad way of dealing with a mid-life crisis. But looking at the ecology of winter I begin to think that maybe this isn't quite true. Animals huddled in their dens during a February blizzard probably think, in whatever way they can, that winter is an awful strategy for making them stronger. Why all the added pressure? Can't you see we're already trying to make it through a dearth? Surely evolution and the seasons could have agreed on something more pleasant than this deranged game of do-or-die! Apparently they could not. To get through the seasonal crisis you have to make your mind go as fast as your body must go and hope that it works as well as it does when it has a little more slack.

This is where the set of tools we call tradition comes in handy. People who think about such things have often recognized a two-handed pattern of repeated holding and reaching as a motive force in human history. (The pattern has imperfect rhymes in the step and stride of walking, the stroke and coast of paddling, and the kick and glide of skiing.) Sometimes the reaching hand goes into the unknown, seeking a new hold, but is burned or bitten and must draw back to the place not yet abandoned by the holding hand. Tradition, made practicable as various kinds of infrastructure, is what enables us to hold and not just reach and gives us something to fall back on when our exploration comes to nothing, as it sometimes will.

But tradition is not simply there. It is handed down through time and is forever being adapted. When we use a tradition we modify it and send it along. I had seen how trails are containers of long experiment and refinement that enable us to use lessons learned by others to get ahead through wild places. What I had not seen was that marriage—which nowadays seems so stuffy because it has taken on the rigidity and unadaptability of bad infrastructure—was another such infrastructure, long in developing and not just pulled out of thin air, for getting through the wilderness of life in society. Like a trail when you lose it and a storm rages around you, it can make you pull your hair out and curse the gods, but when you come out on the other side, if it is a good trail—or a good marriage—it will pick up where it left off.

And so I was walking in the woods in Italy just the other day with Beowulf, who is now twelve years old, when I noticed that although we were walking together along the same trail we sometimes went along at different paces and followed different deviations. Sometimes he dashes up a steep stretch that I take slowly and steadily. Other times he stops to sniff at something or mark it with his scent while I walk onward, or I take a few steps back for a second impression of something I want to remember for later, and Beowulf scoots ahead to drink from a brook he hears rippling in the understory. We always meet again. Unlike the road, where when we have to walk along it we're tethered to each other by a leash and neither of us seems really happy, the trail lets us go together but apart. Trail companionship requires a responsiveness, a sixth sense that is really an ability to synthesize the perceptions of the other five, in which both travelers have a duty. I almost never have to look back when I'm walking with Beowulf, because even when I can't hear him scurrying along I can nevertheless sense that he is there. There is never the least feeling that the distance between us signifies less affection.

This way of moving through the world reflects the shape my marriage has taken after coming through a very long winter. Elena never stopped believing in our relationship and held on even as I reached away from her into the unknown. After a lot of grasping I came away empty-handed and feeling foolish. But Elena was still there, and we adapted. We are together again, after five years apart, but sometimes our togetherness entails a physical separation—just as Elena suggested in Jasper. I have stayed home in North America, ranging between an island in the St. Lawrence River and the New Hampshire of my youth, but spend three or four months a year in Italy with Elena and Beowulf. They are months I look forward to. Elena joins me on this side of the ocean when time off from school permits her to do so. It's a joy every time we come together again, and there's a strange feeling that seems sadly absent from many marriages—some blend of tempered trust, care, devotion, and longing—that spans the space between us when we are apart. It's an adaptation of marriage that works for this time of our lives.

But no matter how any of us chooses to live with those we love, still it's good to be alone sometimes. "All my life people have been telling me you should never travel alone," said wilderness canoeist Bill Mason, "but it's interesting—I've never been told that by anybody who's ever done it." When you go into nature's spaces by yourself, and it doesn't have to be a great wilderness, your ego can melt away as you become absorbed in miniscule facets of the world that in company you might never have noticed. A minute ago I looked up from my paper and pencil to watch an ant scramble under the left front foot of a bright green lizard, then zigzag up the lizard's shoulder. The lizard stood perfectly still, with wide eyes unflinching, except that its torso abruptly expanded and contracted every few seconds, as if it were a granite statue breathing. The air vibrated with a cicada chorus, and I felt a bead of sweat bulge on the nape of my neck until the surface tension broke and it raced down the valley of my bare back. The thick lap of supersaline Mediterranean wavelets nearby beckoned me to plunge into the sea.

When we go to the wilderness alone we are reminded that our human life is itself just a miniscule facet of the world. We are also reminded, especially if we go in winter, that at some point each of us is going to die. Just as the sense of our own smallness next to the totality of nature can give us an ecstatic sense of participation in the greatness of the whole, the reminder of death built into the cycle of the seasons can sharpen our awareness of being alive. An intimacy with winter makes it sometimes unsettlingly apparent that nature is not some volitional force that cares whether we live or die. Caring is what humans do. It's why we make homes, our little refuges in the wilderness, and trails that lead us back to those homes, where we find other people who care for us and need our caring in return. It is this that holds the human center and gives life, that wonderful oxygenating of the coursing blood, the soft warm glow we call meaning.

ACKNOWLEDGMENTS

Many people, over the course of many years, have contributed in ways large and small to the making of this book. Some will inevitably remain unmentioned.

My first thanks go to my parents, David and Margaret, who raised me to love the woods and never burdened me with their worry when I disappeared in them. My father was also vitally instrumental in the logistics of the journey described in these pages, as well as great company during its final days. Thanks are owing to my brothers too—Matthew, David, and Jonathan—who have been my companions in exploration for almost forty years now.

I met countless helpers along the trail, several of whom have remained friends. In British Columbia were Zac Bowland, Ray Robinson, Chris Campbell, Jun Chu, Randy Murray, Lennox Brown, Nick and Mika Meyer, Servaas Mes, the loggers and truck drivers of the Babine District, Paul and Kelley Inden, and especially Edward and Eliza Stanford. In Alberta were Michael Gross, Delwyn Slemp, Christine Jones, Maureen Fisher, Kevin McNeil, Luc and Susan Ouellette, Barry and Heather Boisvert, Joe McWilliams, Theresa Driediger (as well as her parents, Al and Adrian), and Scott McCallum. In Saskatchewan were Harley Nault, John and Pauline of Waterhen Lake, Wally Couillonneur (a.k.a. The Mysterious Stranger), Philip Cardinal, Don Skopyk, Glen McCallum, Curtis Chandler, Earl Stobbe, the wonderful people of Pinehouse, Regan Chell, David and Crystal Fast, and Leon Dorion. In Manitoba were Dave Price, Frank Fieber, Rick Hall, Bill Fulford, Heather Acres, Alan Vowles, Art and Helen Fenner, and Curtis and Colleen Cook.

I am grateful to several companies for their donation of equipment and provisions, without which I could not have afforded to outfit this journey: Crispi, Åsnes, Hilleberg the Tentmaker, Mountain House, Belly Timber, Raw Revolution, and Mountain Equipment Co-op.

I owe an immense debt of gratitude to the staff at Mountaineers Books in Seattle, especially Kate Rogers for championing my book from early days and for her continued encouragement and kindness. Thanks to my project editor, Laura Shauger, for guiding me through all the phases, and most of all to Ellen Wheat, who worked double duty as developmental and copy editor. Without her intervention all but the most patient of readers would doubtless have given up on this book. On a related note, thanks as well to my friends Kerstin Mierke, Priscilla Putnam Martin, and David Allison for their thoughts on early drafts.

I reserve a special thought for the late Trygve Tørud, who put me up during a visit to Norway in the preparatory phases of the journey described here and who alone had the nerve to unequivocally express disapproval of my decision to abandon my marriage to go skiing. He was a man who understood the importance of both skiing and marriage.

Finally, my greatest thanks—and much else—go to Elena, the love of my life, and to Beowulf, our four-legged son and my best friend.

SUGGESTED READING

Allan, Billie Lamb. *Dew Upon the Grass*. Saskatoon, SK: Modern Press, 1963.

Brody, Hugh. *Maps and Dreams: Indians and the British Columbia Frontier*. Vancouver, BC: Douglas & McIntyre, 1981.

Burr, Eric. *Ski Trails and Wildlife: Toward Snow Country Restoration*. Victoria, BC: Trafford, 2008.

de Leeuw, Sarah. *Unmarked: Landscapes Along Highway 16*. Edmonton, AB: NeWest Press, 2004.

Glavin, Terry. *This Ragged Place*. Vancouver, BC: New Star Books, 1996.

Gopnik, Adam. *Winter: Five Windows on the Season*. Toronto, ON: House of Anansi Press, 2011.

Halfpenny, James C., and Roy Douglas Ozanne. *Winter: An Ecological Handbook*. Boulder, CO: Johnson Books, 1989.

Hoagland, Edward. *Notes from the Century Before: A Journal from British Columbia*. New York: Random House, 1969.

Huntford, Roland. *Two Planks and a Passion: The Dramatic History of Skiing*. London, UK: Continuum, 2008.

Ilgunas, Ken. *This Land Is Our Land: How We Lost the Right to Roam and How to Take It Back*. New York: Plume, 2018.

Jiles, Paulette. *North Spirit: Sojourns Among the Cree and Ojibway*. Saint Paul, MN: Hungry Mind Press, 1995.

Johannsen, Alice E. *The Legendary Jackrabbit Johannsen*. Montreal: McGill-Queen's University Press, 1993.

Kagge, Erling. *Walking: One Step at a Time*. Translated by Becky L. Crook. New York: Pantheon Books, 2019.

Karras, A. L. *North to Cree Lake: The Rugged Lives of the Trappers.* Toronto, ON: Paperjacks, 1970.

Langford, Cameron. *The Winter of the Fisher.* Toronto, ON: Macmillan of Canada, 1971.

Lynch, Wayne. *The Great Northern Kingdom: Life in the Boreal Forest.* Markham, ON: Fitzhenry and Whiteside, 2001.

Marchand, Peter. *Life in the Cold: An Introduction to Winter Ecology.* Hanover, NH: University Press of New England, 1987.

McKibben, Bill. *Long Distance: A Year of Living Strenuously.* New York: Simon & Schuster, 2000.

Moor, Robert. *On Trails: An Exploration.* New York: Simon & Schuster, 2016.

Nansen, Fridtjof. *The First Crossing of Greenland.* Translated by Hubert Majendie Gepp. London, UK: Longmans, Green, and Company, 1890.

Olson, Sigurd F. *The Lonely Land.* New York: Alfred A. Knopf, 1961.

Reed, Peter, and David Rothenberg, editors. *Wisdom in the Open Air: The Norwegian Roots of Deep Ecology.* Minneapolis: University of Minnesota Press, 1993.

Rutstrum, Calvin. *Paradise Below Zero.* New York: Macmillan, 1968.

Teale, Edwin Way. *Wandering Through Winter.* New York: Dodd, Mead, 1965.

Wallis, Velma. *Two Old Women: An Alaska Legend of Betrayal, Courage and Survival.* Fairbanks, AK: Epicenter Press, 1993.

ABOUT THE AUTHOR

PHOTO BY ELENA MAZZACCHERA

Anders Morley was born in 1978 and grew up walking and skiing in New Hampshire. He holds degrees in history from Taylor University and St. Andrews University and also studied at the University of Edinburgh, Columbia University, and the Università degli studi di Bergamo. A writer and translator whose work has appeared in *The Globe and Mail, Maisonneuve, Northern Woodlands, The Aurorean,* and *New Hampshire,* he divides his time between northern Italy and northern New Hampshire.

MOUNTAINEERS BOOKS, including its two imprints, Skipstone and Braided River, is a leading publisher of quality outdoor recreation, sustainability, and conservation titles. As a 501(c)(3) nonprofit, we are committed to supporting the environmental and educational goals of our organization by providing expert information on human-powered adventure, sustainable practices at home and on the trail, and preservation of wilderness.

Our publications are made possible through the generosity of donors, and through sales of 700 titles on outdoor recreation, sustainable lifestyle, and conservation. To donate, purchase books, or learn more, visit us online:

MOUNTAINEERS BOOKS

1001 SW Klickitat Way, Suite 201 • Seattle, WA 98134
800-553-4453 • mbooks@mountaineersbooks.org • www.mountaineersbooks.org

An independent nonprofit publisher since 1960

YOU MAY ALSO LIKE:

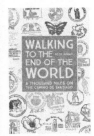